Understanding the market

Andrew Dunnett

By the same author

Understanding the economy

Longman
London and New York

Longman Group UK Limited
Longman House, Burnt Mill, Harlow
Essex CM20 2JE, England
and Associated companies throughout the world

Published in the United States of America
by Longman Inc., New York

First published 1987
Fourth impression 1991

British Library Cataloguing in Publication Data
Dunnett, Andrew
Understanding the market
1. Microeconomics
I. Title
338.5 HB172
ISBN 0-582-29669-2

Library of Congress Cataloging in Publication Data
Dunnett Andrew, 1948—
Understanding the market.

Includes index
1. Economics. 2. Capitalism. 3. Oligopolies.
I. Title
HB171.5.D84 1987 b 330 86—7206
ISBN 0-582-29669-2

Set in 10 on 11 Linotron 202 Times Roman
Printed in Malaysia
by The Commercial Press Sdn. Bhd.,
Serdang Raya, Selangor Darul Ehsan

Contents

Chapter 5 Costs

Chapter 6 Revenue, cost and profit

Chapter 7 Objectives of the firm

Chapter 8 Behaviour in oligopolistic markets

Preface

This book is directed towards first-year students doing economics either as a single discipline or as a part of a broader social science degree (such as business studies); at those students taking professional examinations (for example in accountancy); and at students of A-level economics. As such the market to which it is directed is the same as that for my earlier book *Understanding the Economy* which was an introduction to macroeconomics. *Understanding the Market* is an introduction to microeconomics.

The approach of this book reflects the belief that the teaching of microeconomic theory cannot be divorced from the real world to which that theory can and should be applied. It is thus a mixture of theory and application. Although the microeconomic theory presented is the bare minimum which the student needs to assimilate to appreciate the applied material, it remains an unpalatable fact that this material is often difficult for students to grasp. In writing this book there were two possible strategies I could have adopted. Either I could 'fudge' the issues and spare the reader the mental effort involved in trying to fathom out exactly what was meant by long-run equilibrium, a Pareto optimal allocation of resources, and so on. Or I could do it 'properly' with a degree of rigour appropriate to the discipline of economics, sweetening the bitter pill where possible and rewarding the reader with applied material when the necessary theory had been covered. I took the second option. Notwithstanding this, however, the balance between theory and application in this book is heavily biased towards application, reflecting, I believe, the needs of students and teachers alike.

Chapter 5 epitomizes this approach. The cost concepts therein are treated rigorously but there are numerous applied examples provided as illustrations.

Most markets in the real world are oligopolistic. Paradoxically it is in this area that neo-classical theory has least to say or has the fewest definitive predictions to make. My approach to this in Chapter 8, which is a major chapter, has been to take a number of cases, each one illustrating particular features of oligopolistic behaviour and public policy towards it.

In Chapters 10 and 11 I have presented a welfare-theoretic model of how markets allocate resources. This serves as a useful reference point in Chapter 12 where I consider an alternative way of allocating resources – planning in command economies and in wartime. This chapter is an unusual but, I believe, valuable feature of this book. The welfare framework carries over to Chapters 13 and 14 where I consider state intervention in market economies in the form of the public provision of goods and services and the nationalized industry sector. The approach here is however essentially pragmatic and the issues discussed are those of contemporary relevance.

The theme which develops as the book progresses is the role of the state in mixed economies, a theme which is discussed in the concluding chapter.

The questions which follow each chapter are designed to highlight some of the points in that chapter. They are designed to make the reader think about what he has read and (where this book is being used as a textbook) to stimulate class discussion. There is no particular pattern to these questions, though they are all designed as 'short answer' questions. It must be emphasized, however, that in the multiple-choice type of question there is not necessarily any single correct answer – more than one answer could be considered correct or none could be correct. Complex issues cannot have simple definitive answers.

In writing this book I have received an enormous amount of support from my colleagues at Ealing. They have given freely of their time and much of the empirical material in this book has been contributed by them. Being economists, they understand that knowledge is one of the few things you can give away and still retain, and that social benefits over and above the private benefit flow from a project such as this.

In particular, I would like to thank Phillip Wyatt who is an inexhaustible font of knowledge and cuttings from the *FT*. The debt I owe him is enormous. I would also like to thank David Glen, Carol Rees, John Crowley, Andy Hartropp, Paul Cormack, Brian Ardy and Adrian Bourne. Thanks to all those friends who helped and supported in the critical period during which this manuscript was in preparation.

Acknowledgements

We are grateful to the following for permission to reproduce copyright material:

AGB Research PLC for fig. 8.5 from fig. 3 p 25 Copyright Audits of Great Britain Ltd; Basil Blackwell Ltd for tables 5.4 from tables I, II pp 313, 316, 8.7 from table 2 p 276, 8.8 from table 3 p 281, 14.4 from table 13.1; Cambridge University Press for tables 3.1 from table 5A.1 p 154, 8.3 from table 6 p 18; Gerald Duckworth & Co Ltd for tables 12.1, 12.2 from tables 7, 6 pp 223, 220–1; the editor, Journal of the Economics Association No 83 Vol XIX Pt 3 for fig 4.8; The Economist Publications Ltd for fig. 5.6 from p 90, table 14.2 from p 73; The Controller of Her Majesty's Office for figs. 5.7–5.10 from exhibits 4, 9, 10, 7 pp 92, 96, 95, figs. 8.3, 8.4 and tables 5.2 from table 1, 5.3 from table 4, 8.1, 8.4, 8.5; the author, G L Kouris for table 6.2; Macmillan, London and Basingstoke for table 8.13; Macmillan, London & Basingstoke & Basil Blackwell Ltd for table 8.6 from p 24, table 1 p 275; the editor for table 8.12 from fig 2 p 25 Copyright 'Marketing' magazine; The Observer Ltd for table 9.3 adapted from pp 52–53; Office of Fair Trading for table 8.2 from table 2 p 31; the author, D G Rhys for table 5.5 from table 8.3 p 184; Sussex European Research Centre for fig 5.11 from table 13 p 100; Times Books Ltd for table 9.1 from table 1 p 7.

Chapter 1
Introduction

1.1 What economics is about

Definitions are for dictionaries (or, more correctly, dictionaries are for definitions) but some definitions are so abstract and so conceptual that to the uninitiated reader they convey very little meaning. Economics as a discipline covers a broad spectrum of enquiry and hence its subject matter can only be defined in very broad terms. Using such broad terms, we could say that *economics is about making decisions*. The '*economic problem*' or '*choice problem*' consists, in its widest sense, of two elements. Firstly, there must be a scarcity of resources – money, labour, time, land, and so on – and secondly, because of the scarcity of resources, choices have to be made about how they are used. Defined in this way, of course, the scope of economics appears vast but this is no accident for the scope of economics *is* vast – it is the 'science of choice' and as such its subject matter covers almost every aspect of human activity.

The purpose of this present work is somewhat more modest. It concerns itself with how decisions are made but confines itself to a narrower range of decisions – they are the economic decisions taken by three principal agents, the producer, the consumer and the state. Taken together these decisions shape the sort of society in which we live. The producer decides what will be produced, in what quantities and by what methods, responding to a lesser or greater extent to the wishes of consumers on these same issues. The extent to which the consumer is sovereign, in the sense that ultimately producers merely respond to his wishes, will be an important theme in this book. The second key theme concerns the role of the state, the third member of the triumvirate. The state acts as both producer and consumer but, in addition, it determines the legal and institutional framework within which producers interact with other producers and with consumers. Thus, the role of the state is crucial in determining ultimately how society's resources shall be allocated.

Economics is conventionally divided into macroeconomics and microeconomics. Microeconomics concerns itself with individual decisions – the individual firm, the individual consumer and individual prices. In macroeconomics the subject of enquiry is the economy as a whole – thus problems of inflation, unemployment, the balance of payments and economic growth are studied. The reader will appreciate, however, that the study of macroeconomics is predicated upon a particular analysis of how the microeconomy works. This book provides such an analysis.

1.2 Some key words

One of the difficulties experienced by the student of economics is that certain key words used by the economist have a meaning and significance peculiar to economics itself and different from the everyday usage of the terms. In this section we shall introduce some of these key words while at the same time sketching out how these concepts relate to the wider whole. Our aim is to provide the reader with some sort of perspective – a large-scale map of the landscape of this book.

The word *market* refers to the totality of buyers and sellers (both actual and potential) of a particular *good* or commodity or service. Thus, for example, one can talk about the market for shoes, the housing market, the market for foreign exchange and the market for professional footballers. A few markets have a physical existence (for example, the Stock Exchange is a place where buyers and sellers come together to trade shares) but most markets do not. When talking about a particular market it should be delineated with care. For example, the micro (home) computer market may be quite separate from the mini (business) computer market, or they may overlap.

In any market there are those who wish to sell and those who wish to buy. The buyers constitute the *demand* side of the market, the sellers the *supply* side. The demand for shoes therefore means the total number of pairs of shoes people would be prepared to buy at a given price. Note that one can talk about an *individual's demand* for shoes (normally a few pairs per year) or the *market demand* for shoes (several million pairs per year in Britain). The concept of demand implies both willingness and ability to pay for a particular good – thus it is different from *need.* A poor man may need a new pair of shoes but unless he has the money to pay for them there is no demand in the market.

The supply of shoes similarly implies willingness to sell at a particular price. Note that both demand and supply are dependent upon price. The price is the money or other consideration given when goods or services are exchanged. Note also that *price* rather than *value* is used since price is an objective datum whereas value is a subjective assessment of intrinsic worth.

The prices paid by buyers and received by sellers can be

considered to be *market prices*, that is, determined in some way by the *market forces* of demand and supply. In some situations, however, the price at which a particular good or service is sold is more or less set by the seller, for example, postal charges are set by the Post Office. In such a case where there is little interaction between demand and supply – or in other words where market forces are very weak – it is more realistic to talk about *administered prices*, rather than market prices.

In a Soviet-type *command economy* or *centrally planned economy* most prices are in fact administered prices, set by the state. The term *mixed economy* refers to an economy such as that of the UK, where some productive decisions are taken centrally by the state (for example, in the sphere of the National Health Service and defence) while other productive decisions are left to the market. Thus, some prices are administered while others are 'market prices'. It is important to note however, that even where there is no state intervention, many prices are administered rather than determined by market forces. This is because the supply side of the market is dominated by a few large firms. Such firms set (or administer) prices. These prices can be considered as market prices only in the very general sense that demand conditions will ultimately determine whether the prices set are sustainable.

Markets that are dominated by a few large firms are known as *oligopolies* or oligopolistic markets. In some cases one firm, called a *monopolist*, supplies the whole market for a particular good or service – for example, British Rail is a monopoly seller of rail transportation services. Markets can in fact be classified according to the *degree of concentration* that they exhibit on the supply side. Markets which are highly concentrated on the supply side (monopoly, oligopoly) will typically exhibit different behaviour patterns from those low concentration or *competitive* markets where market forces or the *forces of competition* wield greater sway. That is, the structure of a market will determine to some extent the *conduct* and *performance* of the firms within it. A market structure of extremely low concentration where there are many buyers and sellers, no one of whom is large enough to affect the market price, is known as *perfect competition*. Such market structures are seldom encountered in the real world, except perhaps for some agricultural products, and even here prices are often affected by state intervention.

The foregoing definitions are designed merely to prevent the confusion that might otherwise arise when the terms are encountered for the first time. Short definitions cannot hope to convey the full meanings of some of the terms since many of them carry deep philosophical and ideological connotations, the full import of which will become apparent only as the reader proceeds through the book.

Hopefully, this rather perfunctory introduction has served to steer the reader away from the common areas of confusion. Economics is no different from any other discipline in that it needs its own jargon for its practitioners to function effectively and to communicate with one another. All too often, however, in economic discourse words are used in a confusing way. Like Humpty Dumpty in *Through the Looking Glass*, who said:

'When *I* use a word, I use it to mean what I choose it to mean.' Small wonder Alice was confused.

Chapter 2
Market demand

2.1 Determinants of demand

In this chapter we shall discuss those factors which determine the demand for a good or service. In order to make the discussion somewhat less abstract we shall consider the demand for a particular good, say, lager.

The market demand for lager (which we can measure as so many million barrels per month) will be affected by a number of different factors, including:

1. *The price of lager.* Other things being equal, the higher the price of lager, the less will be demanded.
2. *The price of substitutes*, such as other beers, spirits, soft drinks, and so on. Other things being equal, if the price of substitutes goes up while the price of lager remains fixed, then there will be a tendency for people to switch to lager. That is, they will consume more lager and less of the higher-priced substitutes.
3. *The price of complementary goods.* Again, other things being equal, a rise in the price of complementary goods may affect the demand for lager. A rise in the price of crisps, for example, will tend to reduce the demand for lager. In practice of course only a very substantial increase in the price of crisps would produce a discernible impact on beer consumptions. A priori, however, we could argue that if there is any effect at all we could predict the *direction* of that effect. That is, an increase in the price of crisps will tend to reduce (rather than increase) beer consumption.
4. *Income.* This may affect lager sales but we cannot predict a priori the direction of causation. That is, we cannot say for certain whether an increase in income will increase or decrease (or leave unchanged) consumption of lager. Normally however, we might expect higher incomes to increase demand for most goods including lager.
5. *Tastes.* This term tends to be used in economics to represent all the other factors which influence demand other than those specifically mentioned above. In the context of our example there are many other influences on tastes. Successful advertising, for

example, will increase the demand for lager. The weather may also have some effect (more is consumed in hot sunny weather) and changing social habits (for example, the emergence of wine bars, stricter drink/drive laws and increasing home consumption of alcohol) may also have some long-term influence on lager consumption.

We can summarize what we have said so far in symbols as follows:

$$q_d = f(P, P_s, P_c, Y, T) \qquad [2.1]$$

This is simply a shorthand way of saying that the demand for lager (q_d) depends on or is a function (f) of the set of variables within the brackets, namely, the price of a lager (P), the price of substitutes (P_s), the price of complementary goods (P_c), income (Y), and tastes (T). Equation [2.1] can in fact be used to analyse the demand for any good or service – the demand for cars, foreign holidays, two-bedroom rented apartments, cinema tickets, window cleaners, economics textbooks, and so on. It is a completely general model which is universally applicable. All we have to do is to specify – carefully – what good or service we are considering and eqn [2.1] will provide us with a framework (though nothing more) for considering what factors will influence demand. We must be careful, however, to specify exactly what good is being considered. For example, the demand for

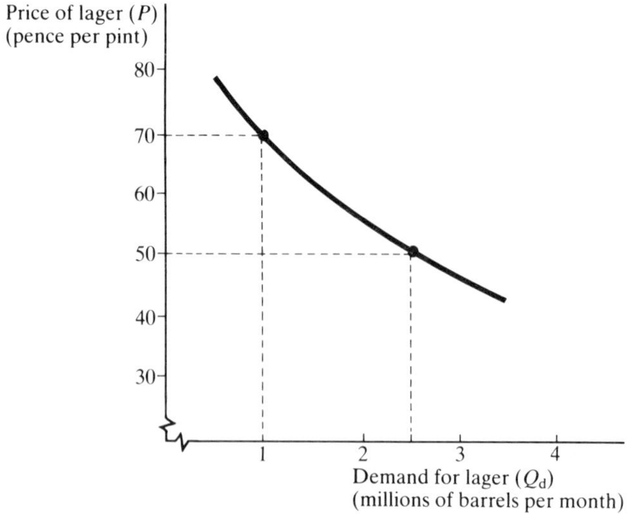

Fig. 2.1

one particular brand of lager will be different from the demand for lager generally.

For the time being we shall just consider the relationship between the demand for lager and the price of lager. That is, we shall assume that all the other factors which influence the demand for lager are held constant. This is known as the *ceteris paribus* assumption, and it is a simplifying assumption which we need to make at this stage.

Ceteris paribus ('other things being equal') demand varies inversely with price – that is, when the price goes up the quantity demanded goes down. An example of this is shown in Fig. 2.1. Figure 2.1 illustrates a hypothetical demand schedule, or demand function, or demand curve (which may often be a straight line). The units of measurement of the axes are for illustrative purposes only. At a price of 70p a pint, market demand will be 1 million barrels per month. At a lower price of 50p, the quantity demanded will increase to 2.5 million barrels. Thus, the demand function shows the relationship between the quantity demanded and price. It is important to emphasize, however, that the demand curve such as that shown in Fig. 2.1 is drawn on the assumption that all the other factors influencing demand are held constant (the *ceteris paribus* assumption). If these other factors are not constant (*ceteris non paribus*) then the demand curve will shift. For example, consider the probable effect of an increase in the price of whisky. Since whisky, in

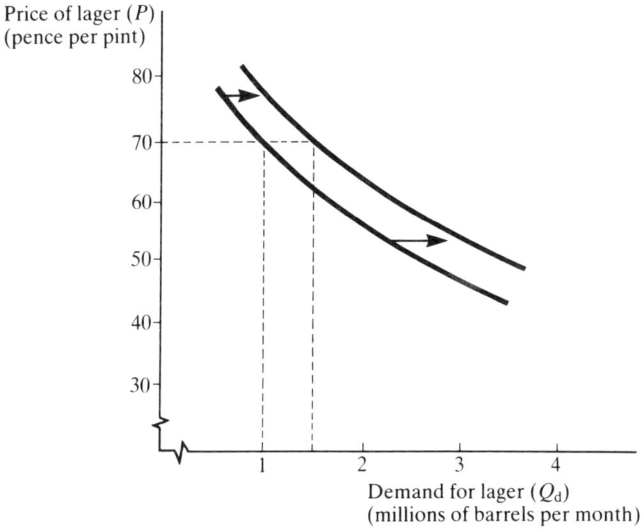

Fig. 2.2

some situations, is a substitute for lager, this will cause some people to increase their demand for lager while reducing their demand for whisky. This is illustrated in Fig. 2.2.

The whole curve shifts to the right, indicating that, at each price, more will be demanded than previously. For example, at a price of 70p per pint, market demand increases from 1 million to 1.5 million barrels. Note that in Fig. 2.2 demand has increased because the whole curve has shifted. Thus we can see that the phrase 'an increase in demand' can mean one of two things. Either:

1. A movement along the demand curve as a result of a drop in price.
2. A shift of the demand curve to the right as a result of a change in one of the non-price factors. For example, we mentioned earlier the probable effect of an increase in the price of whisky. This, we argued, would cause a drop in the demand for whisky (movement along the demand curve for whisky) which, in turn, would cause an increase in the demand for lager (demand curve for lager shifts to the right).

2.2 Demand and elasticity

The knowledge that the demand for lager will fall if the price goes up is not in itself particularly useful. However, it might be quite useful to know the extent of any fall in demand consequent upon a price increase. Economists use the term *elasticity* to describe the degree of sensitivity of demand to price changes.

Elastic demand

If a small increase in price causes a large fall in the quantity demanded, then demand is said to be sensitive to price changes or *elastic*. Similarly, if demand is elastic a small drop in price will result in a large increase in demand.

Inelastic demand

If the quantity demanded changes very little as a result of a change in price, then demand is said to be *inelastic* or insensitive to price changes.

Unit elasticity

If a given percentage fall in price leads to an equal percentage increase in demand then demand is said to be of *unit elasticity*. For example, if the demand for a particular commodity is of unit elasticity this implies that a 3 per cent rise in price will lead to a 3 per cent fall in demand.

Elasticity can be defined as:

$$e = \frac{\text{percentage change in quantity demanded}}{\text{percentage change in price}}$$

Its value (ignoring the sign, which is always negative) varies between zero and infinity, as Table 2.1 illustrates.

Table 2.1 Elasticity definitions

Value of *e*	**Description**	**Meaning**
Less than 1	Inelastic	Demand insensitive to price changes
1	Unit elasticity	Demand changes by the same percentage as the change in price
Greater than 1	Elastic	Demand sensitive to price changes

The concept of elasticity is an essential part of the economist's analytical apparatus – his bag of tools, so called. The measure of elasticity we have just defined is, in fact, only one of a number of differing elasticities. The concept of elasticity just refers to the degree of sensitivity of one variable to another – in this case the degree of sensitivity of demand to price. In order to distinguish this elasticity from others, it is normally known as the *own-price elasticity of demand*.

2.3 Factors influencing the elasticity of demand

The elasticity of demand for any particular good depends primarily on the availability of substitutes. If close substitutes are readily available then demand will be elastic, implying that a small increase in price will cause many consumers to switch to the substitutes, resulting in a large fall in demand. If there are no close substitutes, on the other hand, demand will be much less elastic, that is, it will be much less sensitive to price changes.

This implies, in terms of the example we considered earlier, that the demand for a particular type of lager will be more elastic than the demand for lager in general. We can illustrate this diagrammatically in Fig. 2.3. The *slope* of the demand curve gives an approximate indication of its elasticity. (This is not strictly true because the scale used for the axes will affect the slope and, as we shall see later on, the elasticity varies at each point on a straight-line demand curve; but it will serve our purposes for the present.) For the moment assume that a steep demand curve indicates inelastic demand (as in Fig. 2.3a) whereas a less steep curve indicates a more elastic demand (Fig. 2.3b). We shall, for the purpose of this example, invent a new brand of lager. Any Scandinavian or Bavarian sounding name will do, so we shall call it 'Kronerbrau'. Hence we compare in Fig. 2.3 the effect of a price increase on the demand for Kronerbrau and the demand for lager generally.

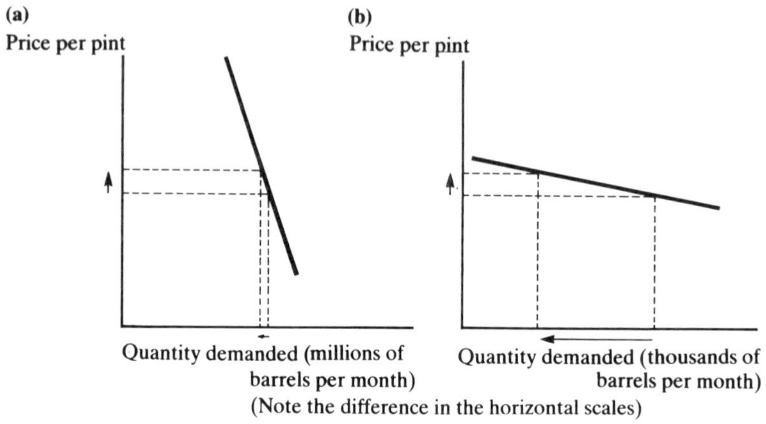

Fig. 2.3 (a) Demand for all lagers **(b)** Demand for Kronerbrau

For the purposes of comparison we have indicated the same percentage price increase in both parts of Fig. 2.3.

The demand for Kronerbrau is much more elastic than the demand for lager generally, since other brands are very close substitutes for Kronerbrau. Hence, if the price of Kronerbrau goes up while the price of other brands remains constant (remember, the demand curve is drawn on the *ceteris paribus* assumption), demand for Kronerbrau will drop sharply (Fig. 2.3b). The same percentage price increase applied to all lagers, however, will produce a much smaller percentage drop in demand since there are no close substitutes available.

2.4 Estimating the elasticity of demand

Economics cannot proceed very far unless it can make *quantitative* predictions based on empirical estimates of parameters such as demand elasticities. For example, it is not very useful to be told that if the price of milk goes up then the demand will go down. However, a prediction that the demand for milk will drop by, say, 5 per cent following a 10 per cent increase in price is a very useful piece of information, always provided of course that it is more or less correct.

To make such a prediction, however, it is necessary to have an (accurate) estimate of the price elasticity of demand for milk, derived from data which records consumers' responses to changes in the price of milk in the past. Obtaining reliable estimates of such elasticities is by no means a straightforward task. What we shall do here is to illustrate how such estimates could, in principle, be derived, glossing over some of the more intractable statistical problems which are beyond the scope of this book.

As the reader will by now be aware, the elasticity of demand is dependent on the slope of the demand function. Hence we shall discuss initially the way in which the demand function is estimated. Suppose you wish to estimate the elasticity of demand for Kronerbrau, and that you have available information from previous months on the sales of Kronerbrau (q_d) which were achieved at a number of different prices (P). This information is given in Table 2.2 and the same information plotted in Fig. 2.4. As you can see, there is a clear tendency for demand to increase as price falls, that is, there is an inverse relationship between price and quantity demanded.

Table 2.2 Price/quantity of Kronerbrau

Price per pint (P)	**Quantity demanded (000's of barrels per month** (q_d))
65	120
55	150
51	200
45	210

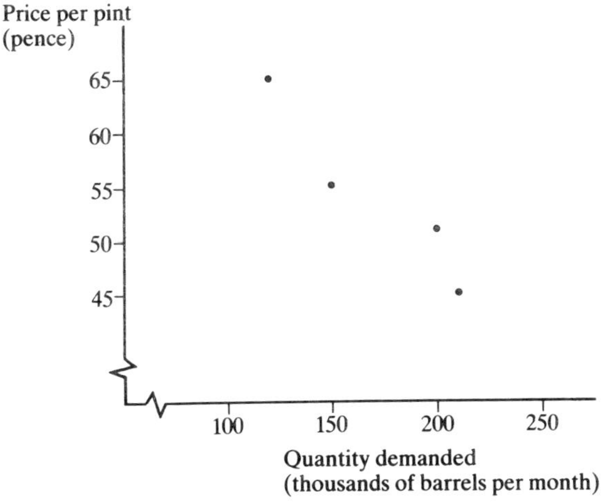

Fig. 2.4

We argued above that demand will depend on price plus a number of other factors. That is:

$$q_d = f(P, P_s, P_c, Y, T) \qquad [2.1]$$

We will therefore have to assume that all these other factors were constant during the period to which our data relates if we are to estimate the relationship between demand and price. The simplest form of such a relationship is a straight-line demand 'curve' of the form

$$q = a - bP \qquad [2.2]$$

where a and b are known as the *parameters* of the equation. It would be nice if we could straightforwardly translate eqn [2.2] into a line on a graph in Fig. 2.4. To do this, however, it is preferable to rotate Fig. 2.4 through 90° so that price is now plotted on the horizontal axis and quantity on the vertical axis, as in Fig. 2.5.

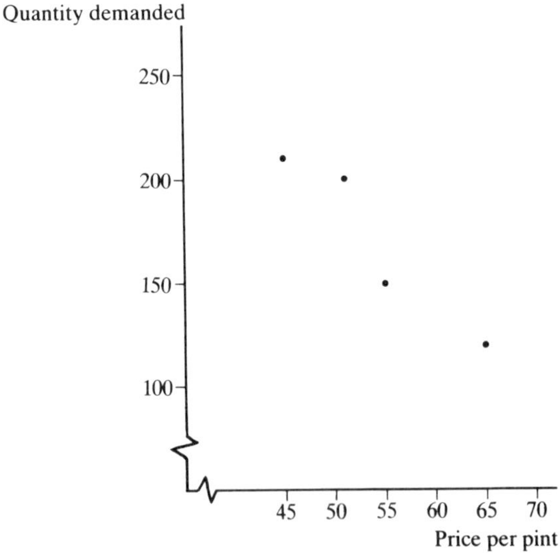

Fig. 2.5

The reason for this is that when we plot functional relationships it is a convention that the *dependent* variable should be measured on the vertical axis and the *independent* variable on the horizontal axis. The quantity demanded depends on (or is a function of) price – hence quantity is the dependent variable and price is the independent variable. It is merely a convention – like driving on the left-hand side of the road in Britain – but Alfred Marshall (1842–1924), one of the founding fathers of modern economics, appears not to have known this. Hence he drew his diagrams the 'wrong' way round as in Fig. 2.4, and since then everyone in economics has followed suit. To be consistent with the way that mathematicians plot functional relationships, however, we shall – in this section only – adopt the mathematical convention as in Fig. 2.5. Thereafter we revert to the normal Marshallian treatment.

To the scatter of points in Fig. 2.5 we can fit a line such as that in Fig. 2.6. The technique used to fit such a line – which we shall not discuss here – is known as regression analysis.

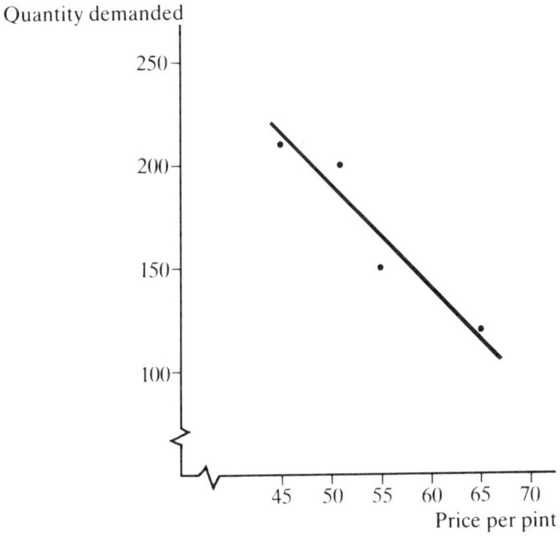

Fig. 2.6

The slope of the estimated demand curve shown in Fig. 2.6 gives us an indication of the elasticity of demand. Consider Fig. 2.7.

The slope of the demand curve $\Delta q/\Delta P$ shows the ratio of the change in quantity Δq to the change in price ΔP. This is not quite the same as the elasticity which shows the ratio of the *proportional* change in quantity to the *proportional* change in price. Because of this it turns out that elasticity is in one way a rather inconvenient measure, because the value of the elasticity is different at each point on a straight-line demand curve.

This is illustrated in Fig. 2.8 (where we have reverted to the standard Marshallian treatment).

The fall in price from P_1 to P_2 is the same in absolute terms as the fall from P_3 to P_4 and it produces the same absolute increase in

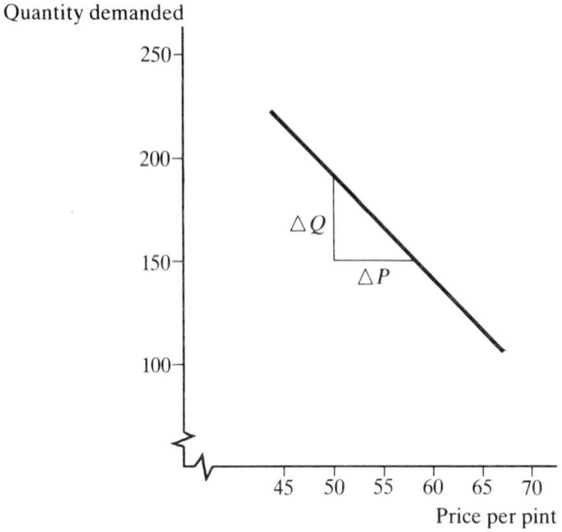

Fig. 2.7

quantity demanded. However, when price falls from P_1 to P_2 the *proportional* fall in price is quite small but it produces a large *proportional* increase in demand – hence the elasticity of demand is high.

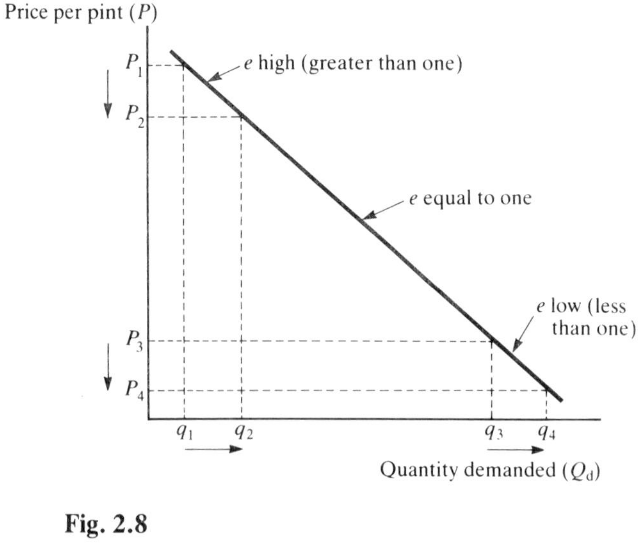

Fig. 2.8

Conversely, the fall in price from P_3 to P_4 represents a large proportional drop in price but it produces a small proportional increase in demand, hence elasticity here is low. Thus, given a straight-line demand curve, elasticity is high (that is, more than 1) at the 'top' (that is, at high prices) and elasticity is low (that is, less than 1) at the 'bottom' (that is, at low prices). It follows that, since the value of the elasticity coefficient falls as we move 'down' the demand curve, there must come a point, roughly in the middle of the curve, where the value of the coefficient is equal to unity.

The fact that the value of the elasticity coefficient is different at different points on the straight-line demand curve is, as we said before, an inconvenient feature. Clearly we would prefer to have a single value for the elasticity coefficient rather than an infinite number of such values. The way that this problem is normally overcome is to model the relationship between demand and price not by a linear demand function such as that in eqn [2.2], but by an exponential demand function such as

$$q_d = aP^b \qquad [2.3]$$

This looks intractable (and indeed it may look incomprehensible to readers without some mathematical knowledge) but it turns out that such an equation can be estimated almost as easily as the linear eqn [2.2.] Moreover, such an equation has a constant elasticity.[1] This is the way in which the estimates of elasticity in section 2.6 have been derived. We have of course glossed over the problems of estimation. In practice these problems are considerable, so the reader is warned to treat any such estimates with caution.

2.5 Empirical estimates of price elasticities

Econometrics is the name given to the statistical estimation of economic relationships, such as demand parameters and elasticities. As the reader will appreciate from section 2.4, econometrics involves rather complicated technical procedures – in fact the process of estimating demand elasticities is more difficult than we suggested in section 2.4 since there are additional statistical problems which have to be overcome. Econometric techniques have however been developed which allow estimates of demand elasticities to be generated, though these estimates should always be treated with care and used with caution.

One area in which copious amounts of data on consumption levels and prices have been collected is that of food. The Annual Report of the National Food Survey Committee publishes estimates of the price elasticity of demand for certain foods and a selection of these is given in Table 2.3. As one would expect, the demand for foods for which there is no close substitute – milk, eggs, potatoes – is rather inelastic. For example, a 10 per cent increase in the price of milk would reduce consumption by only 1 per cent according to this estimate. The demand for beef is, however, rather elastic ($e = -1.90$) since there are plenty of substitutes available – pork, lamb, chicken, and so on. The demand for fresh peas is very elastic ($e = -3.20$) since frozen peas represent an almost perfect – and perhaps superior – substitute. Note also that the elasticity of demand for bread depends upon the type of bread being considered. Demand for the standard white loaf is rather inelastic – again since no good substitute exists. White bread is, however, an adequate substitute for the more expensive wholewheat and wholemeal loaves and demand for these is therefore much more elastic.

Table 2.3 Estimates of price elasticity of demand for certain foods (1975–80) (Figures in brackets are standard errors – see text)

Liquid milk	−0.10	(0.06)	Chocolate biscuits	−0.98	(0.32)
Instant milk	−0.75	(0.56)	Beef	−1.90	(0.28)
Yoghurt	−1.24		Pork	−1.94	(0.23)
Eggs	−0.20	(0.14)			
Sugar	−0.39	(0.12)	Butter	−0.17	(0.10)
Marmalade	−1.29	(0.48)	Margarine	−0.18	(0.22)
Potatoes	−0.16	(0.04)			
Fresh peas	−3.20	(0.79)	Tea	−0.43	(0.09)
Frozen peas	−0.76	(0.32)	Instant coffee	−0.59	(0.11)
Standard white loaves	−0.45	(0.20)	Branded food drinks	−1.66	(0.76)
Wholewheat and wholemeal bread	−2.57	(0.54)			
Biscuits, other than chocolate biscuits	−0.54	(0.20)			

Source: *Household Food Consumption and Expenditure 1980*, Annual Report of the National Food Survey Committee, HMSO (MAFF), App. B, Table 3

The figures in brackets in Table 2.3 are the *standard errors* of the parameters. They give an indication of how reliable the estimates are. If the ratio of the parameter estimate to its standard error is more than about 1.96 then we can be reasonably confident in the estimate.

Thus most of the estimates shown in Table 2.3 appear to be fairly reliable, though the estimates for margarine and to a lesser extent milk products and eggs, appear less so.

2.6 The problem of defining a market: goods and characteristics

Up to now we have glossed over the problems of delineating the market we are studying. The demand for a particular brand of lager is, of course, part of the demand for lager generally, which, in turn, is part of the overall demand for beer. This much is reasonably obvious. What is less obvious is that lager is sold in two quite distinct situations – firstly in pubs for consumption on the premises and secondly in supermarkets and off-licences for home consumption. These two segments of the lager market are sufficiently distinct that we may be justified in treating them as if they were two separate markets. Ostensibly the product being sold is the same in both situations but this overlooks the point that when people buy things they are expressing a demand for certain characteristics which that good possesses. (This was the insight into consumer behaviour provided by the economist K. Lancaster.[2]) People drink lager in pubs as part of a wider social experience – in other words they go to pubs not just to drink but also to meet their friends, to make new contacts, and so on. When they buy drinks in a pub they are purchasing all these attributes or characteristics. When they buy lager in a supermarket they are purchasing different characteristics since the product will be consumed in a different set of circumstances, even though the product itself may be the same wherever it is purchased.

This has important implications. We could argue for example that the elasticity of demand for lager sold in pubs may be different – probably lower – than the elasticity of demand for lager sold in supermarkets. In other words, people are more aware of, and more responsive to prices when those prices are prominently displayed, as in a supermarket. This in itself might tend to increase the elasticity of demand for supermarket lager above that of pub lager. However, the decision to buy drinks in a pub may be taken when one has already 'had a few' which may itself influence the consumption decision. In the cold light of the supermarket shelves you might see things in quite a different way. The fundamental point, however, is that when you go to a pub you are expressing a demand for certain characteristics – company, conversation, pleasant surroundings, a chance to make new friends and influence people. These are, in effect, included in the price of the drinks. One's demand for these things (these characteristics) may be much less elastic than the demand for the thirst- quenching properties of beer.

2.7 Income elasticity of demand

Up to now our discussion has been conducted within the *ceteris paribus* assumption – that is, we have assumed that the other factors which influence demand have been held constant. We now turn to a consideration of the non-price factors which influence demand.

The responsiveness of demand to changes in income is known as the income elasticity of demand. The formula is

$$e_Y = \frac{\text{percentage change in quantity demanded}}{\text{percentage change in income}}$$

The value of the income elasticity of demand (e_Y) can be either positive or negative or zero. If a rise in income results in a fall in the quantity demanded (e_Y negative) then the good in question is termed an *inferior* good. Classic textbook examples of inferior goods are such things as black-and-white television sets, white bread and holidays in

Table 2.4 Estimates of income elasticity of demand for individual foods (1980)
(Income elasticities of quantity purchased)

Liquid milk	0.05	(0.02)
Beef	0.36	(0.12)
Pork	0.43	(0.11)
Canned peas	−0.66	(0.13)
Frozen peas	0.76	(0.08)
Bread:		
white large loaves sliced	−0.48	(0.10)
wholewheat and wholemeal	0.78	(0.15)
Tea	−0.17	(0.06)
Coffee:		
instant	0.42	(0.09)
ground and bean	1.57	(0.34)
Table jellies, squares and crystals	0.01	(0.07)*
Salt	−0.01	(0.12)*
Potatoes:		
'new' (Jan.–Aug.)		
not prepacked	−0.24	(0.09)
prepacked	0.02	(0.17)
'old' (Sept.–Dec.)		
not prepacked	−0.31	(0.11)
prepacked	0.19	(0.16)
Total fresh potatoes	−0.16	(0.05)
Butter	0.22	(0.04)
Margarine	−0.18	(0.03)
Sugar	−0.16	(0.04)

Source: *Household Food Consumption and Expenditure 1980*, Annual Report of the National Food Survey Committee, HMSO (MAFF), App. B, Table 2. (*i.e. not significantly different from zero).

Southend. Actually there is nothing wrong with Southend (apart from the fact that the tide goes out rather a long way) but the argument runs that the result of an increase in income will be to make people buy fewer rather than more holidays in Southend as their increased affluence allows them to switch to higher-priced substitutes (for example, holidays in Spain). Most goods are *non-inferior* – that is, the income elasticity of demand is positive, implying that an increase in income leads to an increase in demand. Table 2.4 gives some empirical estimates of the income elasticity of demand for a number of different foods. As expected, foods like canned peas are inferior (the income elasticity of demand is negative) indicating that when incomes rise consumers switch to a better product (for example, frozen peas). Similarly, white bread and margarine are both inferior. Increases in income produce a switch to more expensive substitutes (wholemeal bread and butter).

Note that for some goods, for example salt, the income elasticity of demand is not significantly different from zero, indicating that people's consumption of salt will not change significantly no matter what happens to their income. This is because salt takes only a tiny fraction of this income. Most other foods have a positive income elasticity of demand – they are non-inferior, and those with a high positive income elasticity, such as ground coffee, could be described as luxury goods. Finally, note that potatoes are not necessarily inferior, since pre-packed new potatoes have a positive income elasticity (though the estimate is unreliable, as judged by its standard error).

It is important to note that the *income* elasticities shown in Table 2.4 measure something quite different from the price elasticities of Table 2.3. Price elasticities show the responsiveness of demand to changes in price. Income elasticities show the responsiveness of demand to changes in income. Price elasticities are always negative. Income elasticities can be positive, negative or zero.

2.8 Cross-price elasticity of demand

The demand for some goods is sensitive to changes in the price of other goods. For example, the price of holidays in Spain will affect the demand for holidays in Greece, Italy and the UK. Such goods are clearly substitutes. The cross-price elasticity of demand measures the responsiveness of demand to changes in the price of other goods. The formula is

$$e_X = \frac{\text{percentage change in the quantity of good A demanded}}{\text{percentage change in the price of good B}}$$

Goods which are *substitutes* have a positive cross-price elasticity of demand. As one would expect, and as can be seen from Table 2.5, the demand for lamb is sensitive to changes in the price of other meats – if the price of beef rises by 10 per cent then the demand for lamb will rise by about 5 per cent.

Table 2.5 Estimates of cross-price elasticities (1973–80)

Cross-price elasticity of demand for	**With respect to the price of**		
Mutton and lamb	Pork	0.22	(0.12)
Mutton and lamb	Beef and veal	0.48	(0.23)
Butter	Soft margarine	0.23	(0.05)
Soft margarine	Butter	0.84	(0.18)
Butter	Total bread	−0.22	(0.10)

Source: *Household Food Consumption and Expenditure 1980*, Annual Report of the National Food Survey Commitee, HMSO (MAFF), App. B, Table 5

Some other pairs of goods have a cross-price elasticity of demand which is negative. Such goods are termed *complements* or complementary goods. Examples of complementary goods are video recorders and video tapes (if the price of video recorders goes down the demand for video tapes will go up) and, as can be seen from Table 2.5, bread and butter.

Notes

1. The equation is 'transformed' by taking logarithms of both sides, thus:

   $$\log q_d = \log a + b \log P$$

   so that linear regression techniques can still be applied. Equation [2.3] has a constant elasticity since

   $$e_D = -\frac{dq}{dp}\frac{p}{q} = -abp^{b-1}\left(\frac{P}{ap^b}\right) = -b$$

2. **Lancaster, K.,** *Introduction to Modern Microeconomics.* Rand McNally, 1974.

Questions

2.1 How would an economist describe the following demand characteristics:
(a) 'quantity demanded fell very little as a result of a substantial rise in price.'
(b) 'a large increase in demand resulted from a small reduction in price.'
(c) 'quantity demanded fell by the same percentage as the rise in price.'

2.2 What are the most important factors affecting the elasticity of demand for a product?

2.3 How elastic do you expect the demand for the following goods to be? Give an inspired guess in each case and explain the basis of your guess.
(a) salt (b) cigarettes (c) Lambert and Butler King Size cigarettes (d) first-class letter services

2.4 Why might the demand for coal be more elastic in the long run than in the short run?

2.5 State whether you would expect the cross-price elasticity of demand between the following goods to be positive, negative or zero, and explain why.
(a) margarine and butter
(b) petrol and motor vehicles
(c) coffee and cocoa
(d) motor cycles and motor cycle helmets

2.6 In the last three years sales of natural gas have risen despite an increase in its price. Does this mean that the demand curve for natural gas is upward sloping? How else could you explain the phenomenon?

2.7 On the Friday of each week a petrol-filling station cuts the price of petrol from £2.00 to £1.90 per gallon. Sales on Fridays rise to 1200 gallons per day, which compares with an average of 1000 gallons per day during the rest of the week. Calculate the price elasticity of demand facing the filling station.
Give two reasons why this estimate may not be valid.

2.8 After Easter most Easter-eggs remaining unsold in the shops tend to be marked down in price. This is not generally true of Cadbury's Creme Eggs (the small chocolate eggs filled with a sweet glutinous mass which sell for about 20p). Can Lancaster's 'characteristics' approach to demand theory help explain this?

Chapter 3
Market supply

3.1 Market structures

In the previous chapter we considered the demand side of the market. We now turn to a consideration of the factors influencing the supply of a particular good or service, the so-called supply side of the market.

In any particular market the degree of concentration on the supply side – that is, the number of firms who together make up the market supply – will be an important influence on the behaviour we can expect to find in the market. Consider two extreme cases, on the one hand atomistic or perfect competition and, on the other monopoly.

3.1.1 Atomistic competition

The term atomistic competition, or perfect competition, refers to a situation in which the market is supplied by many small firms, no one of whom is large enough to have any influence on prices. That is, each individual firm constitutes such a small proportion of total market supply that it cannot affect the price it receives for its product. If it were to substantially increase or decrease the amount it produces, the effect on total market supply would still be neglible because the firm is but a tiny part – a tiny atom – of the overall market supply. Such a firm is known as a *price taker* because it has no influence on market price but must accept it as a given datum. Such a firm, in effect, faces a demand curve for its product which is perfectly elastic, as in Fig. 3.1. It can sell as much as it likes at the market price, P_m, but any attempt to charge a higher price will result in all the firm's customers switching to a rival supplier. It is worth emphasizing that atomistic competition can only exist in markets where the good or service is *homogeneous* – that is, the output of one seller is indistinguishable from that of other sellers.

This condition is more or less satisfied in the market for some agricultural products. If the requirement that there should be a large number of sellers is also satisfied then we can legitimately describe such markets as being atomistically competitive. A better example, however,

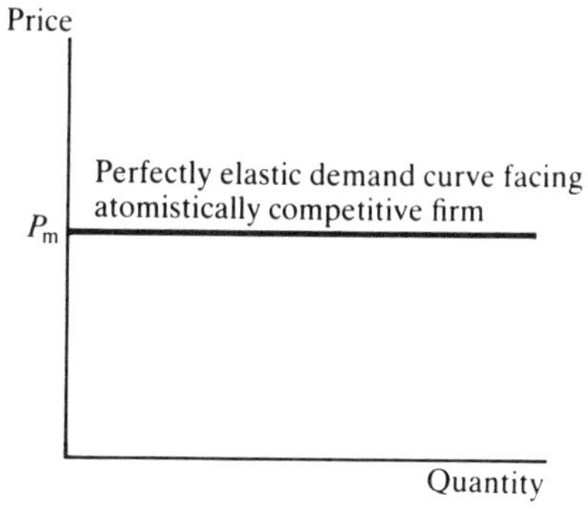

Fig. 3.1

is the foreign exchange market where the commodity being traded is foreign currency. This is completely homogeneous. (Belgian francs being sold by individual A are indistinguishable from those being sold by individual B) and the multiplicity of traders ensures that none of them can have an appreciable impact on market supply (nor, in this case, an appreciable impact on market demand).

The term perfect competition and atomistic competition are here used interchangeably. The use of the term 'perfect' is not meant to imply that there is anything particularly meritorious about this form of market structure. It does imply, however, that this represents an extreme case – or polar case. Perfect competition then, is the most unconcentrated form of market structure that can be conceived of. At the opposite extreme, the most highly concentrated form of market is one in which a single firm supplies the entire market for a particular good or service – monopoly.

3.1.2 Monopoly

Monopoly literally means 'single seller'. Since the firm is the sole supplier of a particular good the demand curve facing that firm is the market demand curve. The degree of elasticity of this demand curve depends among other things on the extent to which substitutes are available even though, by definition, there are no close substitutes. Thus, for example, British Rail is a monopoly seller of rail transportation services, but substitutes do exist in the form of transport by private car, bus, air, bicycle, and so on. The degree to which one or more of these alternative means of transport is an acceptable alternative – that is, a close substitute – will determine the elasticity of the demand curve facing British Rail.

Unlike the perfectly competitive firm which is compelled to accept the ruling price as a given datum, the monopolist is a *price maker*. He is free to charge whatever price he likes though he cannot, of course, force consumers to buy at these prices – the higher the price he sets the less will be the market demand – and in determining what price to charge the monopolist will have regard to the elasticity of demand for his product.

The model of perfect competition and that of monopoly may be seen as representing two ends of a spectrum. They are polar cases. Although there are markets in the real world which approximate closely to one or other of these polar cases, most markets exhibit a degree of concentration which would place them somewhere in between these two extremes. Such market forms are known as imperfect competition (or monopolistic competition) and oligopoly.

3.1.3 Imperfect competition

An imperfectly competitive market is similar to a perfectly competitive market in that a large number of sellers supply the market. However, unlike the perfectly competitive market where the product is homogeneous, in imperfect competition the output of each firm is differentiated in some way from that of other firms – the product is *heterogeneous*. This is achieved mainly through branding which emphasizes in the mind of the consumer the distinguishing characteristics of each firm's product. Thus, for example, soap was at one time sold by weight. It was a homogeneous product in much the same way as salt or sugar are now. In the post-war period, however, soap manufacturers began to differentiate their product from that of rivals by marketing techniques which included distinctive packaging, colour and scent and extensive advertising expenditure designed to accentuate the special characteristics of their product and to promote its brand image. This product differentiation is partly real and partly imaginary. There are real differences between the various brands of soap but these differences are not as great as the advertisers would have us believe. Often the advertising does not emphasize any real distinguishing attribute of the firm's product, since these are minimal anyway. Rather, it seeks to establish in the mind of the consumer a favourable product image by associating it with vitality, luxury or sexual success: 'Use Acme soap and famous film stars will lust after your body.'

Extensive advertising expenditure is a feature of imperfectly competitive markets. It is one of the most important forms of *non-price competition*. Competition by price becomes less of a feature since the product has been rendered non-homogeneous and the fact that it is not sold in standard weights or sizes makes it more difficult for the consumer to compare the value for money he is getting from the various brands.

Imperfectly competitive firms are no longer price takers though the amount of discretion they have in setting prices is not as great as that of the pure monopolist. The demand curve for their product is, however, downward sloping and the elasticity of demand for their product will depend upon how successful they have been in differentiating their product from that of rivals. A successful advertising campaign which convinces consumers that Acme soap (and no other brand) brings vitality, luxury and sexual success will render the demand for Acme soap inelastic since other brands (substitutes) do not have these desirable attributes – at least, not in the mind of the consumer. The important implication of this, of course, is that if the Acme Soap Co. can establish a brand loyalty for its product and thereby render the demand inelastic, it can increase prices without suffering a large drop in demand and can thereby increase its sales revenue and profits.

Such product differentiation through advertising is an important form of non-price competition since it allows firms who are selling what is essentially a homogeneous product to enjoy the same quasi-monopolistic market conditions as those firms selling a heterogenous product. Examples of successful attempts at product differentiation abound. Unsuccessful attempts are less common but one such is the retailing of petrol. In the early 1960s each of the oil companies attempted to differentiate its product from that of their rivals by extensive advertising suggesting that their brand was superior in terms of power generated and miles per gallon delivered. The introduction in the mid-1960s of the star octane rating system (by which the petrol was graded by a star system corresponding to its octane rating) made it more difficult for the oil companies to pursue these claims so that they abandoned the attempts at product differentiation. What advertising still goes on is designed to promote the overall image of the oil company rather than directly to promote its particular brand of petrol.

3.1.4 Oligopoly

In imperfect competition firms are selling similar but differentiated products. Strictly speaking, to be classified as an imperfectly competitive market the number of supplying firms should be large. An oligopolistic market, by contrast, is one in which the number of supplying firms is, by definition, small. (Oligopoly means literally 'a few sellers'). Thus it is a market form in which a few firms supply the entire market for a particular good or service. An extreme form of oligopoly is known as duopoly – that is, just two firms supply the entire market or, at least, the vast bulk of the market. Of necessity oligopolistic firms are large, sometimes very large. Such highly concentrated market structures are common and, in fact, represent the dominant mode of organization in the manufacturing sector of the

Table 3.1 Concentration ratios – random sample of 29 products

	Sales concentration ratios (C_5) (%) 1968	1975
Flour confectionery	60.1	64.2
Blended whisky	91.0	87.1
Organic chemicals	63.2	—
Detergents	79.9	82.8
Steel blooms, billets and slabs	96.6	—
Contractors' plant	39.7	—
Mining machinery	59.1	—
Pulp-making machinery, etc.	83.3	82.5
Boilers and boilerhouse plant	61.7	—
Insulated wires and cables	81.8	—
Telephone installations	96.4	98.9
Line apparatus	99.9	94.9
Washing machines (C_7)	86.9	100.0
Trailers and caravans	44.2	34.6
Flax	55.6	—
Wool sorting, etc.	50.0	72.3
Jute, yarn and cloth	68.9	73.4
Hosiery, etc.	33.2	40.2
Woven carpets	57.5	—
Other carpets	54.4	—
Narrow fabrics (elastic)	74.3	—
Narrow fabrics (non-elastic)	31.3	35.6
Asbestos manufactures	86.2	86.7
Fellmongery	42.2	50.6
Heavy overalls and aprons	27.4	32.6
Hats, caps and millinery	36.1	34.3
Corsets and brassieres	59.0	63.2
Builders' woodwork	23.0	32.9
Wallpaper	89.7	74.1

Source: P. E. Hart and R. Clarke, *Concentration in British industry 1935–75*, NIESR Occasional Paper 32, 1980

economy. The degree of concentration of a particular market can be measured – albeit somewhat imperfectly – by so-called *concentration ratios*. The five-firm concentration ratio, C_5, shows the proportion of the market for a particular good supplied by the five largest firms in the industry. Table 3.1 shows such concentration ratios for a random sample of 29 products.

Before proceeding, we note a number of difficulties associated with the estimation and use of concentration ratios lest the unwary reader be misled into thinking that they provide an unambiguously accurate measure of concentration. Firstly, data on sales is not generally available in the form in which the researcher would like it. He is therefore often forced to use data on *employment* (which is more readily available) as a proxy for sales data and the resulting estimates are known as employment concentration ratios. Whether employment or sales are used as the basis for calculation, the choice of the top five firms, rather than three or seven, is essentially arbitrary. The five-firm ratio is however the most widely used. The second problem with concentration ratios is that they relate to sales of *home-produced* goods only. Some of these home-produced goods will be exported. More importantly, some domestic markets will be supplied partly by importing firms. If an attempt is made to take account of such imports, the measured degree of concentration would fall for most industries. It has been argued[1] however, that to do so would produce an unrealistic picture of the extent of competition. The reasons for this are that, firstly, many imports are inputs into domestic production. For example, Ford makes extensive use of imported components in its 'UK produced' cars. Secondly, many imports which are nominally competitive are, in fact, complementary since they are resold by major domestic firms under their own brand name. For example, Vauxhall (a subsidiary of the American firm, General Motors) imports Cavaliers and sells them under the Vauxhall name. These are both features of the activities of multinational companies, a major theme which will be taken up again in Chapter 9.

The final caveat that one should note in connection with concentration ratios is that *firm* concentration ratios are not the same as *plant* concentration ratios. For example, a given firm, even though it dominates the market for a particular product, may be supplying that market from a number of small plants rather than from one large one. Though there may be considerable economies (for example, savings in transport costs) to be gained from so doing, it is worth noting that the existence of such multi-plant operations significantly weakens the case for the social benefits that are claimed to flow from the existence of large firms with market power. This theme is taken up in section 8.1.

3.1.5 Oligopolistic behaviour

Oligopolistic firms enjoy a protected position in much the same way – though not to the same extent – as monopolistic firms. This protection is afforded by barriers to the entry of new firms (commonly called simply *barriers to entry*) which prevent newcomers entering the industry to take for themselves part of the profits enjoyed by oligopolists by virtue of their protected market position. Such entry barriers take a variety of forms. There may be legal barriers – the Post Office for example enjoyed, until recently, a monopoly position protected by law. Alternatively, the barriers may be conferred by sheer size alone – the oil companies, for example, make large profits which are undoubtedly the envy of other firms. These other firms find it difficult to break into the oil business, however, because it is difficult to start small in the oil business. Large amounts of capital and expertise are needed to compete on equal terms with the existing oil companies.

In oil exploration and exploitation the nature of the entry barrier is essentially technical: the technology involved is such that only very large-scale operations can be profitable since the set-up costs involved are large. In other industries, however, low unit costs can be achieved with quite small production. Oligopolistic firms in such industries are potentially vulnerable to attack from outsiders, but such firms have evolved a number of defensive strategies designed to exclude interlopers by the erection of artificial entry barriers. Advertising expenditure is one such barrier to the entry of new firms since any potential entrant cannot penetrate the market unless he is prepared to spend large sums on advertising. Thus, even though there are no technical reasons on the production side to deter new entrants, they are prevented from entering the industry by the high cost of advertising necessary to gain a foothold in the market.

A particularly effective entry barrier is provided by the marketing strategy known as brand proliferation. This is practised with particular effectiveness by the tobacco industry. The tobacco industry is virtually a duopoly with two firms, Imperial Tobacco and Gallaghers, supplying almost all the market. There is, however, a multiplicity of brands, many of which are heavily advertised and promoted through sports sponsorship. Given the multiplicity of brands, a new entrant into the cigarette industry can hope to pick up only a small fraction of brand switchers at any one time, and then only if his new brand is heavily promoted. Thus new entrants are deterred from attempting to break into the industry.

3.2 Summary: aspects of market structure

We have in this chapter considered a number of different aspects of market structure which are summarized in Table 3.2.

Table 3.2 Degree of concentration, market structure and characteristics

Perfect (atomistic) competition (Many sellers)	**Imperfect (monopolistic) competition (Several sellers)**	**Oligolopy (A few sellers)**	**Monopoly (One seller)**
Example			
Agricultural produce (but marketing boards introduce imperfections)	Eggs	Cars	London Transport (but may be in competition with British Rail) British Gas
Features			
Homogeneous product	Product differentiated by branding	Differentiated product	Exclusive product
← No entry barriers →		← Entry barriers →	
Price taker	← Price maker →		
	← Advertising →		
	← Additional forms of non-price competition →		

The most obvious aspect of market structure is the degree of concentration, but the presence or absence of entry barriers and the degree of product differentiation is also important. These things, then, determine the structure of the industry. The conduct of the firms within the industry will be determined to a large extent by this structure. Thus, for example, in industries of high concentration we would expect to find significant amounts of advertising and other forms of non-price competition. Price competition, if it does occur, will be in industries where the product is homogeneous.

It is important to emphasize at this point that what we have provided is four different *models* of market structure – atomistic competition, monopolistic competition, oligopoly and monopoly. In analysing any particular market situation one should be careful to select the appropriate model with which to analyse the situation. If one considers the market for petrol, for example, then the choice of the appropriate model of market structure will depend upon what aspect of that market we are considering. The major oil companies, once called the Seven Sisters, are clearly oligopolistic. At the retail level, however, since there are many retail outlets – lots of individual filling stations and garages – the market is clearly an imperfectly competitive one. Moreover, we could even argue that since the product being sold is perceived as being homogeneous then the degree of imperfection is slight, that is, the market is almost perfectly competitive. The implication of this is that price competition between garages will tend to result in them all charging the same price, since each garage in effect faces a perfectly elastic demand curve. On the other hand, certain garages may enjoy an element of monopoly by virtue of their geographical location – a garage which is the only one within a fifty miles radius is unlikely to engage in price competition to attract custom.

Notes

1. See: **Hart, P. E. and Clarke, R.**, *Concentration in British Industry 1935–75*. NIESR Occasional Paper 32, 1980, App. 1A; Monopolies and Mergers Commission 1978 Green Paper, *A Review of Monopolies and Merger Policy*, p. 57.

Questions

3.1 Economists are fond of analysing market situations in terms of models which correspond to certain 'ideal types' – perfect competition, monopoly, oligopoly, imperfect competition and duopoly. Which of the above models would you choose to analyse the following markets?
(a) the market for air-travel
(b) food retailing
(c) the foreign exchange market for sterling
(d) the market for ice-cream (in the UK)
(e) the market for rail transport (in the UK)
(f) tobacco and tobacco products (UK)
(g) the 'rag trade'
(h) oxygen and industrial gases (UK)
(i) the market for germanium (a metal)
(j) fireworks
(k) longlife fruit juices (e.g. 'Just Juice')
(l) eggs

3.2 State which of the following firms are price takers and which are price makers.
(a) a perfectly competitive firm
(b) a monopolist
(c) an oligopolist
(d) an imperfectly competitive firm

3.3 Would a firm operating in a perfectly competitive market be likely to:
(a) combine with other firms to advertise the industry's product?
(b) advertise its own product?

3.4 Coca Cola and Pepsi Cola jointly have about 40 per cent of the soft-drinks market. They both spend large amounts on advertising. What form does this advertising take? Why do they not engage in price competition? What is the intended effect (on the elasticity of demand for Coke) of slogans such as 'It's the real thing' and 'Coke is it'?

3.5 Why has the EEC sought to introduce common standards for items such as cauliflowers, apples and sausages?

3.6 An oligopolistic firm suspects that if it cuts prices its rivals will follow suit. How will this action on the part of the rivals affect the elasticity of the demand curve facing the firm?
(a) it will make the firm's demand curve more elastic
(b) it will make the firm's demand curve less elastic
(c) it will not affect the elasticity of the firm's demand curve

Chapter 4
The market price

4.1 The determination of market price

Chapter 2 looked at the demand side of the market. Chapter 3 considered the supply side of the market by looking at those factors affecting the structure of the market for a particular good or service. In this chapter we shall put these two things together to study how prices are determined in competitive markets.

It is possible to conceive of an industry supply curve or market supply curve – in many ways analogous to the market demand curve – such as that in Fig. 4.1.

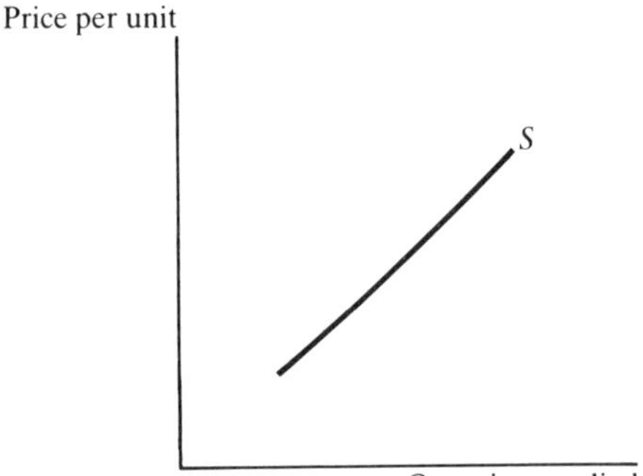

Fig. 4.1

Like the market demand curve it is drawn on the *ceteris paribus* assumption and its upward slope illustrates the general proposition that more will be supplied (that is, offered for sale) at higher prices than at lower prices. This makes sense because the higher the price per unit, the easier it will be for firms to make a profit and more firms will be attracted into the industry, thereby expanding industry supply. A point to be emphasized is that supply conditions in any particular market will depend to a large extent on the structure of that market. Initially it will be convenient to think in terms of perfectly competitive markets for here there are no barriers to the entry of new firms. Moreover, in atomistic competition no one firm is large enough to significantly influence market supply. Thus prices are determined by the market forces of demand and supply and each individual firm is a price taker rather than a price maker. The determination of this market price is illustrated in Fig. 4.2. In the figures *S* denotes the supply curve and *D* the demand curve.

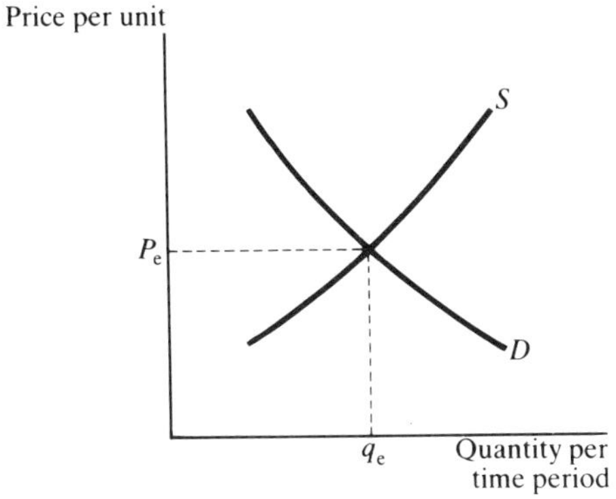

Fig. 4.2

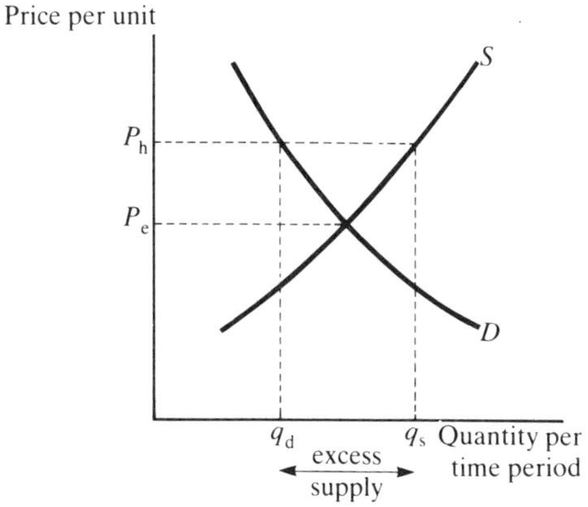

Fig. 4.3

Price P_e is an equilibrium price in the sense that at this price the amount being offered for sale is exactly equal to the amount consumers are prepared to purchase. This is the *market clearing* price at which there is neither excess demand nor excess supply. In Fig. 4.3, however, at price P_h there is excess supply since the quantity which firms would like to sell (q_s) is greater than the amount consumers are prepared to buy (q_d). The existence of this excess supply will tend to depress prices, driving them down towards the market clearing level P_e. Note that there is an automatic tendency for this to happen; that is, in the absence of any factors to prevent it, price will tend to move towards the equilibrium level. Similarly, if there is an excess demand as in Fig. 4.4, the efforts of buyers to secure for themselves the available supply will push up prices towards the equilibrium level where both buyers and sellers are satisfied. Note that as price increases from P_L to P_e two things happen. Firstly, the increase in price encourages firms to supply more; that is, there is a movement along the supply curve from point A to point E. Secondly, the increase in price discourages consumers. In effect some purchasers who would have bought at the lower price P_L are not prepared to buy at the higher price P_e. Thus there is a movement along the demand curve from point B to E.

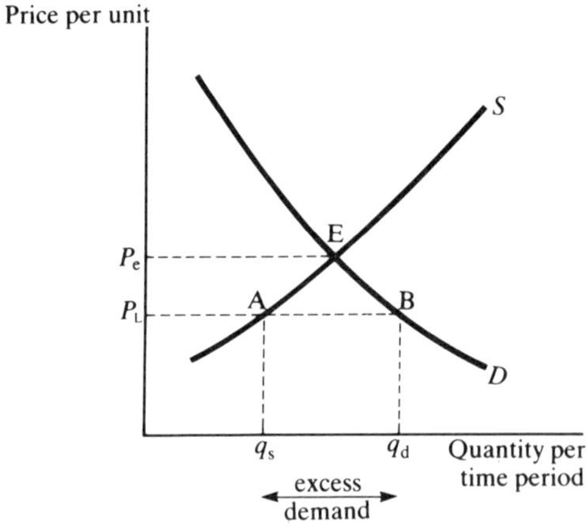

Fig. 4.4

4.2 Shifts in supply

If we continue to think in terms of perfectly competitive markets we can analyse the effect on market price of shifts in the supply curve. As we shall show in Chapter 5, the industry supply curve will depend upon the costs (both production and selling costs) of the firms in the industry. A reduction in costs will cause the industry supply curve to shift to the right, indicating that more will be supplied than previously at each price. Similarly, an increase in costs causes the supply curve to shift to the left. This is shown in Fig. 4.5 as a shift from curve S to curve S'. As a result of the shift in supply, excess demand will emerge at the old equilibrium price and the existence of this excess demand will drive up the price to a new equilibrium.

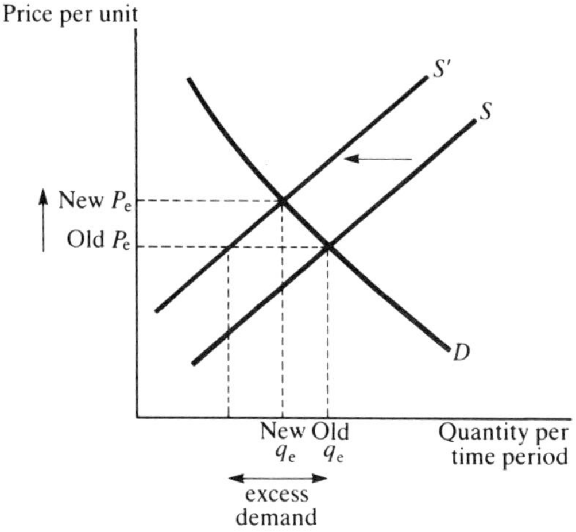

Fig. 4.5

The quantity traded also falls. Thus the market moves from one equilibrium position (old P_e, old q_e) to a new equilibrium (new P_e, new q_e).

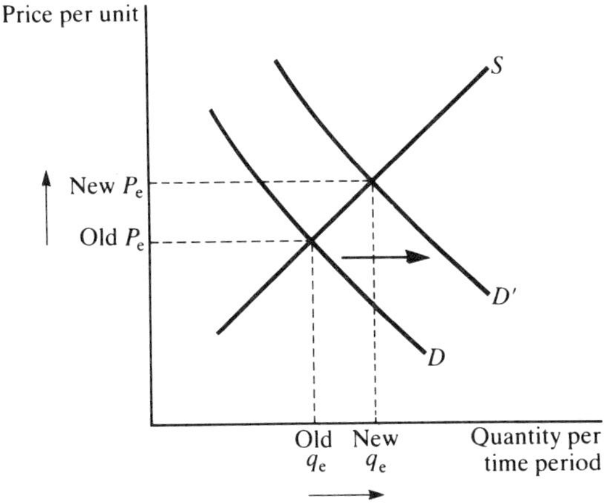

Fig. 4.6

The effect of shifts in demand can be analysed in a similar manner. In Fig. 2.2 on page 7 we showed that the effect of an increase in the price of a substitute would be to make the demand curve shift to the right. As Fig. 4.6 shows, this will result in an increase in market price and an increase in the quantity traded.

4.3 Elasticity of supply

In section 2.2 we introduced the concept of elasticity – the responsiveness of one variable to changes in another. The own-price elasticity of supply is defined as:

$$e_s = \frac{\text{percentage change in quantity supplied}}{\text{percentage change in price}}$$

If supply is elastic, therefore, this means that a relatively small change in price will result in a relatively large change in the quantity supplied. On the other hand, if supply is inelastic it will be relatively unresponsive to price changes. Obviously, supply elasticities are positive, an increase in price leading to an increase in supply and a fall in price leading to a fall in supply.

4.4 Price in non-competitive markets

Strictly speaking, industry supply curves such as those shown in Figs. 4.1 to 4.6 only make sense in the context of perfectly competitive markets where firms are price takers. In markets where a degree of monopoly exists (that is, in all markets other than perfectly competitive ones) we can no longer talk about market price since prices are set by sellers. We shall use the term *administered price* to distinguish this situation from the competitive situation for which we reserve the term market prices. Administered pricing will be analysed in detail in Chapter 8.

There is, however, a less rigorous and more general sense in which to interpret Figs 4.2 to 4.6 This interpretation is that in all markets, regardless of market structure, the price of a particular good or service will depend upon relative scarcity, that is, how much buyers are prepared to pay relative to how much sellers are prepared to accept. In other words, there exists a market clearing equilibrium price which is determined by demand and supply. This proposition is, in a fundamental sense, correct but it is too general and non-specific to take us very far in analysing real-world situations. Moreover, it tends to obscure certain aspects which may be important features of the real world. For example, price may be administered (as it is in non-competitive markets) and any excess demand or supply may be eliminated by quantity adjustments rather than price adjustments.

We have also ignored the possibility of trading taking place at prices other than equilibrium prices, a possibility we explore in the following section.

4.5 The stability of equilibrium

We have assumed up to this point that equilibrium prices are stable equilibria in the sense that the actual market price automatically tends to move towards the equilibrium price. In certain markets, however, for reasons explained below, prices tend to be rather unstable, oscillating from a high price to a low price but never converging on an equilibrium. The markets for certain agricultural products exhibit this tendency, the market for pig meat being a well-documented example.

The market for pigs is fairly competitive on the supply side, though becoming less so as factory-farming methods become increasingly more common with the decline in the number of producers and the increase in the average size of pig unit. In pig production there is a biologically determined production period of a more or less fixed length which means that supply reacts to price changes only after a time lag. In addition, farmers have historically responded to price information in a rather naive way, not realizing that high prices which encourage lots of farmers to move into pig production will, after a certain time lag, lead to a glut of pig meat and hence a slump in pig prices. These two factors can produce cycles in pig prices such as that illustrated in Fig. 4.7.

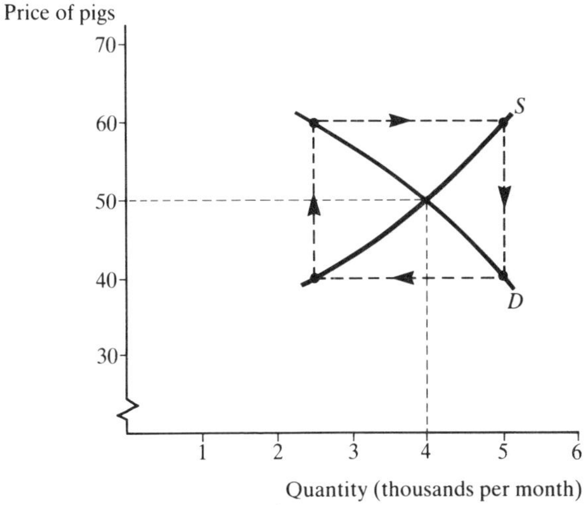

Fig. 4.7

Suppose the initial equilibrium price of £50 is disturbed by some random shock – perhaps an outbreak of foot-and-mouth disease – which causes the quantity supplied to fall from 4000 to 2500. The price immediately jumps to £60 per pig and this encourages more farmers to move into pig production. After a time lag, supply therefore expands to 5000 but the market will only absorb this amount if prices drop to £40 per pig. This causes some producers to switch away from pig production, and after a time lag output therefore drops to 2500, and the cycle starts all over again.

4.6 Market prices and administered prices

In competitive markets, where price is determined by the market forces of demand and supply, prices often fluctuate much more than they do in those markets where prices are administered by firms. That is, markets where firms are price makers will exhibit more price stability than markets where firms are price takers.

Compare, for example, the market for cadmium with that for

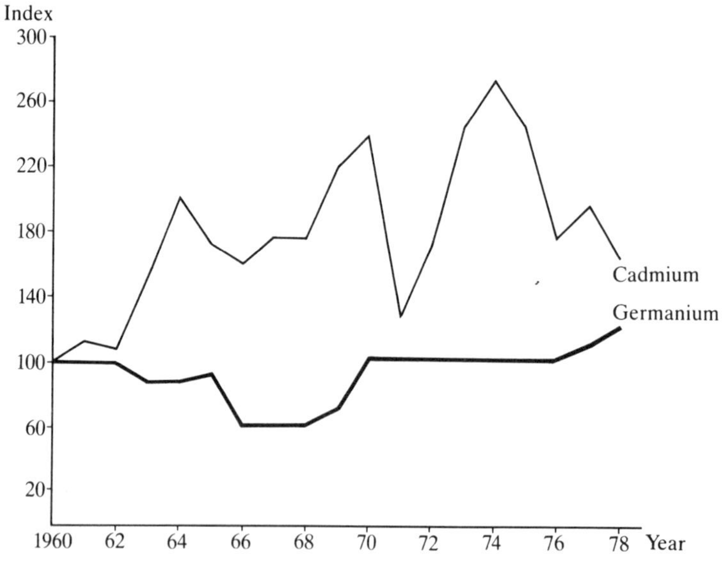

Fig. 4.8 Price-relative index for cadmium and germanium

Source: T. Wilkinson 'The economics of mineral byproducts and co-products, *Economics*, Autumn 1983, p. 85.

germanium. Both metals are in fact produced as by-products in the production of other metals but supply conditions are very different in the two cases. Cadmium is a by-product of zinc production which is fairly widely diffused among a number of firms. Hence the supply of zinc is fairly competitive, with no single producer or group of manufacturers being in a position to control the market. It follows therefore that the market for cadmium is also competitive with each firm being a price taker.

In contrast, the market for germanium is a producer-controlled oligopoly. There are only thirteen producers worldwide, five of whom produced 78 per cent of total world output in 1977/78. The producers of germanium would therefore be in a much better position to control germanium prices than the cadmium producers who would have to accept passively the market prices. Fig. 4.8 shows this to be the case. In the competitive industry (cadmium) prices fluctuated in response to changes in demand brought about by changes in worldwide economic activity. In the oligopolistic market (germanium) producers achieved a much greater degree of price stability over the period.

4.7 When is a market not a market?

Why should there be greater price stability in producer-controlled markets than in competitive markets? There are two possible explanations. The first is that in producer-controlled markets the market is brought to equilibrium by movements in quantity rather than by movements in price. That is, producers affect and control the market price by restricting supply when prices are tending to fall and by expanding supply when prices are tending to rise. The second explanation is rather different. This is that in producer-controlled markets there is *no such thing* as a market price, that is, an equilibrium price determined by the forces of demand supply. The price is simply that determined by the producer. This is clearly the case in monopolistic markets, but the same may also be true for oligopolistic markets, particularly where one producer is a dominant firm within the oligopoly. This possibility is explored in Chapter 8.

Questions

4.1 Consider the market for cocoa beans. What will be the probable effect on equilibrium price and quantity of the following?
(a) a successful advertising campaign for Cadbury's Drinking Chocolate
(b) a drought in the cocoa-producing areas
(c) an increase in the price of coffee and the introduction of a new high-yield strain of cocoa bean

4.2 For a particular week in June, three families – Smith, Jones and Brown – have the demand schedule for strawberries shown in Table 4.1. Assuming these three families comprise the whole market, calculate the market demand for strawberries and plot it on a graph. On the same graph plot the supply function using the data in column A. What are the equilibrium price and equilibrium quantity?

Table 4.1 Strawberries

Price per punnet	**Quantity demanded**			**Market demand**	**Quantity supplied**	
	Smith	**Jones**	**Brown**		**A**	**B**
35	3	5	5		8	11
40	3	5	4		9	12
45	2	4	4		10	13
50	1	4	3		15	18
55	0	3	2		20	23

Now suppose that favourable weather conditions produce a bumper crop. Growers will now be willing to sell more at each of the old prices. This causes a shift of the whole supply function. Plot this new supply function from the data in column B. What are the new equilibrium price and quantity?

4.3 Table 4.2 shows production levels and prices for oilseed rape (used in the production of margarine, etc.).

Table 4.2 Price and output of oilseed rape

	quantity harvested	**price**
1973	31	79
1974	55	172
1975	61	128
1976	111	136
1977	142	162
1978	155	182
1979	198	215
1980	300	230
1981	325	255
1982	581	270
1983	563	310

Source: *Annual Abstract of Statistics 1985*, Tables 9.4 and 18.10

Consider the validity of the following statements, amending or deleting where necessary.

(a) Over the period the percentage increase in output was much more than the percentage increase in price. Therefore the supply of this commodity is shown to be very inelastic/elastic.

(b) The easier it is to switch from growing one crop to growing another, the more elastic/inelastic will be the supply.

(c) Any estimate of the elasticity of supply is valid only if we are prepared to accept the assumption of *caveat emptor/ceteris paribus/per ardua ad astra*. In practice other things may not remain the same. For example, the price of cereals and vegetable crops may also have increased.

(d) Switching from wheat production to rape production depends on relative prices/absolute prices – that is, the price of rape relative to the price of wheat.

4.4 House prices in Ealing, West London, as elsewhere, are determined by market forces. What will be the probable effect on house prices of the following? (Assume *ceteris paribus* throughout and explain your answer.)

(a) The Building Societies adopt a more generous attitude to borrowers when granting loans for house purchase.

(b) Mortgage interest tax relief is abolished.

(c) A new motorway is built linking Ealing with Central London.

(d) The local authority relaxes planning restrictions on new housing development.

(e) House prices in Acton (near Ealing) rise.

(f) The cost of building new houses increases.

(g) Banks start to give mortgages for house purchase.

Table 4.3 Potatoes

	Price (£ per tonne)	**Land in potato production ('000s hectares)**	**Output ('00 000s tonnes)**
1973	20.7	224	68
1974	23.6	216	68
1975	56.8	204	45
1976	143.4	222	49
1977	69.9	233	66
1978	40.0	214	73
1979	58.9	204	65
1980	51.2	206	71
1981	63.3	191	62
1982	78.5	192	69
1983	85.5	195	48

Source: *Annual Abstract of Statistics 1985*, Tables 9.3, 9.4 and 18.10

4.5 Table 4.3 shows for the UK the price per tonne of potatoes, the amount of land devoted to potato production and the annual output of potatoes. Consider the extent to which the data for the mid-1970s shows evidence of a 'cobweb' type reaction in this market, similar to the pig cycle in Section 4.5.

Chapter 5
Costs

5.1 Cost concepts

'Costs', as one of my colleagues once remarked, 'is difficult'. Despite the seemingly ungrammatical nature of this remark, it illustrates that what is apparently an unambiguous and straightforward concept turns out to be much less straightforward on closer examination. To take a simple example: say one wished to know the cost of driving from London to Birmingham in order to make a comparison with the cost of doing the same journey by train. The total cost of car ownership can be broken down into three main headings:

1. *Variable costs*: that is, those costs which are directly related to distance travelled, in this case petrol and oil.
2. *Fixed costs*: those costs which are incurred whether the car is used or not, in this case insurance premiums, road tax and the depreciation in the value of the car that occurs solely on account of its ageing.
3. *Semi-fixed costs* (or semi-variable costs): the depreciation that occurs in the value of the car by virtue of use rather than ageing, for example, tyre and brake pad wear, engine wear and general mechanical deterioration.

In practice it may be quite difficult to measure what we have called semi-fixed costs and to distinguish them from truly fixed costs since the market value (that is, the second-hand value) of a car is determined almost exclusively by age rather than by distance travelled.

What then is the cost of driving from London to Birmingham? If we assume that you already have a car and a current driving licence, then there are essentially two ways of looking at the cost of such a journey. One could argue in a certain context that the only cost that should be taken into consideration is the variable cost, that is, the cost of petrol, since the other costs (fixed costs) would be borne anyway whether or not you drove to Birmingham. The *extra* cost that is incurred as a result of the trip (that is, the cost of 4 gallons of petrol, or whatever) is normally termed the *marginal cost* of making the trip. It is the increase in the total costs of car ownership which results from making the journey.

On the other hand, one could argue, in a different context, that the real cost of driving from London to Birmingham is seriously underestimated if one only takes into account the marginal cost of the journey. If, for example, one is contemplating buying a car in order to make this journey every week for a year, and one wishes to compare the annual cost of travelling by car with the annual cost of doing the same number of journeys by train then, for a valid comparison to be made, the cost of travelling by car should include some, if not all, of the fixed costs. Since these fixed costs constitute a substantial part of the total cost of car ownership this will clearly materially affect one's assessment of the relative cost of travelling by car as opposed to rail. In this context the relevant cost is not the marginal cost but rather the average cost of doing the journey, that is, the total annual cost divided by the number of journeys.

Clearly, therefore, the context in which one is assessing the costs will determine what should be included and what should be excluded. The first context we considered – in which the fixed costs would be borne irrespective of whether the car was used for the trip or not – we will term the *short-run* context. The short run, in economics, is defined as a situation in which there are fixed factors. In this case, the car is a fixed factor. On the other hand, the second context we considered in which one was contemplating the purchase of a car in order to make repeated journeys, we will call the *long-run* context because here there are no fixed factors.

It is very important to note that the terms 'long run' and 'short run' do not refer to time periods. They refer only to the fixity or non-fixity of factors. The long run can, in fact, be extremely short in terms of time. Consider the situation where you are contemplating making a single trip to Birmingham but you do not own a car. The cost of driving to Birmingham then is the cost of petrol plus the cost of hiring a car for a day. Is this a short-run or a long-run context? Well, in terms of our definition (which is the standard definition) this is a long-run context because there are no fixed factors. In this long-run context, however, the marginal cost of the trip will be much higher than it would have been if you already owned a car – that is, the long-run marginal cost will be much higher than the short-run marginal cost.

The concept of marginal cost (along with similar concepts such as marginal revenue) is central to traditional neo-classical analysis, yet, initially it can be a difficult concept to grasp. Marginal cost is the increase in total cost which results from the additional activity being considered. It is not the same as variable cost (though it is similar). Nor is it the same as short-run cost because the short run is a *context* within which various cost concepts are considered. We shall go on in section 5.2 to explain the concept more formally. Table 5.1 may also help to summarize what we have said so far.

Table 5.1 Cost concepts

Context	**Example**	**Relevant cost**	**Features**
Short run	Single trip to Birmingham (already owns car)	Extra cost incurred, i.e. marginal cost. Short-run marginal cost is cost of petrol	Fixed factor, i.e. the car
Long run	Weekly trip to Birmingham for one year	Average cost over 12 months, i.e. total cost divided by number of trips	No fixed factors, i.e. can decide whether or not to buy car and, if so, what type
Long run	Single trip to Birmingham (but has to hire car)	Extra cost incurred, i.e. marginal cost. LRMC more than SRMC	Defined as being a long-run situation because there are no fixed factors
Very long run	Repeated trips to Birmingham (but has to learn to drive first)	Average cost	All factors variable including 'technology' (that is, the skill with which you use those factors). When you have done it once it becomes easier to repeat it. 'Learning effect'

Note that for the sake of completeness we have included in Table 5.1 yet another context in which we could assess costs. This we call the *very long run*. This corresponds to a situation in which not only are there no fixed factors but also 'technology', that is, the skill with which you use those factors, is also variable. Without straining the analogy too much it could, for example, correspond to a situation in which one has neither car nor driving licence, yet one is contemplating the cost of repeated trips by car as opposed to rail. A valid comparison would therefore have to take account of the additional cost of acquiring a driving licence. Once this has been acquired, however, we move from a very long-run context to a different context. This is known as a 'learning effect' and will be explained in section 5.6. In sections 5.2, 5.3 and 5.4 we shall look at cost in a short-run context. In section 5.5 we move to the long run and in section 5.6 we consider learning effects.

5.2 The variation of costs with output in the short run: the special case

What we shall do initially is to describe a special case to illustrate how unit costs (average costs) may vary as output varies in the short run. In the following section we explain the technical relationship between the various cost concepts and then, in section 5.4, consider a more usual example of how unit costs vary with output in the short run.

The special case is taken from the shipping industry and the context we shall consider is a short-run context in which the only variable factor is the amount of fuel used. The rate at which fuel is burnt, of course, determines how fast the ship steams. All other factors – depreciation of the vessel, insurance, crew's wages, and so on – are fixed. So these are fixed costs which remain the same regardless of the speed at which the ship steams. The faster the ship steams therefore, the more these fixed costs can be spread. The 'output' being produced in this example is a service – the transportation of cargo. Output is measured in tonne-kilometres transported and one unit of output is one tonne of cargo transported one kilometre. If the ship steams faster it will therefore be increasing output since it will cover a greater distance in a given time. Since this allows the fixed costs to be spread more thinly, we can say that average total costs (or unit costs) are falling as output increases. This

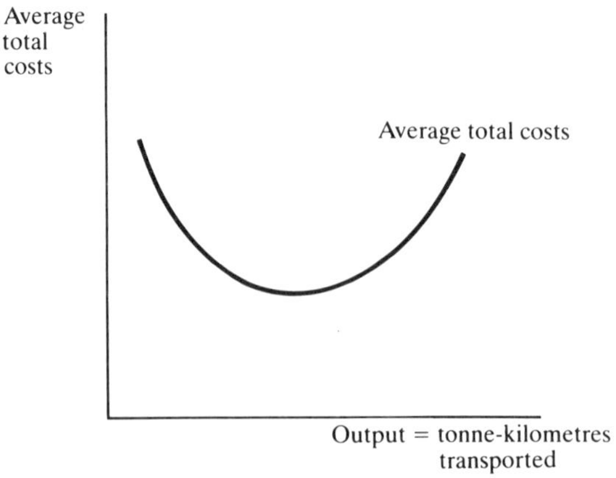

Fig. 5.1

explains the downward sloping part of the average total cost curve, shown in Fig. 5.1.

However, Fig. 5.1 shows that average total costs do not decline continuously as output increases. Rather, they begin to level off after a certain while and then start to increase. That is, in this special case, the short-run average total cost curve is U-shaped. The reason why average costs start to increase beyond a certain point is because the speed of the ship is not linearly related to the amount of fuel used. For example, steaming at 14 knots requires more than twice as much fuel as steaming at 7 knots. In fact there is a sort of 'cube law' governing the relationship between speed and fuel used: the fuel used is proportional to the cube of the speed,

$$F = kS^3$$

A similar physical law applies to the speed at which a car is driven and the amount of fuel used: driving at 60 mph takes more than twice as much petrol as driving at 30 mph, and the reasons are similar in both cases. Water resistance (in the case of the ship) and wind resistance (in the case of the car) is related to speed in a non-linear fashion.

This explains why, beyond a certain point, average costs start to increase as shown in Fig. 5.1. At fairly low speeds the increased fuel cost resulting from faster steaming is more than offset by the cost reduction resulting from spreading the fixed costs more thinly. Thus, as output increases, average total cost falls. However, because of the 'cube law' alluded to above, at higher speeds the increased fuel costs resulting from faster steaming more than outweigh the benefits of spreading fixed costs. The resultant short-run average total cost curve is U-shaped.

5.3 The technical relationship between average cost and marginal cost

This section illustrates graphically the relationship between the various cost concepts. Though useful, it is not essential to an understanding of subsequent sections and could be omitted by those readers wishing to avoid the more technical aspects of the subject. They should proceed to section 5.5.

With a U-shaped average cost curve such as that shown in Fig. 5.1 there exists a technical relationship between total costs, average total costs and marginal costs which owes more to the laws of mathematics than to economic laws (if, indeed, there be any). This is illustrated in Figs. 5.2a and 5.2b. Note that both figures have the same horizontal scale (output) but the vertical scales are different. We have put an (arbitrary) scale on the vertical axes to emphasize this. Fig. 5.2a shows the relationship between average costs (SRATC; short-run average total costs) and marginal cost (MC). Marginal cost is equal to average cost at one and only one point, namely where average cost is neither rising nor falling (that is, at the bottom of the U-shaped curve). The marginal cost curve cuts the average cost curve from below at its lowest point.

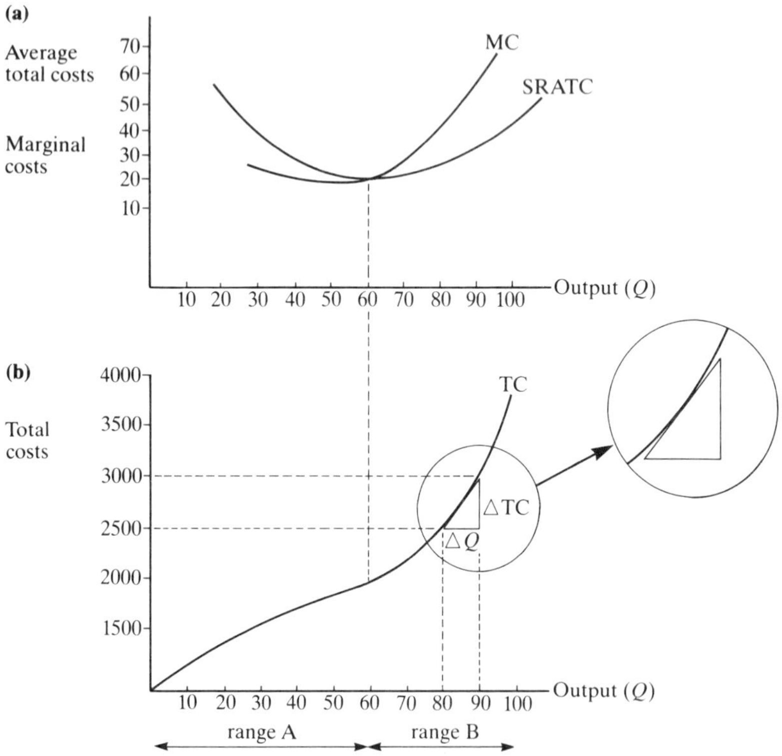

Fig. 5.2 (a), (b)

To appreciate why this should be so, consider an analogous example, namely that of a football team whose average height is six foot. If an extra player comes along (the marginal player) whose height is 6ft 1in. then the average height of the expanded team must rise. Thus if 'marginal' is greater than 'average' then 'average' is rising. Similarly, if the new player is only 5ft 11in. then the average height of the team will fall. Thus, if 'marginal' is less than 'average' then 'average' is falling.

By looking at this in reverse it is clear that if the average is falling then 'marginal' must be less than 'average' and if the average is rising then 'marginal' must be greater than average. As with the football team, so with the cost curves shown in Fig. 5.2a. And, of course, if the extra player's height is exactly 6ft then the average height of the team will not change (that is, marginal and average are equal when the average is not changing).

Figure 5.2b shows how total costs (TC) rise as output rises. The slope of the total cost curve in fact measures marginal cost. To see why this should be so, consider what happens as output rises from 80 to 90 units. (This change in output is marked as ΔQ on the inset diagram). As can be seen, costs rise by 500 (ΔTC = 500).

Thus:

$$\frac{\Delta \text{TC}}{\Delta Q} = \frac{500}{10}$$

This is the change in total costs that results from producing 10 more units of output. Stricly speaking, marginal cost is the change in total costs that results when output increases by a very small amount. As the inset in Fig. 5.2b emphasizes, ΔTC/ΔQ only measures this approximately since with the slope of TC changing the triangle is only tangent to the TC curve at one point. If we make ΔQ small, however (say one unit), then ΔTC will be 50. That is, at this level of output marginal cost is approximately equal to 50 (as can be seen from Fig. 5.2a).

We have drawn Fig. 5.2 so that the slope of TC (that is, MC) falls into two distinct regions. In range A total cost is increasing at a decreasing rate (that is, the slope of TC is decreasing). Hence MC is decreasing. In range B the slope of TC is increasing; hence MC is increasing.

5.4 The variation of costs with output in the short run: the normal case

In section 5.2 we showed how the short run average cost curve would be U-shaped. We emphasized, however, that this was a special case. A more normal short run situation would be one in which average costs stay constant over a range of output before eventually starting to increase. This is illustrated in Fig. 5.3.

Given the relationship between average cost and marginal cost explained in section 5.3, it follows that if average cost is constant then it will equal marginal cost, that is, between output levels A and B marginal cost and average cost are the same, as illustrated in Fig 5.3.

At output levels beyond B, average costs are shown to rise. The reason for this is that we are illustrating a short-run situation, that is, one in which there are fixed factors of production. It is obvious that if more and more units of the variable factor are applied in a situation in which other factors are fixed then, eventually, the returns to this variable factor will start to diminish. For example, suppose in the manufacture of a particular product, the fixed factors are considered

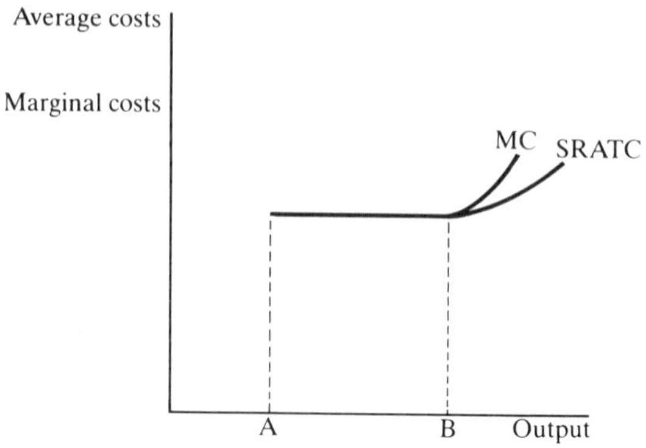

Fig. 5.3

as the floor space in the factory and the machines within it, and the variable factor is the amount of labour employed. If the amount of labour employed increases there is some scope for increasing output without increasing unit costs. Beyond a certain level of output, however, average costs will start to rise because the combination of factors (labour, machines, floor space) is non-optimal. In practice the range of output over which short-run average costs are constant may be quite small because many production processes are characterized by *fixed factor proportions*. For example, say a capstan lathe requires a single operator. The employment of a second operator to take over when the first has a break would probably raise output a little but would add a lot to the costs. Thus average costs would rise sharply. Obviously, with a given technology, in this situation only one combination of factors is sensible (one operative to each machine).

The short-run situation is in fact a very restricted context. In general, the long-run context in which the number and type of machines, the number of men and even the size and number of factories can be varied is a more valid and interesting context in which to investigate the variation of costs with output. This is discussed in the following section.

5.5 The variation of cost with output in the long run

Once all the factors are variable there is no reason to suppose that an increase in output will produce an increase in average costs. Thus the long-run average cost (LRAC) curve in most industries would be downward sloping or horizontal, as in Fig. 5.4.

If increased output results in lower unit costs, we say that there are *economies of scale*. Scale economies, or *returns to scale*, are

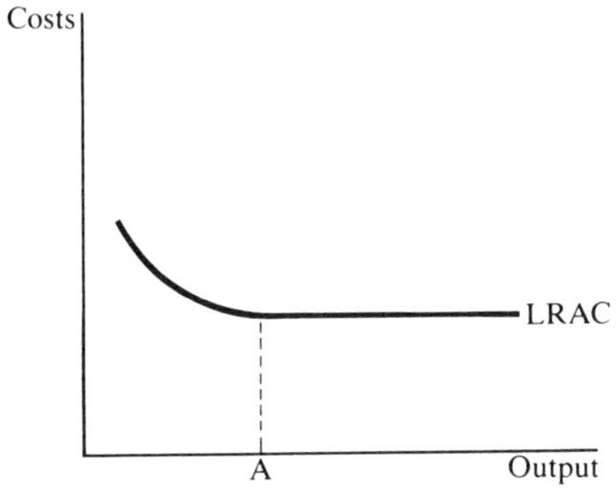

Fig. 5.4

almost universally present. For example, to build a double garage is not twice as expensive as building a single garage. Running a double-decker bus is cheaper than running two single deckers. Two can live as cheaply as one (almost). It may be, however, that beyond a certain level of output all the benefits of economies of scale have been reaped. Beyond this point the long-run average cost curve becomes horizontal. Figure 5.4 illustrates a situation in which there are economies of scale up to point A. Beyond point A there are constant returns to scale.

The level of output labelled A in Fig. 5.4 would be called the *minimum efficient scale* (MES) or *minimum efficient plant size* (MEPS) because firms or plants operating below this level of output are too small to reap all the benefits of economies of scale. One should be careful to distinguish firm size from plant size, since a large firm may, for example, operate a number of small production units. Firm size in itself may confer benefits but these tend to be *financial* economies of scale rather than *technical* economies of scale. For example, by virtue of its size, the large firm may be able to borrow more cheaply or buy its raw materials more cheaply because its buying power enables it to exert influence over suppliers. Unlike technical economies, which benefit society as a whole, these financial economies benefit the firm at the expense of other sections of society. Whereas technical economies of scale may provide a valid justification for the existence of large firms, often with monopoly power, financial economies do not.

Estimates of the MEPS are available for a number of industries and these are shown in Table 5.2. These are so-called 'engineering type' estimates since they attempt to estimate costs which could be achieved in plants of various sizes using the best technology currently available. Note from Table 5.2 that in some industries, for example bread, the MEPS is quite small, or rather it is a relatively small

Table 5.2 Some engineering-type estimates of minimum efficient plant size (MEPS)*

Product	Estimates of MEPS	UK produced sales of product in 1973	MEPS as % of UK produced sales
Bread	30 sacks/hr 12–18 sacks/hr.	2.2 m. tonnes (17.3 m. sacks)	About 1 About 0.5
Potato crisps	30 000–35 000 t.p.a.		About 10
Beer	1 m. bls p.a. 4.5 m. bls p.a. 1–1.5 m. bls p.a. 600 000 bls p.a.	35 m. bls	About 3 About 13 3–4 About 2
Cigarettes	36 bn cigarettes p.a.	276 m. lb (approx: 170 bn cigarettes)	21
Oil refining	10 m. t.p.a.	114 m. tonnes (crude input)	9
	10 m. t.p.a. (200 000 bls per day)		9
	5 m. t.p.a.		4
Sulphuric acid	1 m. t.p.a.	3.9 m. tonnes (production	26
Ethylene	300 000 t.p.a.	887 000 tonnes	34
Soap	10 000 t.p.a.	240 000 tonnes	4
Detergent powder	70 000 t.p.a.	342 000 tonnes	20
Ammonium nitrate	300 000–350 000 t.p.a.	About 1.12 m. tonnes (379 227 tonnes nitrogen)	27–31
Steel	2–3 m. t.p.a.	About 24 m. tonnes (production)	8–12
	4–9 m. t.p.a. 4 m. t.p.a.		17–37 17
Pig iron	2–3 m. t.p.a. from blast furnaces	About 15 m. tonnes (production)	13–20
Aluminium	200 000 t.p.a.	550 000 t.p.a.	36
Semi-manufactures			
Diesel engines (industrial)	100 000 units (engines of 1–100 b.h.p.)	179 000 units	56
Electronic calculators	3–4 m. units	About 0.5 m. units (?)	Probably well over 100
Turbo-generators	6000 MW p.a. 8–10 000 MW p.a.	5000 MW approx.	120 160–200
TV tubes	750 000 p.a.	n.a.	Around 100
White goods	500 000 units	About 2.5 m. units	20
Electric cookers	300 000 units	1.04 m. units	30
Electric refrigerators	250 000–500 000 units 800 000 units	1.13 m. units	22–43 69

Table 5.2 continued

Product	Estimates of MEPS	UK produced sales of product in 1973	MEPS as % of UK produced sales
Automobile storage batteries	1 m. units	About 7 m. units (?)	14
Tractors	90 000 units p.a.	119 000 units	76
Motor cars	0.5–1 m. units p.a.	1.75 m. units	29–57
Commercial vehicles	20–30 000 units p.a.	416 000 units	5–7
Clutch mechanisms	300 000 p.a.	About 2.5 m. units (?)	12
Bicycles	160 000 units p.a.	2 m. units	8
Aircraft	'Substantial economies of scale are available'	2 m. units	At least 100 (?)
Synthetic fibres	80 000 tones p.a. polymer manufacture 40 000 tonnes p.a. extruded filament yarn	454 000 tonnes (production)	18
Cotton and synthetic textiles	37.5 m. sq.yd (288 Sulzer looms) 1000 conventional looms	771 m. sq. metres (production)	6
Shoes	300 000 pairs p.a. 1 m. pairs p.a. 1200 pairs/day	189 m. pairs	0.2 0.5 0.2
Building bricks	25 m. p.a. 50–62.5 m. p.a.	7000 m. bricks (5580 m. ?)	0.4 0.7–0.9
Cement	200 000 t.p.a. (kiln capacity) 2 m. t.p.a. 1.2 m. t.p.a.	17.8 m. tonnes	1 11 7
Plasterboard	18–20 m. sq.metres	104 m. sq.metres	17–19
Rubber tyres	5000 tyres/day	30.3 m. tyres (car and van)	About 6
Rubber contraceptive sheaths	500 000 gross p.a.	About 1 m. gross	About 50

*For several of the products listed more than one estimate is given.
Source: The Monopolies and Mergers Commission Green Paper, 1978. *A Review of Monopolies and Mergers Policy*. A Consultative Document. HMSO, 1978, Annex C, p. 87.

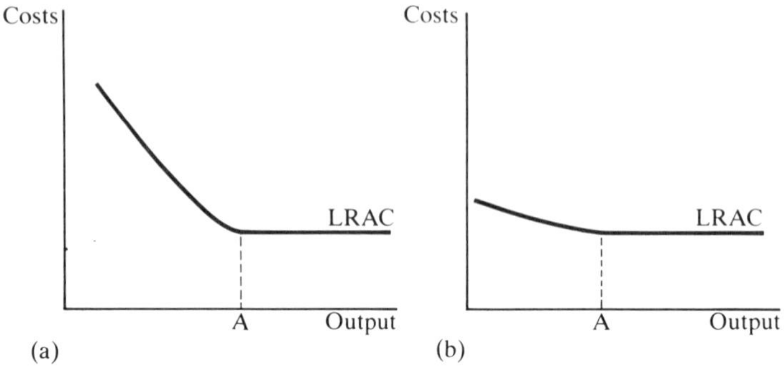

Fig. 5.5

proportion of the total UK produced sales. In other industries however, the MEPS is a large proportion of UK produced sales. In ethylene production, for example, the MEPS represented over one-third of total UK produced sales.

In assessing the benefits of large size, one must take into account not only the estimated MEPS but also the cost penalty incurred from operating below this MEPS. For example, any firm operating in an industry with the cost conditions illustrated in Fig. 5.5a would be at a clear disadvantage if its plant size were less than that producing

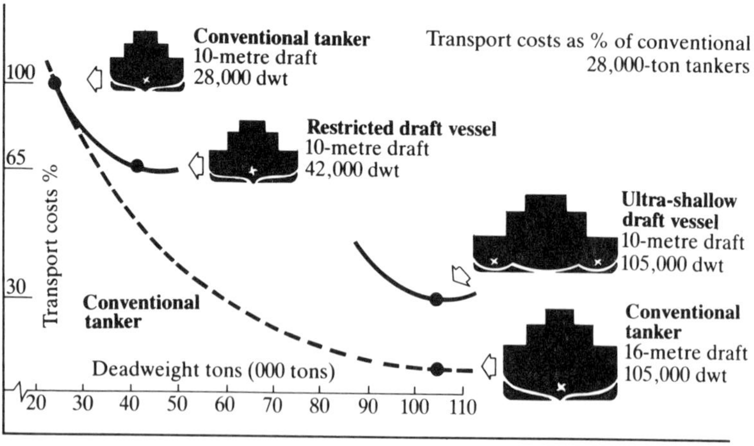

Fig. 5.6 Transport costs as percentage of conventional 28 000 ton tankers

(Source: *The Economist* 20 Feb. 1982)

output level A. In Fig. 5.5b however, although the MEPS is the same, the cost penalty for operating below it is minimal.

There may be some instances in which the MES is so large that it may be difficult to operate at such a scale. An example of this is provided by the tanker industry. Other things being equal, the larger the tanker, the lower the unit costs of transporting crude oil. This is illustrated in Fig. 5.6, where the dotted line shows the LRAC curve of conventional tankers. Unfortunately, when conventional tankers become very large their increased draught prevents them from entering shallow ports and this tends to restrict their usefulness. As can be seen from Fig. 5.6, a compromise solution is the proposed ultra-shallow draft vessel (USDV) which is as large as a conventional supertanker but being much wider has a smaller draught. The costs per ton of oil transported of such a vessel would be higher than a conventional supertanker but much lower than conventional small tankers, and it would be able to enter ports previously restricted to small vessels.

5.6 Learning effects

Large firms may have significant cost advantages over small firms not just because of the current scale of their activities, but also because of the accumulated experience they have in a particular industry. This experience can only be gained by operating in the industry and it gives rise to what is known as *learning by doing*. Such learning effects produce cost savings, the magnitude of which is well documented in a number of studies. So-called learning curves have been drawn up for a number of different industries and three examples are shown in Figs. 5.7, 5.8 and 5.9.

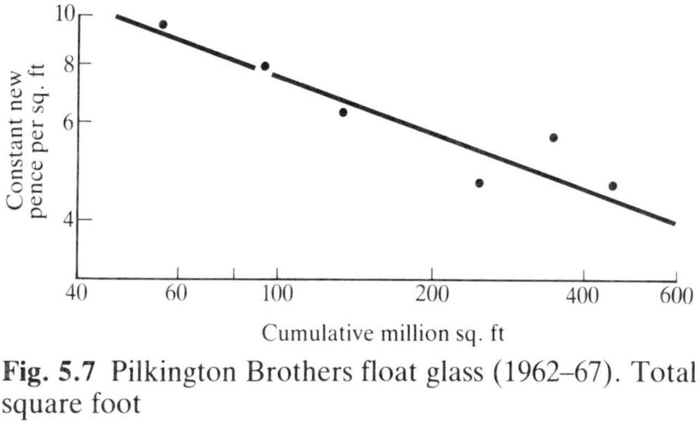

Fig. 5.7 Pilkington Brothers float glass (1962–67). Total cost per square foot

(Source: The Monopolies and Mergers Commission Green Paper, 1978, *A Review of Monopolies and Mergers Policy*)

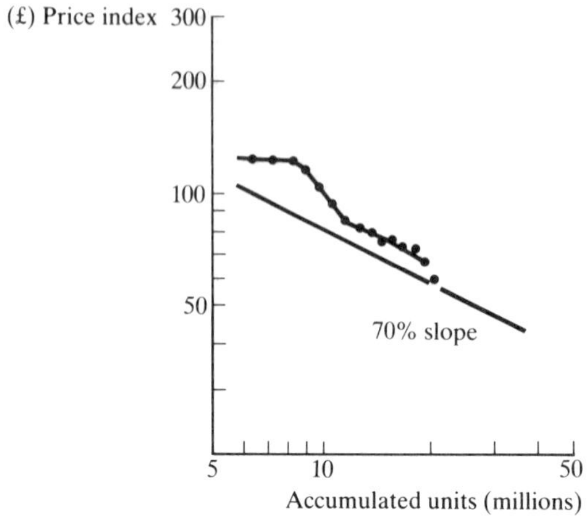

Fig. 5.8 Refrigerators UK, 1957–71 (Source: The Monopolies and Mergers Commission Green Paper, 1978, *A Review of Monopolies and Mergers Policy*)

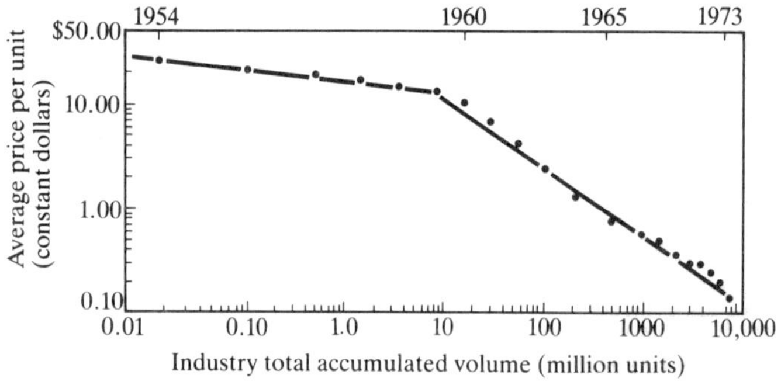

Fig. 5.9 US silicon transistors (Source: The Monopolies and Mergers Commission Green Paper, 1978, *A Review of Monopolies and Mergers Policy*)

Note that unlike the LRAC curves of Figs. 5.4 and 5.5 which measure the current scale of output on the horizontal axis, the learning curves of Figs. 5.7–5.9 relate unit costs to *accumulated* output.

Accumulated experience and scale tend to go hand in hand of course, the one reinforcing the other so that large firms have a cost advantage by virtue of the large scale of their plants, but the ability to design and run such plants in a cost-effective way only comes with experience. Fig. 5.10 shows the combined effects of scale and experience in the manufacture of a plastic resin. The learning effect is embodied in the acquired technology necessary to construct and run larger plants.

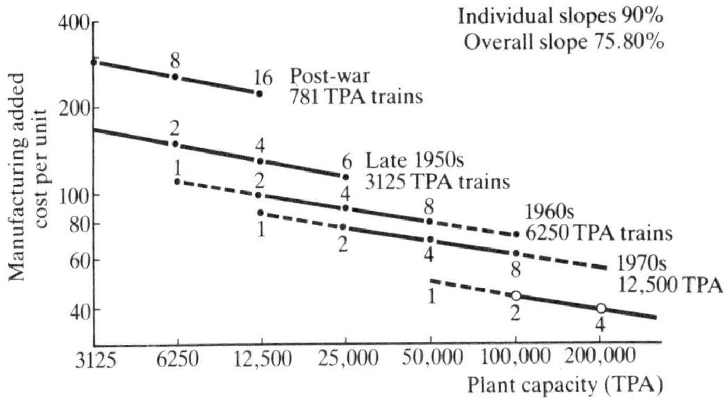

Fig. 5.10 Scale evolution over time – A plastic resin

(Source: The Monopolies and Mergers Commission Green Paper, 1978, *A Review of Monopolies and Mergers Policy*)

Fig. 5.10 is very much a hybrid. It illustrates the short-run, the long-run and the very-long run contexts which we considered at the beginning of this chapter. At any particular time, for example in the late 1950s, with a given plant size we are in a short-run situation since we have a fixed factor (the size of the plant). Even with a given plant size, however (for example, the 3125 TPA trains typical in the late 1950s), cost reductions can be achieved by operating the plant at a higher level of capacity utilization (each of the short-run average cost curves is downward sloping). However, for a given plant capacity (measured along the bottom axis), for example, 12 500 TPA, experience enables it to be run more efficiently. For example, the four firms operating plants of this size in the 1950s had average costs of 140p per unit whereas the single firm operating a plant of this size in the 1970s had average costs of 90p per unit. This is the effect of learning. Learning also enables bigger plants to be built, and this is the effect of scale.

5.7 A case study on costs: the motor industry

Some of the cost concepts we have introduced in this chapter will be illustrated in this section in the context of the British and European motor industries. The data is drawn from a variety of sources but the reader should be reminded that data on costs is no more reliable –

and in some cases may be less reliable – than data in the social sciences generally. It is not so much the case that, as Disraeli claimed, 'there are lies, damned lies and statistics'; rather the reader should try to develop *respect for the data*, a respect which is only gained by a careful consideration of how the data involved could have been collected and what it is intended to show. For example, many studies of minimum efficient plant size cite the pioneering but now somewhat dated work of Pratten whose estimates of the variation of costs with output were of the 'engineering' type. That is, they were not based on the costs of plants actually in existence but, rather, they were based on the estimates of engineers, skilled in their particular field, of the costs of operating plants of various sizes. Figure 5.11, adapted from the evidence presented by Pratten, shows the cost advantages enjoyed by the larger firms in the motor industry. As can be seen, severe cost penalties would be incurred by firms producing less than 500 000 units per year. A firm producing only 100 000 units, for example, would have average costs some 25 per cent higher than one producing 500 000 units. Beyond this level, however, the

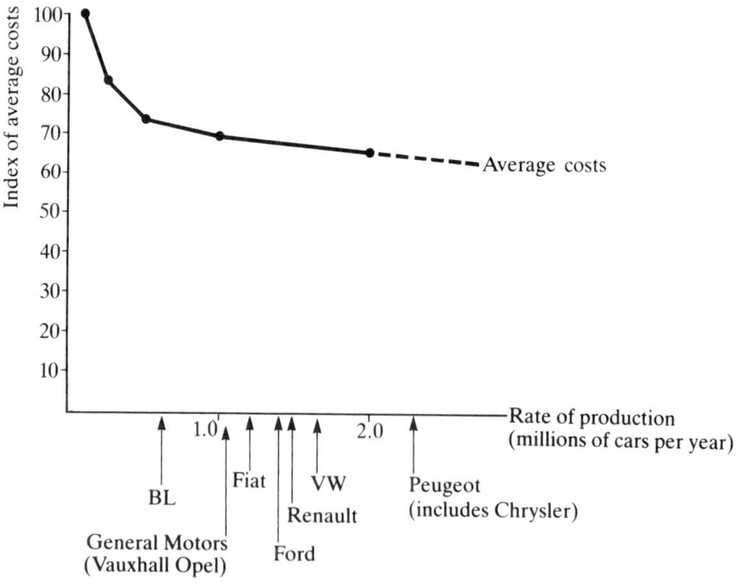

Fig. 5.11 Economics of scale in the European car industry 1978

(Sources: Cost data derived from Pratten's (1971) estimates cited by D. G. Rhys in P. S. Johnson, *The Structure of British Industry*, Granada, 1980. Volume figures for individual manufacturers which relate to 1978, are derived from D. T. Jones, *Industrial Adjustment and Policy; I. Maturity and Crisis in the European Car Industry: structural change and public policy*, Sussex European Research Centre, 1981

cost advantages of large-scale production are not so marked. Figure 5.11 also shows the production levels achieved by the major European producers in 1978. Note that Fig. 5.11 should not be interpreted as conclusive evidence that Peugeot, the largest producer, does have lower costs as a result of scale economies than BL, the smallest producer. Pratten's engineering estimates coupled with the data on production levels are nevertheless suggestive of this conclusion.

The total number of cars produced by a particular manufacturer may however be a poor indicator of the potential for scale economies. The number of units of any particular *model* and the extent to which common components can be fitted to a number of different models should also be taken into account. This is because the volume required to achieve the potential cost reduction varies considerably from one operation to another, as Table 5.3 illustrates.

Table 5.3 Minimum efficient scale (MES) of different manufacturing operations

Manufacturing operation	MES (identical units per plant per year)
Casting of engine block	100 000
Engine and transmission machining and assembly	500 000
Final assembly	250 000

Source: *The Future of the British Car Industry*, Central Policy Review Staff. HMSO 1975, p. 16.

Note particularly from Table 5.3 that the MES of engine and transmission production is double that of final assembly, a fact which explains why manufacturers prefer to install the same basic engine in a number of different models, to collaborate with other manufacturers in the production of major components, or even to buy in major components from other manufacturers (BL, for example, uses Volkswagen gearboxes in its Maestro range).

Bearing in mind the information of Table 5.3, we can now consult Table 5.4. Note first that the first row shows the estimated capacity which in most cases is considerably less than production levels actually achieved (Fig. 5.11 shows production levels for 1978). Given the number of basic models planned (shown in the second row of Table 5.4) this produced an estimate, shown in the third row, of the potential output per model. Note that for several manufacturers this is less than, or very close to, the estimated MES of 250 000. Similarly, the fourth row shows that several manufacturers were

Table 5.4 European car producers and MES

	Chrysler	**BL**	**General Motors**	**Renault**	**Peugeot-Citroen**	**Ford**	**VW**	**Fiat**
Estimated capacity 1976–80 (millions of cars per year)	1.0	1.2	1.55	1.55	1.65	1.65	1.8	1.85
Number of basic models (planned)	3–4	4–5	4–5	8	7	5	5	6
Potential output per model (thousands)	250–330	240–300	310–388	194	236	350	360	308
Planned output per basic engine (thousands)	220–270	185–260	420	800	425	570	610	650

Source: D. G. Rhys, 'European mass producing car makers and minimum efficient scale: a note', *Journal of Industrial Economics*, June 1977, vol. XXV, Table 1

operating below the MES of 500 000 in engine production. In the third and fourth rows output levels below the MES are shown in italics.

The information presented so far explains the rush to 'rationalize' car production in the late 1970s and 1980s when a decline in the world demand for cars highlighted the exposed position of the less efficient producers. In particular it helps to explain the reasons for the successful takeover of Chrysler by Peugeot-Citroen, joint engine production by Peugeot and Renault, collaboration between BL and Honda, and a number of other joint ventures between competing firms.

The discussion so far has been about minimum efficient scale. That is, in terms of the nomenclature we introduced earlier, it has been about cost in the long run. However, in the short run, costs also vary according to capacity utilization. Table 5.5 gives estimates of the cost breakdown for the manufacture of an average car at two levels of capacity utilization, the break-even volume (that is, the minimum volume needed for total revenue to cover total costs) and the standard output level (that is, the average level of capacity utilization – about 80 per cent of maximum). Note that fixed costs include capital costs and fixed overheads and also labour, which in the modern car industry is only regarded as a variable factor in the long run. Higher levels of capacity utilization allow these fixed costs to be spread more thinly so that the cost per car produced declines as volume increases towards full capacity levels.

Table 5.5 Unit cost breakdown for an average car

<table>
<tr><th></th><th>At break-even volume (%)</th><th>At standard output (%)</th></tr>
<tr><td>Variable:</td><td></td><td></td></tr>
<tr><td>Materials</td><td>53</td><td>62</td></tr>
<tr><td>Warranty</td><td>2</td><td rowspan="2">14</td></tr>
<tr><td>Variable overheads</td><td>7</td></tr>
<tr><td>Fixed:</td><td></td><td></td></tr>
<tr><td>Direct labour</td><td>12</td><td>8</td></tr>
<tr><td>Fixed overheads</td><td>21</td><td rowspan="2">16</td></tr>
<tr><td>Capital costs</td><td>5</td></tr>
</table>

Source: D. G. Rhys, in P. S. Johnson, *The Structure of British Industry*. Granada, 1980

Questions

5.1 A firm finds that the total cost of producing 1000 units is £400. The cost of producing 1001 units is £405. Therefore marginal cost at this level of output is:
(a) £1 (b) £5 (c) £405 (d) £1000

5.2 If British Rail is running half-empty trains, what is the marginal cost of carrying extra passengers?

5.3 Which of the diagrams in Fig. 5.12 are logically incorrect?

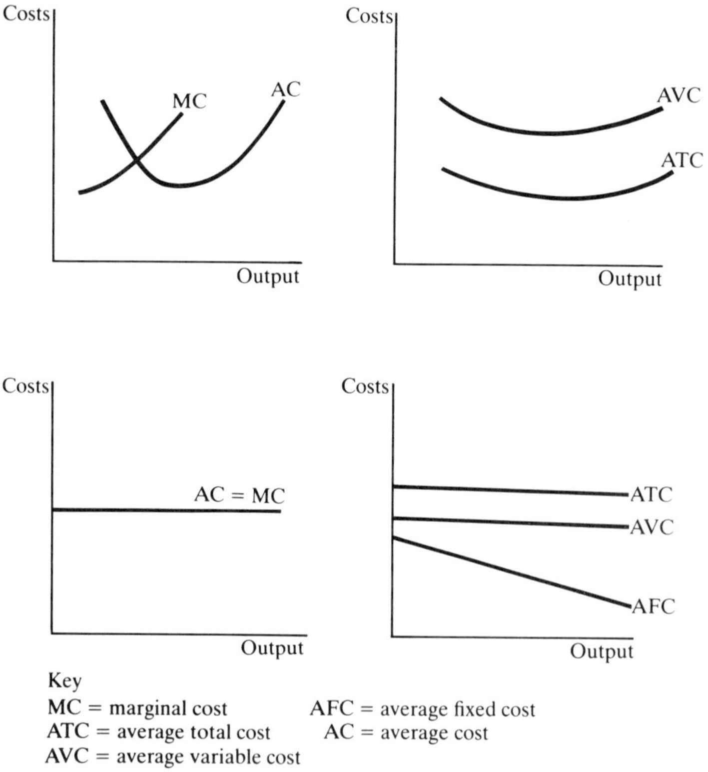

Fig. 5.12

5.4 Give examples of the following types of scale economy:
(a) technical
(b) financial
(c) managerial
(d) marketing and research and development
(e) risk bearing

Which of the above do not represent real savings of resources from society's point of view?

5.5 A seaside hotel has fixed costs of £1000 per month. During the winter it makes a loss since in addition to its fixed losses it has variable costs (heating, lighting, staffing, food) of £5000 per month, whereas its revenues from guests is only £5100 per month. Should the hotel close during the winter?

Chapter 6

Revenue, cost and profit

6.1 Elasticity and revenue

The Gotham City Transport Executive was worried. A meeting had been called to discuss the future of the city bus service which was in crisis again, as it had been every year for the past few years. The number of people using its services was dwindling and it was again unable to meet its operating costs.

Two opposing views were emerging in the Transport Executive. One view advocated an increase in fares, possibly accompanied by the excising of the unprofitable routes from the system. The other view was diametrically opposed to this.

'What we need to do' said one advocate of the opposing view, 'is to *cut* fares, not increase them. Then more people will use the City buses and our total revenue will go up. If you raise fares again it will only make matters worse and more people will switch to using their private cars and the net result will be that our fare receipts will go down. It's a cut in fares we need, not an increase.'

'With the greatest respect, Mr Chairman,' said one of the other members of the Executive, 'that is complete and utter nonsense. If we cut fares the numbers of extra passengers we shall attract onto the system will be minimal. Since all the existing passengers will be paying less than before the net result will be a fall in our revenue. Anyway, people like using their cars. It's more convenient so that even if the bus were cheaper they would still use their cars.'

'Rubbish' said the first speaker. 'For most journeys the bus is a perfectly acceptable substitute. I say cut fares and increase revenue.'

At that very moment Batman and Robin arrived in the nick of time to prevent the members of the executive coming to blows.

'Well, Caped Crusader,' said the chairman of the executive, 'What's the answer? If we want to increase our revenue should we cut fares or increase them?'

'It depends,' said Batman, 'on the elasticity of demand.' If demand for bus services is inelastic, he went on to explain, this means that it is insensitive to price changes so that an increase in fares will result in only a small drop in demand. Hence total fare receipts will rise. If, on the other hand, demand is elastic, an increase in fares will cause lots of people to switch to their cars and total fare receipts will fall.

Table 6.1 Variation of revenue in price

Q	*P*	TR	MR
0	40	0	
			36
1	36	36	
			28
2	32	64	
			20
3	28	84	
			12
4	24	96	
			4
5	20	100	
			−4
6	16	96	
			−12
7	12	84	
			−20
8	8	64	
			−28
9	4	36	
			−36
10	0	0	

Q = quantity ***P*** = price
TR = total revenue **MR** = marginal revenue

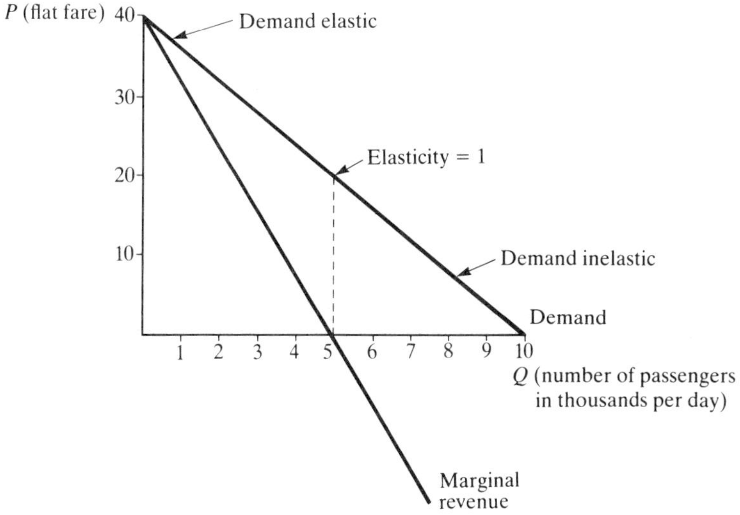

Fig. 6.1

This can be illustrated with a numerical example. Table 6.1 shows the number of passengers (*Q*) who would be prepared to travel at each of the flat fares (*P*). The data from Table 6.1 is plotted in Fig. 6.1. As can be seen, if the bus service was free ($P = 0$) then the number of passengers who would use it would be 10 (that is, ten thousand passengers per day). At the other extreme, a flat fare of 40 pence ($P = 40$) chokes off demand completely ($Q = 0$). From the data given in columns one and two of Table 6.1 we can work out the total fare receipts (total revenue) which will accrue at each price. This is shown in column three. As can be seen, revenue is maximized at a price of 20 pence, where the number of passengers will be 5000 per day. This corresponds, not coincidentally, to a point half-way down the demand curve shown in Fig. 6.1 where elasticity is equal to unity.

This can be further illustrated by considering the *marginal revenue* that results when output is increased. Marginal revenue is a concept similar to the concept of marginal cost introduced in section 5.1. It measures the change in total revenue when output is increased by a small amount (in our example this small amount is one unit of one thousand passengers). As can be seen, marginal revenue declines as output increases but as long as marginal revenue is *positive* this means that the increase in output has increased total revenue. As soon as marginal revenue becomes negative, however, this means that the increased output results in a reduction of total revenue. The data in column 4 of Table 6.1 is also plotted in Fig. 6.1 and it traces out the marginal revenue curve. As can be seen, the marginal revenue curve cuts the 'quantity' axis at $Q = 5$. At this point, marginal revenue is zero. This point on the marginal revenue curve corresponds to a point on the demand curve where price is equal to 20. This, as we saw before, is the point at which revenue is maximized.

It is worth noting a few technical details illustrated by our numerical example. Firstly, marginal revenue measures the change in revenue when output changes by a small amount. Hence, for example, we have shown marginal revenue to be equal to 36 when output increases from 0 to 1 and this can be read off from the graph ($\text{MR} = 36$ when output $= \frac{1}{2}$). Secondly, note that the marginal revenue curve cuts the quantity axis half-way along from where the demand curve cuts the axis. This is not an accidental occurrence but results from the mathematical relationship between the two curves.

Summarizing the main points:

1. If marginal revenue is positive this implies that demand is elastic and that therefore a cut in price will lead to a more than proportional increase in demand, thus increasing total revenue.
2. If marginal revenue is negative this implies that demand is inelastic and that therefore a cut in price will lead to a less than proportional increase in demand, thus decreasing total revenue.

3. Where marginal revenue is zero, elasticity is equal to unity. At this point revenue is maximized since a change in price will lead to an equal proportionate change in demand.

Thus, a firm wishing to increase, or maximize, its sales revenue has only to estimate the elasticity of demand for its product and then apply the simple rules set out above. Unfortunately, when we leave Gotham City and return to the real world we have to recognize that the problem of estimating the elasticity of demand may be inordinately difficult, for reasons sketched out in section 2.4. Often an indication of the elasticity of demand can only be obtained by trial-and-error experimentation. This yields estimates after the event which, had they been available before the event, would probably have led the firm not to undertake the experiment. For example, in 1981 London Transport cut fares on its bus and underground services by 30 per cent, anticipating that this would lead to a sizeable increase in traffic (measured by passenger–miles). However, traffic increased by only 11.5 per cent, leading to the eventual abandonment of the policy.[1]

In practice, of course, the demand curve would not be defined over its entire range as it is in Fig. 6.1. Rather an estimate of the demand curve (and hence of its elasticity) may be available for only a small range of price/output combinations near to the existing price/output combination.

6.2 Elasticity in the short run and the long run

It is also worth noting that the elasticity of demand in the short run may be less than that in the long run. Note that here we are using the terms short run and long run to refer to periods of time rather than to situations in which there are fixed factors (short run) or in which all factors are variable (long run). In a sense, however, the two definitions run together, that is, the elasticity of demand for a particular good tends to be low in the short run (time period) because of the existence of fixed factors; and higher in the long run (time period) because there are no fixed factors. Consider, for example, the elasticity of demand for petrol. An increase in price will lead to only a small drop in demand initially (that is, the elasticity of demand is low in the short run) because people's consumption patterns are to a large extent determined by their own particular circumstances. For example, if they live a long distance from their work and no public transport is available they will have no alternative but to drive to work, at least in the short run, because of the existence of the fixed factors – location of home and job and type of car. In the long run, however, they could get another job nearer their home, or move nearer to their work, or buy a smaller, more fuel-efficient car. In the still longer run of course the increased demand for fuel economy in cars will result in manufacturers developing more fuel-efficient vehicles, thereby further reducing the demand for petrol. Thus, in the long run, the elasticity of demand for petrol is lower than in the short run.

Estimates of such elasticities are of course difficult to obtain in practice because *ceteris non paribus*, that is, other factors have a nasty habit of not remaining constant. The demand for petrol will obviously be affected by income so that, over time, if incomes rise this will induce a rise in the demand for petrol which will partially or totally offset the effect of the price increase. Statistical techniques are, however, available which can separate out the effects of a price change from the effects of an income change. Thus, estimates of both price and income elasticities for both the short run and long run can be obtained. One such set of estimates is shown in Table 6.2.

Table 6.2 Elasticities of demand for petrol in the EEC

Short run	Price	−0.23
(1 year)	Income	0.53
Long run	Price	−0.75
	Income	1.73

Source: G. J. Kouris, 'Price sensitivity of petrol consumption and some policy implications', *Energy Policy*, vol. 6 No. 3, Sept. 1978

Note that, as one might expect, the demand for petrol is rather unresponsive to price changes in the short run, but rather more responsive in the long run. Even in the long run, however, demand is still price inelastic – a 10 per cent increase in price will lead to a fall in demand of only 7.5 per cent.

6.3 Profit maximization

In section 6.1 we showed how a firm would maximize its sales revenue. However, most firms take account not only of the revenue to be gained from a certain level of output but also of the costs of producing that output. Thus, profit, which is the difference between revenue and costs, will be an important consideration. In this section we shall illustrate the rule that should be applied by the firm wishing to maximize profits.

In Fig. 6.2 we take the example of a firm facing a downward-sloping demand curve for its product (that is, any firm other than a perfectly competitive firm). The associated marginal revenue curve is also shown (the relationship between the demand curve and the marginal revenue curve was explained in section 6.1). We have assumed that the cost conditions facing the firm are such that average costs remain constant over a wide range of output. Thus the average cost curve is shown as being horizontal over the relevant output levels. It is important to note that this implies that marginal cost will also be constant and equal to average cost over this same range (for reasons explained in section 5.3).

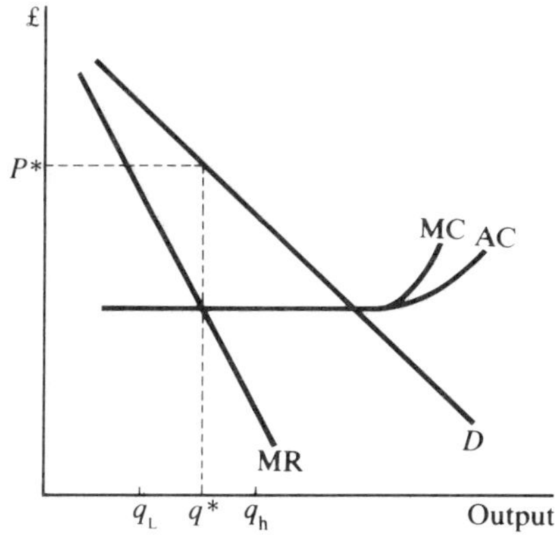

Fig. 6.2

A firm facing these demand and cost conditions has to decide two things – how much to produce and what price to charge, but the two decisions are not independent. Once the level of output has been determined, demand conditions, as summarized in the demand curve facing the firm, will determine the maximum price the market will be prepared to pay to take up this level of output.

First the firm decides on the profit-maximizing level of output. This is q^* in Fig. 6.2. At this level of output marginal cost equals marginal revenue. The reason why this level of output should yield maximum profit can be demonstrated by considering other possible output levels – a lower level of output (q_L) and a higher level of output (q_h). At q_L marginal revenue is greater than marginal cost (the MR curve is above the MC curve). This means that, if one considers a small increase in output, the resultant increase in revenue (MR) will be more than the resultant increase in cost (MC). Since revenue is increasing more than costs, profit must also be increasing. The same must be true for all levels of output below q^* – an increase in output adds more to revenue than to costs, hence increasing profits. For similar reasons, at levels of output greater than q^*, such as q_h, the opposite is true. MC is above MR, hence a *reduction* in output reduces costs more than it reduces revenue, and hence profits increase. Thus q^* is the profit-maximizing level of output.

Having decided on the level of output, the profit-maximizing firm then charges the maximum price per unit that the market will bear. This is given by the demand curve and is labelled P^*.

Fig. 6.3 illustrates the amount of profits achieved by such a firm. Profits are the difference between total revenue and total costs. The rectangle OP^*Bq^* represents total revenue since it is the price per unit (Op^*) multiplied by the number of units sold (Oq^*). Total costs are represented by the rectangle OACq^* since this is the average cost per unit (OA) multiplied by the number of units sold (Oq^*). The difference between the two – the shaded rectangle AP^*BC thus represents profits.

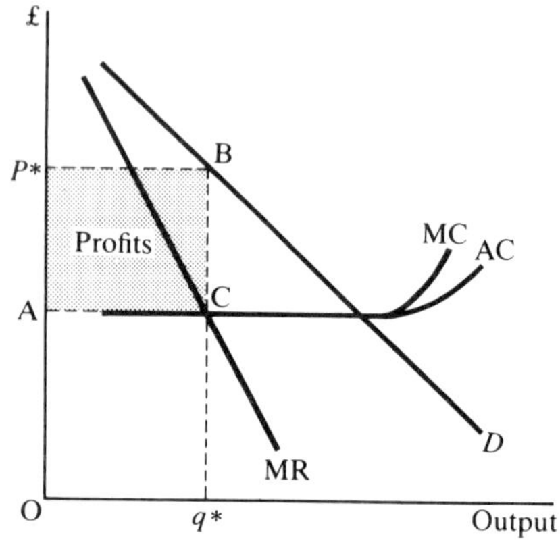

Fig. 6.3

6.4 Profit maximization in perfect competition (short run)

Unlike the monopolist and the monopolistically competitive firm, the perfectly competitive firm faces a demand curve for its product which is perfectly elastic – that is, a horizontal line. The perfectly competitive firm is a price taker. It can sell as much as it likes at the prevailing market price. This means it can sell additional units without reducing the price on all units sold. Thus marginal revenue and price are the same thing. In Fig. 6.4 therefore we show the demand curve facing the competitive firm and label it to indicate that it is equal to price, marginal revenue and, also, average revenue.

The profit-maximizing level of output for the perfectly competitive firm, like any firm, is where marginal cost and marginal revenue are equated. This level of output is only defined therefore if the marginal cost curve is upward sloping since a horizontal marginal cost curve such as that in Figs 6.2 and 6.3 would have no point of intersection with the marginal revenue curve (or an infinite number of points if MC and MR happened to coincide).

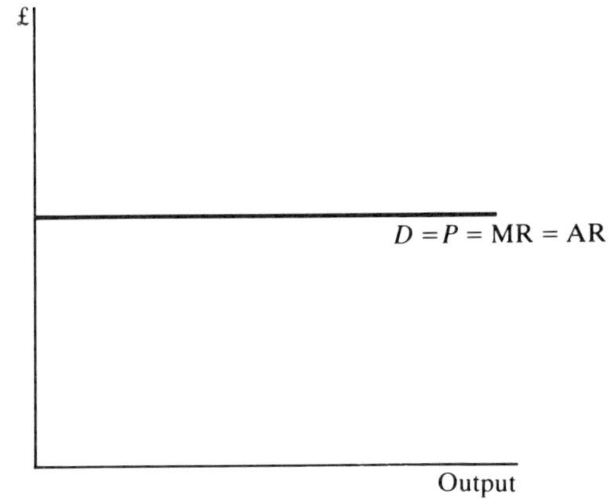

Fig. 6.4

In order to arrive at a solution value for the profit-maximizing level of output for the perfectly competitive firm we will therefore have to assume that the marginal cost curve is upward sloping. In effect, therefore, we are considering a short-run (fixed factor) context such as that of section 5.2. In such a context a U-shaped short run average total cost curve implies that marginal cost will eventually start to rise as in Fig. 6.5. The profit-maximizing level of output – the level of output where marginal cost equals marginal revenue – is again labelled q^*. As before, the level of profits is AP^*BC since this is the difference between total revenue (OP^*Bq^*) and total costs (OACq^*). (Re-read the relevant parts of section 6.3 if you are unsure of the reasoning behind this.)

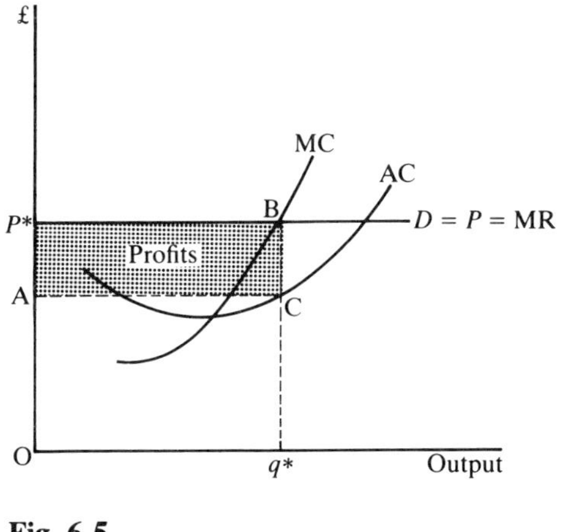

Fig. 6.5

6.5 Super-normal profits and the entry of new firms

In Fig. 6.5 the level of output labelled q^* is an equilibrium level in the sense that there will be no tendency for it to change. It is important to emphasize, however, that it is a short-run equilibrium in two senses of the term 'short run'. Firstly, it is a short-run context in the sense that there are fixed factors of production. Secondly, it is a short-run situation in the sense that the existence of these 'profits' can only be a transient phenomenon. The reason for this is because these 'profits' are above average, or *super-normal profits*. This, in turn, is due to the fact that the costs we have been talking about include a normal return to capital. In other words, part of the legitimate costs of the firm, from the economist's point of view, is the return which the capital tied up in the firm could earn in an alternative use. Economists call this the *opportunity cost* or *transfer price* of capital. For example, if the amount of capital tied up in the firm is, say, £10 000, then any evaluation of the firm's costs should include the interest that could be gained by investing this sum of money in some alternative way – for example, by purchasing government securities or other securities which yield a relatively riskless return.

In this respect the economist's treatment of costs may differ from that of the accountant. For example, if a firm is owned by an individual who has invested his own capital in the firm there will be no monetary cost attached to the use of that capital. He will not, for example, have to pay the bank interest on money he has borrowed since no loan is involved. This is the way that accountants treat cost. For the economist, however, even though there is no monetary cost involved in the use of the capital, there is an opportunity cost – the return which the capital could earn in the best alternative use.

Therefore, since costs include the opportunity cost of capital, the profits shown in Figs 6.3 and 6.5 should be regarded as super-normal profits – that is, profits in excess of those generally earned. Now, in a perfectly competitive market these super-normal profits can only be short-lived because their existence will encourage other firms to enter the industry. This will cause an expansion of market supply, and the market price will drop. This process, in theory, will continue until all the super-normal profits have been eliminated by the entry of new firms. This is illustrated in Fig. 6.6. Industry supply increases from S to S' with the entry of new firms, and equilibrium market price thus falls from P_1 to P_2. Each firm in perfect competition takes the market price as a given datum and equates marginal cost to marginal revenue in order to maximize profits (or minimize losses). When market price has been driven down to P_2 this therefore is at a level of output of q_2^*.

The shaded area represents both total costs and total revenue: thus there are no super-normal profits. Thus, Fig. 6.6b shows a competitive firm in equilibrium when all super-normal profits have

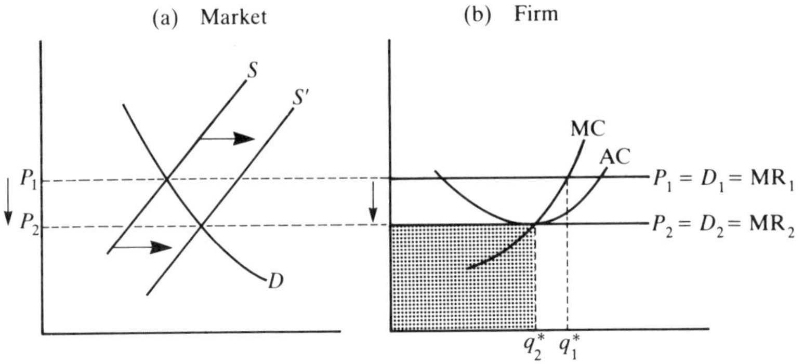

Fig. 6.6

been eliminated. This is sometimes called a *post-entry equilibrium*, that is, the equilibrium that results after new firms have entered the market to earn for themselves some of the super-normal profits. It could also be termed a long-run equilibrium where the term 'long run' refers to the absence of super-normal profits. Thus we have yet another interpretation of the terms 'long run' and 'short run'. We now have three different definitions of the terms short run and long run, and they are summarized in Table 6.3.

Table 6.3 Summary – short run and long run

As applied to	Short run	Long run
Time period	Less than 1 year or whatever arbitrary cut-off point is chosen	More than 1 year
Costs	Fixed factors	All factors variable
Equilibrium	Presence of SNP (also called 'pre-entry' equilibrium)	Absence of SNP (also called 'post-entry' equilibrium)

SNP = super-normal profits

6.6 The elusive long-run equilibrium

To recap, the profit-maximizing level of output, q^*, shown in Fig. 6.5, is a short-run equilibrium level of output both in the sense that it exists in a short run (fixed factor) cost context and also in the sense that it gives rise to super-normal profits, the existence of which triggers off responses from other firms which will eventually undermine this equilibrium, that is, change it from an equilibrium to a disequilibrium position. What of the long-run equilibrium position? Like the pot of gold at the end of the rainbow, the long-run equilibrium position does not exist. From a certain spot you can see the rainbow but you can never reach the crock of gold. The reason for this is not because of the ephemeral nature of the rainbow but because it only exists when viewed from afar. Close to, it vanishes. The same applies to the 'long run'. From a particular short-run perspective you can contemplate the long run, but when you arrive at what you thought was the long run you find you are in another short-run position. You are always in the short run in the sense that the factors you are using are fixed at that particular point in time. You can change these factors but in so doing you do not move to the long run; you merely move to another short-run position.

Consider the example of a farmer producing, say, oil-seed rape, the raw material of margarine. If he is a profit maximizer he will expand production up to the point where the cost of the last tonne produced equals the market price. With a given area under cultivation (that is, in the short run) this is a profit-maximizing equilibrium level of output. If the demand for margarine and hence for oil-seed rape is high this may result in super-normal profits being earned, and if it does, then next season other farmers may switch into rape production, expanding supply, depressing market price and eroding the profitability of rape production – a process which will continue until all the super-normal profits have been eliminated. Each individual farmer, however, always operates in a short-run context, aspiring to a short-run (profit maximizing) equilibrium position. The concept of long-run equilibrium therefore should be seen as a description of a process (involving the entry and exit of other firms) rather than as a static point of equilibrium. Figure 6.6 therefore should be seen as a description of this process.

6.7 The industry supply curve in perfect competition

We talked in section 4.1 about how price is determined in perfect competition by the intersection of the demand curve and the supply curve, and we showed in Fig. 6.6 the interaction between the market and the individual perfectly competitive firm. We are now in a position to describe formally how that market supply curve is formed. This is merely an extension of the process described in Fig. 6.6. Suppose the industry is composed of just two firms, as in Fig. 6.7 – clearly a contradiction in terms since we assumed that in perfect competition there are many small firms, but an expedient assumption that we must make for purposes of exposition.

At a price of P_1, firm A will produce nothing since it has a higher cost structure than firm B and, at this price, it cannot produce at a profit. Only firm B will supply, at an output level of q_1, and this therefore is the market supply at this price. At a higher price of P_2 however, firm A will also find it profitable to produce (at output level q_2) and firm B will expand its output to q_3. Thus market supply at price P_2 is equal to the sum of firm A's production plus firm B's production ($q_2 + q_3$).

In a similar way, by considering other prices we can trace out a market supply curve. This market supply curve is the horizontal summation of each individual firm's marginal cost curves – or, at least, that portion of the marginal cost curve which is above the average cost curve.

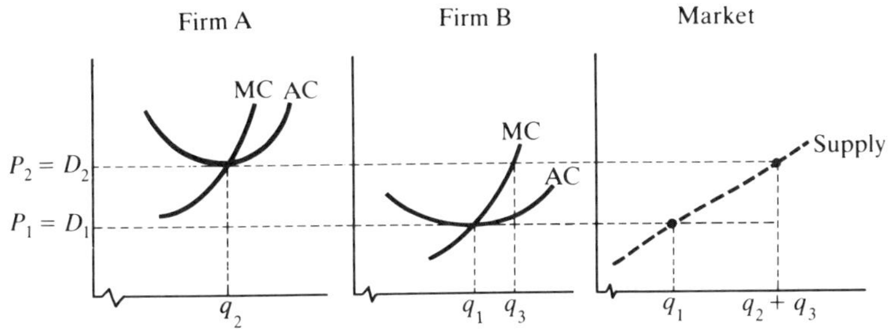

Fig. 6.7

It is worth emphasizing two points. The first is that each firm is in a position of short-run equilibrium. Thus, the industry supply curve should properly be interpreted within a short-run context – that is, we have derived a short-run market supply curve. The second point which should be reiterated is that an industry supply curve is only defined in the context of a perfectly competitive market structure. In other market structures the 'supply curve' is the firm's marginal cost curve as shown in Figs 6.2 and 6.3.

Notes

1. London Transport Executive. Annual Reports.

Questions

6.1 A monopolistic firm can affect the price at which it sells. If it wishes to increase total revenue will it raise, lower or leave unchanged its price if it believes that demand for its product is elastic?

6.2 If a price-making firm wants to maximize its sales revenue it should:
(a) set the highest price it can get
(b) set the lowest price which covers its costs
(c) choose a selling price at which the elasticity of demand for its product is unity

(d) choose a selling price where the extra revenue received from the last unit sold exceeds the extra cost of making that unit

6.3 'London Transport should cut fares to increase its revenue.' Do you agree? What effect might an increase in demand have on London Transport's costs?

6.4 How does the concept of opportunity cost help to evaluate the cost of a training scheme which uses skilled workers to train apprentices?

6.5

Table 6.4

	Price (£/p)	Marginal revenue (£/p)	Output	Total revenue (£)	Total cost (£)	Profit	Average costs (£/p)	Marginal cost (£/p)
A	1.00	0.80	3000	3000	2500			0.75
B	1.50	1.20	5000				1.50	1.20
C		0.90	5000			Zero SNP	1.00	0.90
D	1.20	1.50	4000					1.50
E	1.00		4000	4000	2500		62.5	1.00
F	0.90	0.75	4000	3600	2000		At a minimum	

Table 6.4 contains information on six firms, all of whom are monopolists who wish to maximize profit. Complete the table and advise in each case whether the firm should:

(a) increase price (and reduce quantity produced and sold)
(b) reduce price (and increase quantity produced and sold)
(c) remain at present position
(d) none of the above: the figures supplied cannot be correct

Chapter 7
Objectives of the firm

7.1 Do firms maximize profits?

In Chapter 6 we set out the rules to be followed by the profit-maximizing firm: expand output up to the point where the last unit sold adds as much to revenue as it does to cost – that is, equate marginal revenue (MR) and marginal cost (MC) – and then charge the maximum price the market will be prepared to pay for this level of output. The question which occurs to everyone sooner or later is – do firms actually behave in this way? Do they maximize profit? Do they equate marginal cost and marginal revenue?

The notion that firms maximize profits seems on the face of it to be an overly simplistic view of behaviour. Moreover, it apparently fails to take account of certain important features of firms in the real world. The first of these is the so-called *divorce of ownership from control*. The dominant form of industrial organization, as we have already noted, is the large firm. Such firms are run by managers who are not themselves the owners of the firm. The owners of the firm are shareholders and it is to this group that profits accrue. Since the shareholders are a widely dispersed group they will find it difficult to exert effective influence on the managers who will therefore be able to pursue whatever objectives they see fit. Therefore, it is said, there is no logical reason to argue that the objectives pursued will be those of profit maximization since profits *per se* do not benefit the individuals who make the pricing and output decisions. Thus the divorce of ownership from control makes the assumption that firms maximize profits seem less plausible.

Secondly, the process of profit maximization apparently requires firms to equate marginal cost with marginal revenue – two magnitudes which the firm may find it difficult or impossible to measure. In other words, firms will typically not possess the information necessary for them to follow the rules for profit maximization; nor can they acquire such information except, possibly, at prohibitively high cost. We shall investigate the implications of these two points below, in sections 7.2 and 7.3.

7.2 The implications of the divorce between ownership and control

If the managers of large firms are not motivated by the desire to maximize profits – because they themselves do not receive such profits – then what does motivate their behaviour and what are the implications of this for their pricing and output decisions? A number of plausible hypotheses exist. One such is that firms (in the person of the managers who make the decisions in such firms) attempt to maximize something other than profit. They may, for example, attempt to maximize the firm's sales revenue or the long-term growth of the firm. Such hypotheses are associated respectively with Baumol[1] and Marris.[2] Generally speaking a firm which pursues sales revenue maximization as an objective will sell a larger quantity at a lower price than the profit-maximizing firm (the rules for achieving sales maximization are explained in section 6.1). However, their basic objective may have to be tempered by the necessity to attain a certain minimum level of profitability, so that in practice the price and output level may be somewhere between the profit-maximizing level and the sales revenue maximizing level. Note also that sales revenue maximization as an objective is similar – though not identical – to the maximization of market share.

The growth of the firm is the objective pursued by managers in the Marris model. By considering the fortunes of the firm in the longer term, Marris attempts to lift the theory of the firm from its traditional static context into a more dynamic setting. The implications for price and output decisions are by no means clear cut, however. The necessary finance to fund the long-term expansion of the firm can most readily be obtained internally through retained profits. Thus growth maximization is not necessarily inconsistent with profit maximization. It could also be consistent with the Baumol model of sales revenue maximization, however, since the managers could equate the growth of sales with the growth of the company.

A slightly different approach associated with Williamson[3] is to argue that managers attempt to maximize their *utility*, that is, the intrinsic satisfaction they get from their work. Managers derive utility from a number of different aspects of their job. They may, for example, derive satisfaction from the status that they have within the company and from the company's status within the wider corporate environment (that is, relative to other firms) and in society generally. Their personal status within the company will depend on their position within the hierarchy as exemplified by their salary and the number of staff for whom they are responsible – the size of their department within the company – and the amount of managerial perks they can acquire – company car, expense account, trips abroad, and so on. Thus one might expect that, if such managers attempt to maximize anything, they would, within the limits of their discretion, attempt to maximize expenditure on staff and managerial 'slack' (that is, perks). Their standing in the world outside the company, however, will depend on the image that the company presents. Thus, other things being equal, one would expect the managers to promote not just the growth of the company but, more importantly, to promote those activities designed to enhance its corporate image. Thus sports sponsorship, sponsorship of the arts and expenditure on lavish office buildings can be seen as having a dual role. Not only do such expenditures assist the company in marketing its products by promoting a favourable image of the company to the consumer, they also increase the utility of its managers – the status of the manager depends on the status of the firm. Such expenditures would be termed *discretionary investment*. They are expenditures over and above that necessary to maximize the firm's profits or its sales revenue.

Williamson formalized his model of managerial behaviour in terms of a utility function. Subject to a minimum profit constraint, managers attempt to maximize their utility (U) which depends on expenditures on staff (S), discretionary investment (I_D) and managerial slack (M).

$$U = f(S, I_D, M)$$

Because of these expenditures such firms have operating costs in excess of those which are strictly necessary to promote the firm's growth or profitability. In a sense, therefore, such firms are inefficient, but they are deliberately inefficient through choice. The term *X-inefficiency* was coined by Leibenstein[4] to describe such a situation in which a firm suffered from – or enjoyed – a cost structure which had built into it an allowance for these non-necesary expenditures. X-inefficient firms can still be profit maximizers, however, so in this sense the Leibenstein model is rather different from that of Williamson.

Up to now all the models we have discussed have an explicit maximand: profits, sales revenue, growth or utility. Some authors would argue, however, that typically firms do not attempt to maximize anything. These are the so-called *behavioural theories of the firm*. Such theories, associated with a number of writers including Cyert and March,[5] and Simon,[6] analyse or describe the process by which decisions are arrived at in the firm. It is important to recognize, they argue, that the firm is an organization composed of a number of groups with different and possibly opposing interests. For example, the sales department may be pursuing market share or sales revenue as an objective: the stock control department may be anxious to avoid stock-out situations even if this means the maintenance of uneconomically high levels of stocks; the marketing department may be concerned with product innovation; the director and shareholders with the profitability of the company; and the technical department (if there is one) with the technical excellence of the product. The decisions which emerge from behind the closed doors of the company are the net result of the interplay between these various interest groups, the outcome obviously being influenced by the relative strengths of each group.

Managers working within such an organization, it is argued, may display *satisficing* rather than maximizing behaviour. That is, they will aspire to certain target levels of profitability, sales, market share, and so on. If these levels are not attained, managers will both revise downwards their aspirations and seek other ways of attaining them. In summary, the behavioural theories of the firm describe the process by which decisions are taken. Clearly, this process does not involve equating marginal cost and marginal revenue or anything remotely like it.

This brings us back to the second feature of firms in the real world that we mentioned in section 7.1: firms are (apparently) prevented from maximizing profit by a lack of the requisite information on marginal cost and marginal revenue. Instead of attempting to maximize profit therefore, they may simply set prices according to some arbitrary mark-up principle – that is, they work out what their costs are, add on a bit for profit, and that is the price they charge. This is known as 'cost-plus' pricing and is the subject of the next section.

7.3 Cost-plus pricing

Hall and Hitch,[7] two American economists working in the 1930s, set out to test the empirical validity of the profit-maximizing model of the firm. They did so in a rather naive way by questioning businessmen about how they arrived at their price and output decisions. The businessmen questioned denied strenuously that they equated marginal cost with marginal revenue or that they maximized profit. One is tempted to quote Mandy Rice-Davis's remark when asked by the Press to comment on a denial made in somewhat different circumstances: 'Well, they would say that, wouldn't they?'[8] In other words, it was a naive question to ask. Businessmen will not use the same words to describe their actions as economists do. Thus phrases like 'profit maximization', 'marginal cost' and 'marginal revenue' are not within the businessman's vocabulary. We have already noted that information on marginal cost and revenue is unlikely to be available, and profit maximization, as an objective, is not something to which firms would readily admit. Somehow it does not fit in with the image of the company they would like to promote as a socially responsible and caring organization. What Hall and Hitch's enquiries failed to take into account is the fact that the phrase 'profit-maximizing objective' is merely a shorthand way of saying that profitability is the criterion by which firms judge success, and that they seek success. Put in this somewhat less stark way, many firms would agree that this is indeed their objective. However, very few, if any, would agree that the procedure they use to pursue their objective involved unmeasurable magnitudes like marginal cost and marginal revenue.

Most firms when questioned in fact described a process which has subsequently come to be called cost-plus, or full cost or mark-up pricing. They first work out their average cost which is reasonably constant over quite a wide range of output, as in Fig. 7.1. They then add on a (possibly arbitrarily determined) mark-up of a certain percentage in order to arrive at the price to charge. They then sell what they can at this price. (Sales will, of course, be determined by the demand curve facing the firm, but firms will typically have no knowledge of this curve.)

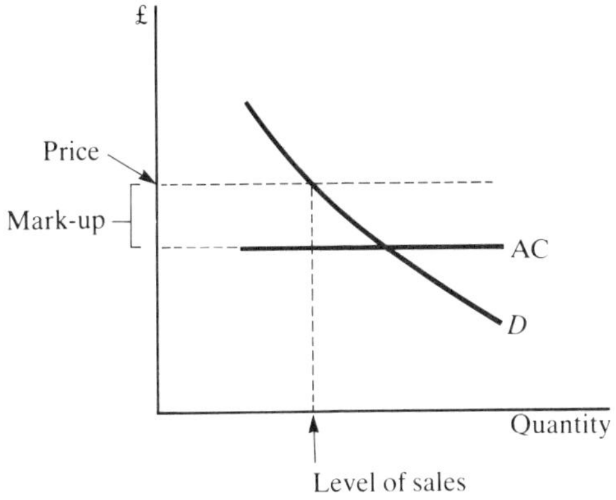

Fig. 7.1

The major deficiency with this explanation of how firms set prices is that it does not attempt to explain how the magnitude of the mark-up is determined. In practice it may be based on the average rate of return of similar firms in the industry or on some target rate of return. But the theory cannot explain how these average or target rates of return are set. What may well happen in practice is that the size of the mark-up is adjusted and its effect on sales and profitability noted, until by a trial-and-error process the firm arrives at the mark-up, and hence the price, which gives it most profit. In other words, the firm charges the profit-maximizing price, but it arrives at that price via an iterative process rather than by a process which involves equating marginal cost and marginal revenue.

Thus, in common with many of the other behavioural models, full cost pricing is not necessarily inconsistent with the models of behaviour which take profit maximization to be the objective. The purpose for which the two models are constructed is rather different, however. The cost-plus pricing model is a description of a process: its weakness is that it has little predictive or analytical power. The marginalist (profit-maximizing) model is not meant to be a realistic description. Rather it is an analytical tool and to criticize it for its lack of realism is to misunderstand the purpose behind its construction.

7.4 Pricing and objectives: some evidence

There are two methods in principle of obtaining evidence about firms' objectives. The first is to ask firms (the Hall and Hitch method) but this is basically unsatisfactory because even if firms were disposed to give truthful answers, they are probably themselves unaware of precisely what criteria they use in setting prices or what ultimate objectives they pursue. The second method is to make inferences from published prices (that is 'hard data') about how those prices are arrived at and therefore the overall stategy on which they are based. This is the general technique we explore here. We shall look at the market for sailboards, a relatively straightforward market but nevertheless one which displays some interesting pricing behaviour from which it is possible to make inferences about firms' strategies.

The sport of boardsailing, or windsurfing, originated in the 1960s but it was not until the late 1970s that one could begin to talk in terms of a clearly defined industry. The market for sailboards is a maturing oligopoly, with a small number of major manufacturers – mostly German, French and Swiss – dominating the market worldwide, and a number of small manufacturing firms producing specialist boards, often restricting their activities to their home market. The market is international in the sense that the major manufacturers sell worldwide. Most boards sold in the UK are imported from Western Europe but there is now growing competition from the nascent UK producers. On the demand side the UK market is small and immature in comparison to that of Western Europe – the sport having been slower to develop here than in other Western European countries.

The aspect of the industry which concerns us here is the pricing behaviour of the firms within the industry. In particular, boards sold on the UK market are typically 20 to 30 per cent more expensive than identical boards sold on those European markets where sailboarding is a major recreational activity. The price differential cannot be explained in terms of transport costs (which are minimal anyway), nor can it be explained in terms of fluctuations in the exchange rate between the pound sterling and other European currencies. Table 7.1 illustrates the price differentials for a random selection of boards sold on the Dutch market and on the UK market.

Table 7.1 Price differentials for sailboards sold on the Dutch and UK markets

Board model	Country of origin	Typical price in Holland (£)	Typical price in UK (£)	Price differential (per cent of UK price)
HiFly 300CS	W. Germany	318	399	20
HiFly 700CS	W. Germany	398	525	24
Wayler Breez	Holland	305	499	39
Sailboard Vario	W. Germany	374	498	25
Mistral Superlight	Switzerland	515	795	35
Bic Star 250	France	256	385	33
Mistral Maui	Switzerland	469	695	32

Source: Research carried out by the author based on published prices in *De Telegraaf*, 2 June 1984, and *Boards Magazine* No. 15, July 1984. Guilder prices converted at 4.25 = £1

Production costs are clearly the same irrespective of where the boards are sold and the variation in transport costs is small – perhaps smaller than one might imagine since many of the companies involved are merely design and marketing agencies, the actual manufacture of the boards being contracted out to major plastics companies and the manufacture of the sails to specialist companies in the Far East. Clearly, then, the price differentials reflect not a difference in costs but a difference in the mark-ups applied.

A mark-up is applied at two stages: when the manufacturer sells boards to the retailer and when the retailer sells boards to the final consumer. The size of both of these mark-ups is in fact much smaller in Holland than in the UK. What inferences can be drawn from this? One possible interpretation is that manufacturers pursue different objectives in different markets – profit maximization in the UK where prices are high, and some other objective in Holland where prices are lower. Such schizophrenic behaviour is extremely implausible, however. What is more likely is that the cost-plus pricing model (introduced in section 7.3) is flawed in arguing that firms base their prices on costs alone without any regard to demand conditions in the market for their product. The evidence of Table 7.1 suggests that firms do take account of demand conditions and that the mark-up they apply reflects this. Thus, although firms may not consciously set out to maximize profit and may not be aware of the elasticities of demand for their product, nevertheless they set prices which cannot be explained solely in terms of costs.

The differences between the market for sailboards in Holland and in the UK can only be fully appreciated after a rather lengthy study of the industry. A few key differences can be noted, however. Most importantly we could argue (by inference from the data of Table 7.1) that the elasticity of demand must be less in the UK than in Holland. The reason for this is related to the degree of maturity and the size of the market. In Holland sailboarding is a major sporting activity which has been popular for a number of years; in the UK it is much less popular. Hence in Holland low prices can be expected to persuade many people to buy a new board who would otherwise not have done so. In Britain the dedicated few are prepared to pay high prices for the board of their choice, but price cuts will not persuade others to take up sailboarding in preference to badminton or bowls. The large size of the Dutch market means that the retailer there can typically expect to sell perhaps ten times as many boards as his UK counterpart. This difference in sales volume in turn affects the extent to which the retailer's overheads can be spread. Thus higher sales volume implies lower unit selling costs, which, in turn, mean that dealers can offer larger discounts thereby encouraging still higher sales volume. This therefore is a self-reinforcing process – higher sales volume makes possible lower unit selling costs, which in turn makes possible lower prices, which encourages still higher volume. Thus one could argue that the lower prices in Holland are partly due to lower selling costs; but note that such a strategy only works because demand is relatively elastic.

Even within the model range of a particular manufacturer, there exist price differentials which cannot be explained in terms of cost differences and which must therefore reflect differences in demand elasticities. For example, as Table 7.1 shows, the German HiFly manufacturer charges a higher price for the 700 model than the 300 model (regardless of where they are sold). However, the rigs (mast, sail and boom) on both boards are identical, and in all other respects the boards are almost identical save for the fact that the 700 is a smaller board and therefore cheaper to produce. If prices were based on cost therefore, the 700 would be a cheaper board to buy. Why is it more expensive?

The reason is to do with the elasticity of demand. The 300 is a first-time buyers board, an all-purpose board, whereas the 700 is a board for the more experienced sailor 'who knows what he wants and is prepared to pay for it'. Demand for the 300 therefore is elastic and lower prices can be expected to result in substantially increased sales. Demand for the 700 is more inelastic so that the manufacturer charges higher prices (applies a higher mark-up) in this segment of the market.

Similar behaviour can be found in the market for cars, a market which has been extensively studied by economists. It is now quite well known that prices on the UK market are significantly higher than prices of identical models sold on the Continental European market.

Again, this has nothing to do with differences in costs. Rather it reflects differences in the elasticity of demand between Britain and Europe. In Britain the demand for cars is relatively inelastic, partly because such a high percentage of cars are sold to companies rather than individuals. Thus mark-ups, and therefore prices, are high. Where demand is more elastic, as in Europe, prices tend to be lower. Moreover, within the model range of a particular manufacturer, mark-ups tend to be higher for larger cars. That is, manufacturers make more profit on large cars than small ones, since large cars are not much more expensive to produce than small ones. Price differentials within a model range owe much more to differing elasticities than to differences in the cost of production.

Notes

1. **Baumol, W. T.**, *Business Behaviour, Value and Growth*. Harcourt, Brace and World Inc., 1967.
2. **Marris, R. L.**, *The Economic Theory of Managerial Capitalism*. Macmillan 1964.
3. **Williamson, O.**, *The Economics of Descretionary Behaviour: Managerial Objectives in a Theory of the Firm*. Prentice-Hall, 1964.
4. **Leibenstein H.**, 'Allocative-Efficiency versus X-efficiency', *American Economic Review*, 1966.
5. **Cyert, R. M. and March, J. G.**, *A Behavioural Theory of the Firm*. Prentice-Hall, 1963.
6. **Simon, H. A.**, *On the Concept of Organisational Goal*, reprinted in Ansoff H. I. (ed.) *Business Strategy*. Penguin, 1969.
7. **Hall, R. L. and Hitch, C. J.**, *Price Theory and Business Behaviour*, reprinted in Wilson, T. and Andrews, P. W. S. (eds), *Oxford Studies in the Price Mechanism*. OUP, 1951.
8. For those readers too young to remember or otherwise out of touch with British political scandal in the 1960s, Mandy Rice-Davis was a high-class call-girl who claimed to have had an affair with a cabinet minister, John Profumo. He initially denied the allegation. Miss Rice-Davis, when asked by the Press to comment on his denial, replied 'Well he would say that, wouldn't he?'

Questions

7.1 What do you understand by the following terms?
(a) divorce between ownership and control
(b) satisficisng behaviour
(c) utility maximizing behaviour
(d) managerial slack
(e) a 'mark-up' model of pricing behaviour
(f) marginalist theories of the firm

7.2 (a) Why might the managers of a firm be more interested in growth of the firm than its profitability?
(b) What constrains these managers in their attempt to maximize growth?
(c) Why don't firms who base their prices on their full costs of production pay more attention to the demand conditions for their product?

7.3 Is the following statement true or false? Explain why. 'If a firm bases its price on full costs of production it will not be maximizing its profits.'

7.4 Why do economists insist on using models of the firm which assume profit maximization when it is so patently unrealistic?

Chapter 8
Behaviour in oligopolistic markets

8.1 Concentration and the public interest

A long-standing debate in economic centres around the question of whether highly concentrated market structures (monopoly, oligopoly) are detrimental to the public interest. The idea that competition is good and monopoly is bad is founded on the proposition – based on rather shaky analysis – that price will be higher and output lower under monopoly than they would be under competition. The validity of this proposition can be easily demonstrated; but only if we make two crucial assumptions, one of which is clearly unrealistic. The assumptions are, firstly, that firms attempt to maximize profits irrespective of the market structure and secondly, that cost structures are the same whether the market for a particular good is supplied by one monopoly seller or by a large number of smaller competing firms. While the first assumption may be a reasonable approximation to reality (the reader can judge for himself having read Chapter 7), the second is clearly not, since large firms can almost always benefit from scale economies which will give

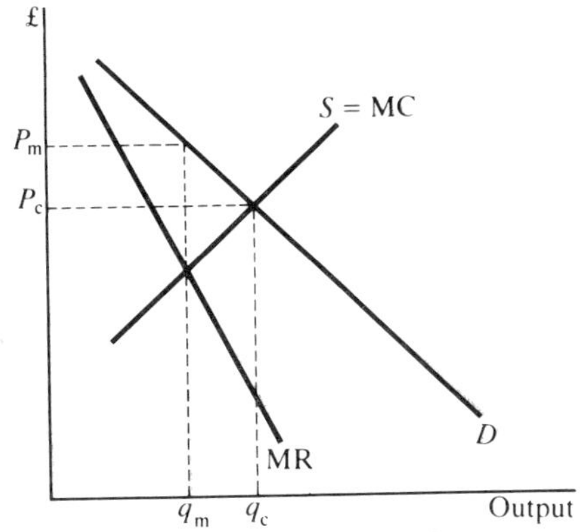

Fig. 8.1

them a cost advantage over smaller firms. If we do make these two assumptions however, then we can see from Fig. 8.1 the correctness of the proposition that monopoly price (P_m) is higher than the competitive price (P_c) and monopoly output (q_m) is lower than the competitive output (q_c).

Note that in Fig. 8.1 the industry supply curve (S) is assumed to be equivalent to the monopolist's marginal cost curve (MC). This follows from the assumption we made that cost conditions are the same whether the industry is composed of one firm or is fragmented into a number of smaller competing firms. In competition, price is determined by the intersection of this supply curve and the demand curve, whereas the monopolist equates marginal cost to marginal revenue to arrive at an output level (q_m) and a price (P_m). In practice, of course, the monopolist would enjoy scale economies which would reduce his costs relative to those of smaller competing firms. If these scale economies were substantial the monopoly price would be less than the competitive price and the monopoly output level higher than the competitive output level. Figure 8.2 illustrates this possibility.

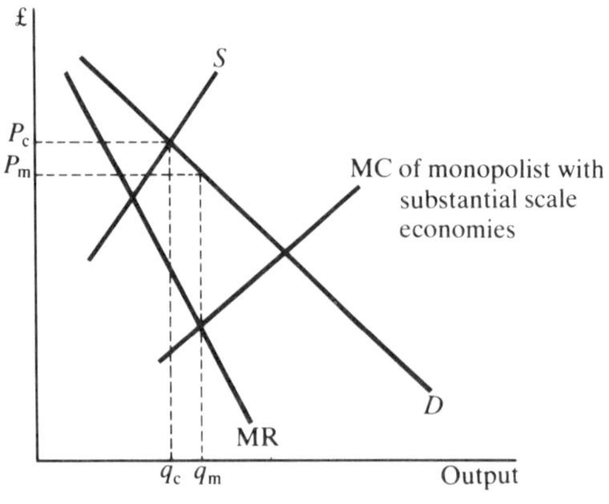

Fig. 8.2

Thus the major justification for monopoly – or market concentration generally – rests on the proposition that large firms will enjoy cost advantages over smaller competing firms and that these lower costs will ultimately result in lower prices to the consumer. That is, the benefits of lower costs more than outweigh any possible dis-benefits which might result from the abuse of monopoly power.

However, we have already noted (in section 3.1.4) that firm size and plant size are not the same thing. Although large firms with substantial market power may enjoy scale economies as a result of the concentration of production in a few large plants, they often engage in *multiplant operation*, preferring to decentralize their production into a number of smaller plants. For example, it has been estimated[1] that in 1968 in Britain the average ratio of plants to firms for the five largest firms was over 10 : 1 (that is, on average each firm operated over ten plants). The existence of multiplant operation weakens the claim that market concentration is in the public interest. Concentration is only in the public interest if large firms enjoy technical cost advantages over smaller firms. Often, however, the advantages they have result from their market power rather than from technical economies of scale.

While bearing this point in mind it is nevertheless true that large firms do benefit from scale economies. This is born out by the evidence of Chapter 5 and, in particular, Table 5.2 which gives engineering estimates of minimum efficient plant sizes (MEPS) for a number of industries. It would clearly be inefficient and against the public interest to insist that such industries operate below the MEPS merely to ensure a degree of competition in the industry, if significant cost penalties resulted from this.

In Britain the agency charged with the responsibility of investigating industries where firms have substantial market power is the Monopolies and Mergers Commission (MMC). In addition to the merger activity which it is required to investigate (discussed in section 8.7), the MMC is empowered to investigate market situations in which a single firm controls over 25 per cent of the market for a particular product (or where a group of firms, acting together so as to restrict competition, jointly controls over 25 per cent of the market). Thus the MMC's terms of reference are very much wider than might have been imagined from the definition of a monopoly as a single seller. In fact the expression 'a monopoly situation' used in this context is merely a convenient shorthand for some rather more cumbersome phrase about 'an oligopoly situation in which the dominant firm's market share exceeds 25 per cent.' The MMC's remit is to consider whether monopoly situations such as these are in the public interest, and in carrying out its remit the MMC has due regard to the evidence on scale economies it can obtain from the firm under investigation. In deciding whether a particular monopoly situation is in the public interest, however, this is only one aspect of such situations which is taken into account. Additionally the MMC investigates the firm's pricing behaviour, aspects of price and non-price competition and any alleged restrictions on competition. Further examples of this are given in sections 8.3, 8.4, 8.7.2 and 8.9.

8.2 Traditional and modern views about monopoly

It is possible to discern a shift of emphasis (which some writers[2] have described as a revolution) in the way that economists view the whole question of monopoly and the public interest. The traditional view outlined in section 8.1 has two aspects:

1. A monopoly situation is a market structure which is defined purely in terms of the degree of concentration.
2. Monopolies, so defined, may or may not act against the public interest. This depends on the objectives of the firm, its ability to reap scale economies, and so on.

In contrast, the modern view can be characterized as follows:

1. A monopoly situation is a market structure which cannot be defined purely in terms of the degree of concentration. Rather, the ease with which new firms can enter the market (and leave it) should be taken into account.
2. A monopoly situation therefore can be defined as a situation in which a firm has a dominant position and is protected against the entry of new firms by effective barriers.
3. It is highly probable that monopolies, so defined, will act against the public interest so that it is appropriate that anti-monopoly investigations concentrate on the alleged anti-competitive devices employed by a firm (that is, devices designed to bolster the firm's monopolistic position by erection of entry barriers).
4. In addition, the modern view emphasizes that ease of exit is an important determinant of ease of entry. New firms will not commit themselves to high levels of capital expenditure (that is, they will not enter) if that capital equipment cannot subsequently be turned to an alternative use (that is, if they are unable to leave if they wish to do so).

To express these modern views in a slightly different way we can say that if (real) monopoly power exists it will probably be abused, that is, prices and profits will be higher. The existence of these profits will, however, invariably attract other firms into the market to secure some of the profits for themselves, provided that there are no barriers to entry. The threat posed by the potential entry of new firms will cause the existing firms to react in one of two ways. They may moderate their pricing behaviour, limiting themselves to the sort of prices and profits that would be found in a competitive market, thus eliminating the incentive for other firms to enter. Such firms therefore are not true monopolists because any attempt to exercise market power results in its eventual erosion. Alternatively, the threat of new entrants may cause the monopolist to react by indulging in tactics the sole purpose of which is to restrict competition. The erection of entry barriers, which take many different forms, is the most important of these anti-competitive tactics. Only if such anti-competitive tactics are successful in excluding new entrants does a true monopoly situation exist which requires some government intervention to limit its power and prevent it acting against the public interest.

In summary, we can say that the degree of concentration is not the only criterion by which to define monopoly situations. Of equal importance is the degree to which the firm enjoys a position protected from the threat of new entrants. The modern approach, sometimes labelled the 'contestable markets' approach, is thus more dynamic as opposed to the more static traditional approach. It draws attention to the likely future developments which may occur when and if new firms enter the market.

8.3 The Kellogg's Corn Flakes case

To illustrate the ideas outlined above we shall in this section study the way in which the MMC approaches the question of the abuse of monopoly power. The example we shall look at is the case of the market for ready-to-eat breakfast cereals – the Kellogg's cornflakes case – which was the subject of an MMC report[3] in 1973. Quotations in the following text are from this report.

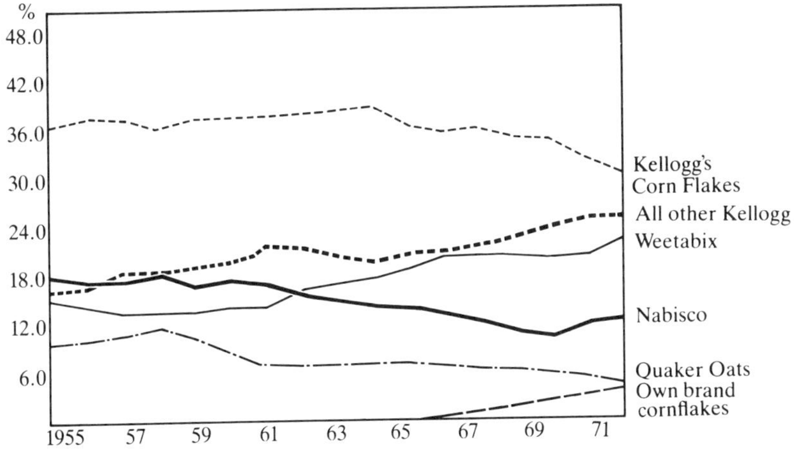

Fig. 8.3 Shares by weight of ready-cooked breakfast cereals

(Source: Monopolies Commission Report 1973, *Breakfast Cereals: A Report on the Supply of Ready-cooked Breakfast Cereal Foods*, HMSO, App. 4)

As can be seen from Fig. 8.3, Kellogg had a dominant position in the market for breakfast cereals. During the period from 1955 to 1971 Kellogg's Corn Flakes had an average market share of over 36 per cent and all Kellogg cereals taken together had a market share of 57

Table 8.1 Breakfast cereals

The products supplied were as follows:

Kellogg Company of Great Britain Ltd

Corn Flakes	Rice Krispies	30% Bran Flakes
Raisin Bran	Coco Krispies	Sugar Smacks
Bran Buds	All-Bran	Frosties
Special K	Ricicles	Puffa Puffa Rice
Variety	Wheatamins	

Weetabix Ltd

Weetabix

Nabisco Ltd

Shredded Wheat	Shreddies	Golden Nuggets
Cubs spoon-size shredded wheat		

Quaker Oats Ltd

Sugar Puffs	Oat Crunchies	Puffed Wheat

Viota Foods Ltd

Corn Flakes	Wheat Bisk

Source: Monopolies Commission Report 1973, *Breakfast Cereals: A Report on the Supply of Ready Cooked Breakfast Cereal Foods*. HMSO, App. 4

per cent. In addition, the three-firm concentration ratio (Kellogg, Weetabix, Nabisco) was about 90 per cent. Clearly a monopoly situation existed according to the criterion then in operation. Kellogg was the dominant firm and thus determined prices in the industry generally. The question which the MMC set out to investigate, however, was whether Kellogg was guilty of the abuse of their monopoly position.

After investigation the Commission concluded that there was no price competition as such in the market. Rather, manufacturers preferred to compete by extending their product ranges, a strategy which Kellogg seems to have taken to extravagant proportions (see the list of products in Table 8.1). This strategy could be considered as an attempt to erect entry barriers through brand proliferation (see section 3.1.5). Kellogg's expenditure on advertising, though high, was not however considered excessive. The ratio of expenditure on advertising to sales fluctuated around 12 per cent during the late 1960s and early 1970s, somewhat less pro rata than two of the other major suppliers and about equal to that of the third. The Commission did, however, state that 'advertising and promotion have helped to create and tend to maintain the kind of market in which it is possible for manufacturers to have substantial freedom to determine their prices as they wish'. (para. 88.)

The Commission noted the introduction of own-brand cornflakes, which occurred in 1966 when Viota Ltd acquired a cornflakes factory and started producing an own-label product for Tesco. In their submission Kellogg said that 'the advent of own-brand cornflakes had substantially sharpened price competition in relation to Corn Flakes' and Viota saw the market for cornflakes as very price competitive (para. 97). The Commission also noted the growing bargaining strength of the major retailers and their ability to exert influence on Viota's prices and thus on cornflake prices generally. Somewhat surprisingly, however, the Commission took the view that this was unlikely to exert a significant restraining influence on Kellogg's prices in the future, a judgement which with the benefit of hindsight appears somewhat questionable. The Commission considered that for most of the period under review, Kellogg's profits had been excessive when compared with manufacturing industry and the food industry generally. However, in the years immediately preceding the Report, Kellogg's profits had suffered a decline (as can be seen from Fig. 8.4).

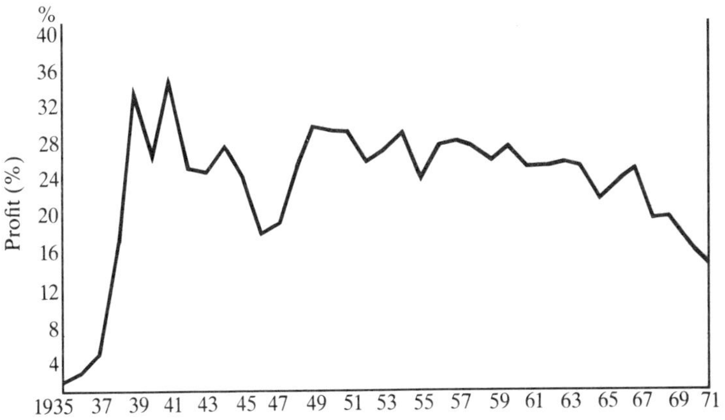

Fig. 8.4 Kellogg's ratio of operating profit to net sales on total domestic business 1935–71 (Source: Monopolies Commission Report 1973, *Breakfast Cereals: A Report on the Supply of Ready-cooked Breakfast Cereal Foods*, HMSO, App.4)

The Commission assumed that this was likely to continue and it was this which, it seems, persuaded the Commission to state that 'We are not prepared to conclude that Kellogg's profits are excessive at present.' (para. 96) In a report full of contradictions and hedged around with ifs and buts, the Commission finally came down firmly on the fence, stating 'Our conclusion is that the determination by Kellogg of the level of prices at which breakfast cereals are supplied does not operate against the public interest but that it may be expected to operate against the public interest.' (para. 101)

What is apparent, however, is that the Commission was unhappy about the lack of price competition in the industry and the dominant and protected position of Kellogg, bolstered by what the Commission saw as anti-competitive tactics (that is, non-price competition). Although Kellogg contended that many of the major food manufacturers had the technical and marketing expertise to break into the market if they so wished, the Commission took the view that new firms were unlikely to risk the heavy expenditure necessary to launch into the market dominated by Kellogg, particularly with a copy of an existing product. Thus, effectively, barriers to the entry of new firms existed.

In addition, the Commission clearly felt that there was 'no practical means of changing the structure of the industry or the nature of competition in the industry in such a way as to ensure the maintenance of price restraint on Kellogg' (para. 102), a conclusion which did little to satisfy the critics of excesses within the industry.

8.4 Anti-competitive tactics: replacement body panels for Ford

Section 8.3 was based on an investigation by the Monopolies Commission whose remit was to decide whether the behaviour of Kellogg acted against the public interest. That is, to condemn Kellogg it was not sufficient to demonstrate merely that they were indulging in anti-competitive tactics. Rather the Commission had to decide, taking into consideration all the relevant information, whether the situation as a whole was or was not in the public interest. In contrast, the case studied in this section is more modest in its scope. It is based on a report published by the Office of Fair Trading in 1984[4] following its investigation of the market for replacement body panels for Ford cars. Quotations in the following text are taken from this report. The Office of Fair Trading is empowered to carry out an investigation where it appears that a firm is pursuing a course of action which is designed to, or does, restrict competition. It has to reach a decision on whether the alleged behaviour constitutes an anti-competitive practice. If it decides that it does, and the firm in question gives no undertaking to amend its behaviour, then the whole matter may be referred to the Monopolies Commission.

The market for replacement body parts for Ford cars was estimated (in 1984) to be worth between £35 million and £45 million a year, of which Ford's share (by value) was over 85 per cent. The remaining market share was filled by independent manufacturers. The OFT investigation was prompted by the legal action taken by Ford against these independent suppliers who, Ford claimed, were in breach of the laws relating to artistic and design copyright. Ford claimed, with some justification under the relevant statutes relating to copyright and registered designs, that the independent suppliers were in breach of the copyright laws, and served notice on them that Ford intended to prosecute if they continued with their action. The independent suppliers in reply offered to pay Ford a royalty on the parts manufactured, an offer which Ford refused.

The market for replacement panels arises from two main sources. Firstly, panels are required for the repair of vehicles subject to accident damage. Secondly, panels are required to replace sections damaged through corrosion, this obviously being more important for older cars which need to be repaired to bring them up to the standard required for the MoT test. The price differential between panels manufactured by Ford and those manufactured by independent suppliers was considerable. This differential was particularly marked for those panels used to repair corrosion damage where the independent suppliers sold 'part panels' particularly suitable for repairing this type of damage cheaply. Ford, up to the time of the OFT investigation, did not supply 'part panels' and repairers were therefore compelled to purchase 'full panels' even though only part of the panel might be used in a repair, the rest being cut away and discarded. Table 8.2 shows the price comparison between the independent suppliers' part panels and the equivalent full panels supplied by Ford. Although not as marked, a sizeable price differential ranging between 6 and 400 per cent also existed for panels commonly used for crash repairs.

The most cogent arguments adduced by Ford in defending its policy are reproduced below verbatim from Ford's submission:

1. *The design of Ford's body panels enjoy protection under the law of copyright. As the legal owner of the copyright in its designs, Ford is entitled to utilise the designs itself, or to license others to do so, or to do both. Any of these courses would be an entirely normal exercise by Ford of the right granted by the law of copyright.*

   (section 5.13)

2. *To produce a new model Ford makes massive investments in design, engineering and tooling. (For example, the total design costs for the Sierra model were about £90 million and the total*

Table 8.2 Prices of corrosion part panels

Model	Independent supplier Part panel name	Price (£)	Ford Full panel of which corrosion panel forms part	Price (£)
Escort Mk1	Rear lower corner	2.61	Rear quarter panel (4-door)	41.98
	Rear wheel arch	1.75	Rear quarter panel (2-door)	73.40
	Front footwell	2.40	Floor pan	78.39
	Sill with extension (2-door)	2.25	Full sill (2-door)	12.66
Escort Mk2	Rear lower corner	4.45	Rear quarter panel (4-door)	62.35
	Rear wheel arch	3.25	Rear quarter panel (2-door)	69.75
	Sill (2-door)	2.50	Sill (2-door)	10.32
	Rear valance	2.90	Lower back panel	19.77
	Full sill (4-door)	4.04	Front and rear sill (2 parts)	15.69
Cortina Mk3	Front wing repair panel	3.73	Front wing	25.00
	Rear lower corner	2.66	Rear quarter panel (4-door)	31.43
	Rear wheel arch to door shut	1.64	Rear quarter panel (2-door)	41.55
	Rear wheel arch to door shut (section only)	0.70	Rear quarter panel (2-door)	41.55
Granada	Rear wheel arch	3.58	Rear quarter panel	53.08
	Rear lower corner	3.93	Rear quarter panel	53.08
Fiesta	Rear wheel arch	3.73	Rear quarter panel – 1981 1981 –	 44.40 46.84
	Rear lower corner	2.10	Quarter panel rear section	34.20

Table 8.2 continued

Model	**Independent supplier** Part panel name	**Price (£)**	**Ford** Full panel of which corrosion panel forms part	**Price (£)**
Transit	Rear door skin (part)	2.40	Full rear door skin	13.42
	Rear wheel arch	3.80	Body side panel	64.97
	Door sill	1.60	Rocker step	10.35
	Skin sill lower	3.00	Body rocker panel extension	5.19

Source: Report by the Office of Fair Trading, *Ford Motor Co. Ltd: Licensing for the manufacture or sale of replacement parts*, 21 Mar. 1984

costs of developing the model and putting it into production about £560 million.) Those who manufacture infringing panels are able, without any investment in original design work, to copy the Ford part and to produce sufficiently close dimensional replicas for an expenditure of some tens of thousands of pounds. Thus the copier, who contributes nothing to the design of the panel, is able to benefit from all the design and development undertaken by the manufacturer of the original panel.

(section 5.37 para. 2 and section 5.10)

3. *Suppliers of infringing panels are concerned only to supply the fast moving, high volume panels. The typical supplier of infringing panels offers 25 panels for each Ford vehicle, making a total for all Ford vehicles of 150 panels, of which some 80%–90% are corrosion part panels which are not offered by Ford. By contrast Ford has a responsibility to purchasers of its vehicles to make available a comprehensive range of spare parts including panels. In consequence Ford stocks around 150 panels for each of its models, and a total for all models of 4000 panels. Ford's responsibility for the supply of a full range of parts for all its vehicles entails maintenance by Ford of a massive warehousing and distribution system. (section 5.37 para. 3 and 4)*
4. *If a manufacturer's prices for its body panels and other parts are not competitive with those of other vehicle manufacturers, its sales of new vehicles will be affected. Over 40 per cent of Ford's car sales in the UK are to fleet purchasers and Ford's success in selling to such operators is of particular relevance. The managers of fleet purchasers are professionals with expert knowledge of the cost of car ownership, including the competitive costs of spare parts. (section 5.35)*

In considering Ford's submission the OFT acknowledged that Ford was acting legally. This was not the point at issue, however. The point at issue was whether the exercise of this right produced a situation in which a firm was able to wield monopoly power. In a well-argued case the OFT concluded:

> *The effects on competition arising from the exercise of copyright depend on the market in which the particular good is supplied. Where there are reasonable substitutes for a particular good, the exclusive rights of supply do not confer monopoly rights in the market and the exercise of copyright is unlikely to have an anti-competitive effect.*
>
> *For example, in the new vehicle market Ford's rights prevent others from manufacturing and supplying copies of its vehicles but other manufacturers are free to, and do, design alternatives to Ford vehicles. (paras 8.5 and 8.6)*

In other words, although the law of copyright applies to the new vehicle market this does not confer monopoly power on Ford since there are substitutes available.

In contrast, the market for replacement body panels is different in competitive terms from the new vehicle market because there are no adequate substitutes. For example, the only part which is suitable for replacing a Cortina bonnet is a part which is identical in design to the original. It follows that a law which confers on Ford the exclusive right to supply such parts in the replacement body parts market confers monopoly powers on Ford in that market. Thus the OFT concluded that Ford's behaviour did constitute an anti-competitive practice. Shortly before the publication of the OFT report Ford announced that they had reviewed their policy and had recently decided to sell a range of corrosion part panels, comprising some 50 individual panels, and planned to extend their range. However, this development was insufficient to persuade the OFT not to refer the case to the Monopolies Commission and it was duly referred in May 1984. The Commission reported in February 1985. Recall however that the Monopolies Commission considered a different and a wider question to that considered by the OFT – namely whether Ford's behaviour was against the public interest. As such the Commission paid more attention to Ford's arguments summarized in the preceding quotations in paragraphs 2, 3 and 4 than the OFT did.

To summarize this case, there are three questions at issue. Was Ford's behaviour legal? Did it constitute an anti-competitive tactic? And was it against the public interest? The first question, though of interest to lawyers, is of no relevance for our present purposes (remember that there was no suggestion that Kellogg was at any time acting illegally). The second question has definitively been answered in the affirmative by the OFT and this was confirmed by the Commission. On the third question the Commission ruled that Ford's behaviour was against the public interest, but it concluded that no suitable remedy existed under the present law. It took the view that while it was feasible for the Commission to compel Ford to grant licences to independent suppliers to supply body panels, it was not part of its function to adjudicate between the parties in deciding what constituted a reasonable royalty. It was likely, it decided, that what Ford would consider a reasonable royalty would not be considered reasonable by the independent suppliers. The Commission therefore advocated detailed changes in the law of patent which would have the effect of limiting the period of copyright on body panels to a maximum of five years. It noted however that changes in the law would take time to implement and that in the interim – which might be very extended – the preservation of competition in the supply of body parts would 'depend upon Ford's readiness to respect the public interest'. If Ford were not willing to do this 'competition . . . might be impossible'[5].

8.5 Pricing strategies in oligopolistic markets

The pricing behaviour exhibited by the firms in the market for cornflakes which we looked at in section 8.3 was relatively straightforward to analyse because there was one firm (Kellogg) which was clearly the market leader. Kellogg's pricing behaviour was not designed to oust the smaller companies, nor did the smaller firms engage in the sort of price competition designed to steal market share. Rather the firms competed through non-price competition in ways which had the effect of reinforcing the status quo. Generally, however, pricing behaviour in oligopolistic markets can be a very complex phenomenon. Before we go on to investigate some further examples of oligopolistic pricing behaviour it will be useful in this section to examine the range of behaviour which could be found in such markets.

In a monopoly situation, as the reader is now aware, there is an incentive for the monopolist to raise prices above the competitive level and thus earn monopoly (super-normal) profits. In an oligopoly, particularly a tight-knit oligopoly in which the number of firms with a significant market share is very small, there will be an incentive for the firms to act in concert as if they were a single monopolist, jointly maintaining prices in the industry above the competitive level in an attempt to maximize industry profits. Such behaviour is known as *joint profit maximizing* behaviour. It involves *collusion* since prices in the industry are set and maintained by a tacit agreement among the major suppliers not to indulge in competitive price cutting. Although the incentive to collude is strong there will also be an opposing tendency: to compete actively by cutting prices in an attempt to steal market share away from the other firms in the industry. Unfortunately for the firm instigating the price competition however, it is likely to provoke a response from its rivals within the industry. If the rivals match the price cuts of the instigator then the net result will be that prices in the industry will fall. The consumer benefits as prices fall below the joint profit-maximizing level.

Short-term considerations must also be tempered by the desire to maximize profits in the longer run. High super-normal profits will provide an incentive for new firms to enter the industry. The entry of these new firms will weaken the monopolistic position of the existing firms and reduce their ability to earn super-normal profits in the long run. To prevent the possibility of this happening, existing firms may forgo some of the super-normal profits they could earn in the short run, opting instead for lower prices as a way of deterring new entrants. Such a policy is known as *limit pricing* since the prices set are just low enough to discourage other firms from entering the market.

With an eye to the longer term the firm may even attempt to drive its existing rivals out of business by engaging in *predatory pricing*. As the name implies, a market leader whose costs, by virtue of its size, are lower than its rivals, may prey on its rivals by forcing prices down. Faced with such an attack, the firm which is being preyed upon has only two defences. It can try to match the market leader's price cuts which it will probably be unable to do since its costs (including marketing costs) per unit are higher. Alternatively, it can stick to a higher price, in which case it will lose customers to the aggressive market leader. Whichever of these two options is pursued, it may fall victim to the aggressive competition of the market leader and be forced out of the market. This leaves the surviving market leader in a stronger monopolistic position where it can raise prices and reap the monopoly profits which are its reward.

Such actively aggressive behaviour is, however, rare, particularly in oligopolies where no clear market leader exists. Even where one firm does have a dominant position in the market, it is likely to tolerate the existence of its smaller rivals. In such situations the dominant firm often assumes the role of a *price leader*, dictating the pace in the market, while the smaller firms assume the role of *price followers*. This brings considerable benefits to the firms in the market. If each of them 'knows their place' and acts in accordance with their allotted role then much of the uncertainty can be removed. Firms in oligopolistic markets live in a very uncertain world since the outcome of any particular action depends on the reaction of rivals. A *modus vivendi* which allows the uncertainty to be reduced brings benefits to all the firms concerned. Such an arrangement is, of course, a form of collusive behaviour.

In summary we can say that the choice the oligopolistic firm makes is not simply one between competition and collusion. Short-term considerations must perforce give way to long-term ones, for the corporate time horizon is very long and survival and growth a most important objective. The way in which firms grow is an aspect of their behaviour we consider in the next section.

8.6 Security and growth: diversification and integration

Firms are in business to do business, and it makes but little difference what business they do. There is no reason therefore why they should limit the range of their activities to those currently undertaken. Firms, particularly large firms, can move into new markets or withdraw from existing ones; they can move into or out of areas connected in some way with their main trading activities; they can even develop interests in areas which are totally alien to their existing activities. Normally, however, firms expand by developing in areas in which they already have some expertise. For example, DIY ('do it yourself') is a rapidly expanding sector of the retail market which has recently been entered by two firms – Sainsbury and W. H. Smith – who previously had no knowledge of DIY but did have plenty of expertise in retailing other products – food in the case of Sainsbury and books in the case of W. H. Smith. Both firms tackled the market in a similar way, by building very large supermarkets (hypermarkets) devoted to DIY products. When firms grow by expanding into new areas in this way it is known as *diversification*. The reason for choosing this development strategy is twofold. Firstly, it increases security since the overall risk is lessened by being spread: the old adage about not putting all your eggs in one basket (clearly relevant in the case of Sainsbury). Secondly, it allows the firm to grow as fast as its internal finances and its borrowing ability allow, rather than being constrained to grow at the same speed as the market in which it is currently operating (which may, of course, be stagnant or even declining).

Growth and security can also be achieved by a different form of expansion: *integration* (often known as *vertical integration*). Integration is a special form of diversification where the firm expands either backwards towards its source of raw materials or forwards towards its retail outlets. For example, if Sainsbury acquires a pork pie factory (and sells the pork pies in its supermarkets) this is an example of backwards integration. Similar examples of backwards integration are the chocolate manufacturers, many of whom own cocoa plantations, and the major rubber manufacturers who own rubber plantations. Forwards integration occurs when the brewers acquire public houses – the 'tied houses' – in which to sell their beer.

British Airtours, a wholly owned subsidiary of British Airways, provides a further example of forwards integration. British Airways' main business is running a scheduled airline service but the establishment of British Airtours, a company which sells package holidays by air, provides a useful (captive) retail outlet for its services.

Note that integration, both forward and backward, can often serve to provide the firm with barriers to the entry of new firms into its existing markets. As such, these developments could be viewed as forming part of an anti-competitive strategy.

Both diversification and integration are examples of expansion into areas related in some way to the firm's existing activities. Some firms, however, are what is known as *conglomerates*; that is, they have interests in a number of unrelated areas. Lonrho, for example, is a major international company with interests in mining, newspapers (*The Observer*) and retailing. Similarly, Trafalgar House has interests in shipbuilding, publishing, property and mining. The archetypal conglomerate, however, was a fictitious company invented by the economist J. K. Galbraith. His company – Universal Global Enterprises or UGE for short (to emphasize its size) – was an amalgam of several real American corporations. UGE had subsidiary companies operating in every conceivable sphere of human activity, from cola to computers and from detergents to defence. The activities of conglomerates like UGE will be discussed in greater detail in Chapter 9 when we consider multinational corporations.

It should be clear that the three avenues of expansion we have identified – diversification, integration and conglomeration – are different ways in which the firm attempts to achieve both a more secure future for itself and faster growth of sales and profits. What is also clear is that the three types of expansion normally result from merger activity between two companies or takeover activity. Since mergers and acquisitions are such an important aspect of the growth of firms, they are considered in greater detail in the following section.

8.7 Mergers

An important element in the growth of firms is merger activity. Mergers may be motivated by the desire to diversify the firm's activities – so-called conglomerate mergers. They may involve the firms in vertical links (forward or backward vertical integration). Finally, they may take the form of the acquisition of former competitors.

Merger activity involving the acquisition of competitors will clearly result in increased concentration in the industry in question, together with a concomitant rise in the market power of the newly merged companies. Vertical integration by merger will often also result in an increase in market power even though it does not increase concentration *per se*. Of course, mergers may also result in improved efficiency through rationalization and through an improved ability to reap the benefits of economies of scale. Indeed, this is the major justification which is put forward for merger activity.

Part of the remit of the Monopolies and Mergers Commission is to decide whether a proposed merger is 'in the public interest'. Its remit allows it to investigate any proposed merger where:

1. The merger would lead to an increase in market concentration.
2. The merger would increase the ability of firms to engage in anti-competitive tactics (as a result of increased concentration or through vertical links).
3. The value of assets taken over exceeds a certain sum, set at £30 m in 1984. This condition allows the MMC to investigate conglomerate mergers.

In recent years public policy towards mergers as carried out by the MMC has tended to evolve, albeit slowly, in two ways. Firstly, the 1980 Competition Act (which concerned itself with competition rather than with mergers) encouraged the MMC to pay more attention to anti-competitive behaviour, both actual and potential, rather than with market concentration *per se*.

The second shift in emphasis in public policy towards mergers has been away from a presumption that mergers are in the public interest (unless the MMC can prove otherwise) and towards a more neutral attitude towards mergers. This results partly from accumulated evidence which shows that the claim that mergers increase efficiency is non-proven. Some of the evidence is contained in the 1978 Green Paper, *A Review of Monopolies and Mergers Policy*. Table 8.3, reproduced from the Green Paper, summarizes the results of a study by Meeks of the post-merger profitability of 213 larger quoted companies which merged in the period 1964–72. Meeks's method was to compare the profits of the combined company in the six years following the merger with the profits of the acquiring and acquired firms in the three years prior to the merger. As Table 8.3 shows, average profits declined after the merger. Only in the year of acquisition did recorded profits rise and too much weight should not be attached to that finding since measurement problems are particularly acute in that year. Although Meeks's findings may seem surprising they are in fact in accord with the weight of evidence (in the Green Paper and subsequently), both for the UK and internationally.

Notwithstanding these findings, merger activity continues unabated. Acquiring companies often claim that the proposed merger will lead to synergy – the profits of the merged company will be more than the sum of its parts. This may occur (although the evidence does not support this) but even if it does, one may question whether the increased profitability results from higher prices made possible by market power, or from lower costs stemming from increased efficiency. It is on this basis that the MMC has to decide whether a proposed merger is 'in the public interest'.

Table 8.3 Post-merger profitability and the proportion of firms showing a decline in profits

Year after merger	Number of firms	Change in profitability*	Per cent of firms with lower profits
0	213	+0.15	34
1	192	−0.02	54
2	174	−0.01	52
3	146	−0.06	53
4	103	−0.10	66
5	67	−0.11	64
6	44	−0.07	52
7	21	−0.07	62

*Change – relative to the average of the three pre-merger years – in the ratio of the profitability of the merged companies to the profitability of the industries to which they belonged.

Source: G. Meeks, *Disappointing Marriage: a study of the gains from merger*. CUP, 1977 (quoted in 1978 Green Paper)

8.7.1 European Ferries and Sealink

To illustrate the sorts of issues involved we shall look at the merger proposal between European Ferries and Sealink which was considered by the MMC in 1981.

In 1981 European Ferries operated nine routes (trading under the name of Townsend Thoresen) and owned a number of ports. Sealink, at that time a subsidiary of British Rail, operated similar routes, either independently or in association with state operators in France, Belgium and Holland. It also owned a number of ports. European Ferries had the largest share of the most important route – that between Britain and the Continent. Sealink, together with its partners, was the other major operator. In addition there were a few other operators, the largest of which was P & O Ferries.

In the years prior to the merger proposal the growth of capacity had outstripped the growth of demand. This is illustrated in Table 8.4. This excess capacity had led to cutthroat price competition in order to attract passengers and as a result European Ferries profits

Table 8.4 Vehicle deck load factors

	Routes	Load factors[1] 1979	1980
Short routes			
Sealink	Dover/Folkestone–Calais/Boulogne	36	29
EFL	Dover–Calais	45	36
P & O	Dover–Boulogne	45	38
Longer routes			
Sealink	Dover/Folkestone–Ostend	72	66
Sealink	Newhaven–Dieppe	72	72
Sealink	Harwich–Hook of Holland	66	65
EFL	Dover–Zeebrugge	62	53
P & O	Southampton–LeHavre	73	60
P & O/NSF	Hull–Europoort	75	70
Unweighted average of short routes		42	34
Unweighted average of longer routes		70	64

[1]Percentage of total space available for vehicles which is actually occupied.

Source: *The Monopolies and Mergers Commission Report on European Ferries/Sealink Proposed Merger*, HMSO, 1981

had been depressed and Sealink had made losses. European Ferries stated that they wished to acquire Sealink in order to rationalize the services and eliminate excess capacity. Failure to do so, they argued, might result in the withdrawal of services as a result of losses or continued low returns on investment. European Ferries were so keen to acquire Sealink that they even offered to give an undertaking on price restraint.

Earlier in the year the MMC had allowed a merger to go ahead between the only two hovercraft operators on the cross-channel route. The Swedish-owned HoverLloyd took over British Rail's Seaspeed. Although this gave the newly merged company, Hoverspeed, a 100 per cent monopoly of cross-channel hovercraft services, the merger had been allowed because the MMC accepted the submission that without a rationalization of capacity, hovercraft services might be withdrawn completely.

The MMC took a different view of the European Ferries' bid for Sealink, however. The merger would have produced a monopoly (using the MMC's criteria) as Table 8.5 shows. Even without

Table 8.5 European Ferries/Sealink proposed merger: combined market shares

	Accompanied tourist vehicles		Freight	
	EFL plus Sealink UK only (%)	**EFL plus total Sealink* carryings (%)**	**EFL plus Sealink UK only (%)**	**EFL plus total Sealink* carryings (%)**
All routes to France, Belgium, and the Netherlands	53	71	50 40	59 51
Routes to Northern Ireland	83	—	65	—
Routes to the Republic of Ireland	60	—	35	—
Routes to the Channel Islands	100	—	100	—
Routes to the Isle of Wight	77	—	69	—

*'Total Sealink' means Sealink together with its European partners

Source: From the *Monopolies and Mergers Commission Report on European Ferries/Sealink Proposed Merger*, HMSO, 1981

Sealink's partners the merged company would have had over 50 per cent of the whole cross-channel market and an even larger market share on the other routes. In addition, their ownership of many of the Channel and North Sea ports might have been used to discriminate against existing competitors and new entrants into the market.

In the event the MMC concluded that the proposed merger was against the public interest. The reduction in competition, they argued, might lead to higher prices and a reduction in consumer choice. Increased vertical integration (the ownership of many of the relevant ports) would also have conferred a disturbing amount of market power on the new company. In coming to this decision the MMC clearly took the view that any benefit resulting from rationalization and increased efficiency would be outweighed by the costs to consumers of increased market power.

Some writers have pointed to the inconsistency in allowing the Hoverspeed/HoverLloyd merger to go through while blocking the European Ferries/Sealink merger. The reason for the MMC's decision is partly to do with the way in which a market can reasonably be defined. The hovercraft merger produced 100 per cent concentration in hovercraft services, but hovercraft accounted for a relatively small amount of cross-channel traffic, and there were good substitutes available. The European Ferries/Sealink merger would have increased concentration (but to much less than 100 per cent) and increased market power (because of the ownership of ports) in a much more important and clearly defined market for which there was no substitute at all (apart from air transport).

This case has a postscript. In 1984 Sealink UK was officially put up for sale as part of the Government's privatization programme. European Ferries asked to be allowed to bid, promising to cut cross-channel ferry prices by 15–20 per cent if it were allowed to buy Sealink. However, both European Ferries and P & O were barred from bidding for Sealink, which was eventually purchased by Sea Containers (registered in Bermuda and operating from London). In 1985 European Ferries bought the Anglo-French services of P & O, increasing its market share of the cross-channel route.

8.8 Petrol: a case of oligopoly pricing

At the wholesale level the market for petrol in the UK is an oligopoly. Unlike the market for breakfast cereals, however, which exhibited a reasonably stable structure over the period studied, the market for petrol has witnessed a reduction in seller concentration over the last 25 years. Moreover, in the market for petrol no firm is now the undisputed price leader, a role comparable to that played by Kellogg in the breakfast cereal market. Table 8.6 shows changes in the degree of seller concentration in the market for petrol since 1953, a convenient starting point since this date marks the abolition of wartime price controls and the reintroduction of branding. Market share in Table 8.6 is measured by the percentage of the total retail outlets supplied by each firm. An alternative measure of market share is gallonage, and this is shown in Table 8.7. As can be seen from Table 8.6, in 1953 five firms supplied virtually the whole market with two firms standing head and shoulders above the rest – Shell/BP (which at the time shared a joint retailing organization known as Shell-Mex and BP Ltd) and Esso. By 1979, however, although Shell, BP and Esso still had over 50 per cent of the market, a sizeable number of smaller firms, some of whom were 'majors' on a world scale, had entered the UK market. Together with the splitting-up of Shell-Mex and BP in 1976, the growth of these 'others' was the most significant factor in reducing the degree of concentration in the industry.

The reduction in concentration was a key aspect of the change in

Table 8.6 Shares of the UK retail market for petrol (%)

	1953	1960	1964	1970	1975	1976	1979
Shell	51.4	49.4	45.0	41.9	40.8	22.9	16.9
BP						17.4	19.4
Esso	28.4	29.8	27.4	22.5	21.8	22.0	20.1
Regent/Texaco	14.0	12.5	11.1	8.9	8.0	7.7	8.0
Mobil	1.1	4.2	5.9	4.0	4.3	4.4	4.8
Petrofina	2.2	2.5	2.5	3.6	3.8	3.7	3.8
Others	2.9	1.6	8.1	19.1	21.3	21.9	27.0

Note: Shell and BP shared a joint retailing organization, Shell-Mex and BP Ltd, until 1976, after which their respective market shares are shown separately.

Source: Early years' figures quoted in R. W. Shaw and C. J. Sutton, *Industry and Competition*, Macmillan, 1976, p. 24. Later years' figures from R.M. Grant, 'Pricing Behaviour in the UK wholesale market for petrol 1970–80: a "structure–conduct" analysis, *Journal of Industrial Economics*, vol. XXX, Mar. 1982

The Figures are for the percentage share of total retail outlets, an approximate indication of sales.

the structure of the industry, which in turn brought with it a change in the conduct of the firms operating there. Note the wording of the previous sentence. It says that the change in structure *brought with it* a change in conduct. We could have said that the change in structure *led to* a change in conduct which implies a definite causal link, but this would have been too strong since the causal link, though hypothesized, is by no means firmly established. We could, alternatively, have said that the change in structure *was accompanied by* a change in conduct but this would have missed the whole point, which is that the conduct (and performance) of an industry is influenced, if not determined, by its structure, the most important, but not the only aspect of which is the degree of concentration.

As we saw in section 8.5, the behaviour of firms in oligopolistic markets is uncertain because they are torn between the desire to compete and the opposing desire to collude. At any one time a firm's decision as to which of these two strategies to pursue will be influenced by the following considerations.

1. Seller concentration

Other things being equal, the smaller the number of firms in an industry the easier it will be for them to collude if they wish to do so.

The recognition of mutual interdependence will be that much greater and communication, both direct and implied, between the firms will be easier. The extent to which firms recognize their mutual interdependence will depend on the degree of cross-price elasticity of demand for their products. In other words, if the output of one firm is a very close substitute for the output of another, the cross-price elasticity, and therefore the recognition of interdependence, will be high. This condition is clearly satisfied in the market for petrol, since petrol is viewed by the consumer as a more or less homogeneous commodity. The introduction in 1969 of the star-rating of petrol by octane level reinforced this.

2. Demand conditions

At the firm level the price elasticity of demand is likely to be high because of the perceived homogeneity of the suppliers' petrol. At the industry level, however, the price elasticity of demand will be an important influence on the extent to which monopoly profits can be earned. If demand is inelastic, price increases will not reduce demand significantly, so that revenue and profits will increase. The demand for petrol appears to be highly price inelastic in the short run – the price of petrol rose by 75 per cent between the beginning of 1974 and the end of 1975 yet consumption fell by only 0.6 per cent. Thus, to the extent that the demand for petrol is inelastic, the incentive for firms to collude in raising prices and reaping monopoly profits is that much higher.

3. Entry barriers

Entry barriers are a way of protecting in the long term the monopoly profits discussed above. In the market for petrol, barriers to the entry of new firms existed by virtue of the fact that at the beginning of the period under consideration existing firms – the 'majors' – were vertically integrated backwards towards the source of their raw materials. The majors were of course active in oil exploration and production and they also had, and still have, a virtual monopoly on UK refinery capacity. This was not an insurmountable barrier to potential entrants, however, since there was an alternative source of supply, the Rotterdam spot market (and in fact many of the smaller independent firms secured supplies through contracts with the majors, though at prices which allowed little scope for price cutting). During the period under review the existing firms also sought to strengthen their position by forward integration. This was achieved by buying up existing retail outlets, particularly those in prime positions, and by exclusive supply contracts with retailers (so-called 'solus site' arrangements).

Thus, the existence of these entry barriers discouraged new firms from entering the market but did not, as it turned out, prevent it. The

Table 8.7 Wholesalers' shares of the UK retail market for petrol (by gallonage)

Company	**Market share (%)** 1964	**1970**	**1974**	**1975**	**1976**	**1977**	**1979**	**1980**
Shell-Mex and BP Limited	45.0	39.6	38.1	35.0	—	—	—	—
Munster Sims & Company Limited	—	—	—	—	—	—	—	—
Shell UK Limited	—	—	—	—	19.3	19.5	21.3	22.6
Esso Petroleum Company Limited	27.4	23.4	21.2	19.2	18.7	19.3	19.3	19.6
Agip Limited	0.2	—	—	—	—	—	—	—
BP Oil Limited	—	—	—	—	14.7	14.6	15.1	15.1
Texaco Limited	—	8.0	9.3	9.4	9.1	9.2	8.2	8.2
Regent Oil Company Limited	11.1	—	—	—	—	—	—	—
Mobil Oil Company Limited	5.9	7.1	6.8	6.6	7.0	7.1	8.4	7.1
Bowen Petroleum Limited	0.1	—	—	—	—	—	—	—
Conoco Limited	—	3.8	3.1	4.1	4.2	4.6	4.9	5.4
Jet Petroleum Limited	3.5	—	—	—	—	—	—	—
Total Oil Great Britain Limited	1.1	3.1	4.7	4.8	4.5	4.6	2.4	2.8
Gainsborough Petroleum Company Limited	0.2	—	—	—	—	—	—	—
Aero Petroleum Company Limited	0.2	—	—	—	—	—	—	—
Elf Oil Great Britain Limited	—	—	—	—	2.8	2.9	2.4	2.8
Isherwoods Petrol Company Limited	0.8	—	—	—	—	—	—	—
VIP Petroleum Limited	—	2.1	1.9	2.3	—	—	—	—

Petrofina UK Ltd	2.5	2.4	2.8	2.8	2.9	2.8	2.1	2.2
Burmah Oil Trading Limited	—	2.6	2.3	2.9	3.1	2.6	2.5	1.6
Lobitos Oilfields Limited *Curfew Petroleum Limited* *Major & Company Limited*	0.8	—	—	—	—	—	—	—
Imperial Chemical Industries Ltd	—	0.9	1.7	2.6	2.7	2.5	3.1	2.7
Gulf Oil (Great Britain) Limited	0.2	1.0	1.8	1.9	2.5	2.5	2.6	2.3
Amoco (UK) Limited	—	1.2	1.3	1.8	1.8	1.7	2.1	2.5
Chevron Oil (UK) Limited	—	0.7	1.0	1.1	1.1	1.1	1.0	0.7
Murco Petroleum Limited	0.3	1.7	1.3	1.3	1.3	1.1	1.0	1.0
Others	0.5	2.4	2.7	4.3	4.4	3.9	3.5	3.4
	100.0	100.0	100.0	100.0	100.0	100.0	100.0	100.0

Companies whose names are shown in *italic* type were taken over during the period.

Source: R. M. Grant, 'Pricing behaviour in the UK wholesale market for petrol 1970–80: a "structure–conduct" analysis', *Journal of Industrial Economics*, vol. XXX, Mar. 1982

Table 8.8 Inner zone scheduled wholesale prices for 4-star motor spirit

Date	Shell	Esso	Texaco	Mobil
16.1.70	6/0	6/0	6/0	6/0
31.7.70	6/0½	6/0½	6/0½	6/0½
6.11.70	6/1½	6/1½	6/1½	6/1½
21.2.71	31.75	—	—	—
22.2.71	—	31.75	31.75	31.75
28.4.72	—	—	—	31.15
29.4.72	32.15	—	—	—
1.5.72	—	32.15	32.15	—
9.9.72	32.65	—	—	—
11.9.72	—	32.65	32.65	32.65
29.4.73	33.65	33.65	—	33.65
15.5.73	—	—	33.65	—
4.10.73	34.65	34.65	34.65	34.65
15.12.73	37.35	37.35	37.35	37.35
12.2.74	45.25	45.30	45.25	45.27
18.12.74	52.20	52.15	52.20	52.20
2.12.75	55.00	—	—	—
3.12.75	—	55.00	—	55.02
8.12.75	—	—	55.00	—
*9.4.76	13.74	13.745	13.74	13.75
29.10.76	14.51	—	—	—
30.10.76	—	—	14.63	—
3.11.76	—	—	—	14.52
6.11.76	—	14.51	—	—
21.12.76	—	—	—	14.74
1.1.77	—	—	14.76	—
10.1.77	—	14.73	—	—
*29.3.77	15.61	14.83	15.86	15.84
26.4.77	16.08	—	—	—
27.4.77	—	—	16.08	—
29.4.77	—	16.08	—	16.08
8.7.77	15.49	—	—	—
*8.8.77	14.39	14.95	14.98	14.98
27.10.77	—	—	—	14.65
1.12.77	—	14.14	—	—
8.2.79	14.97	—	—	—
12.2.79	—	—	—	15.21
16.2.79	15.08	15.17	15.08	—

Table 8.8 continued

Date	Shell	Esso	Texaco	Mobil
6.4.79	—	15.82	16.08	15.82
9.4.79	15.73	—	—	—
26.5.79	—	—	18.58	18.42
12.6.79	18.45	—	—	—
18.6.79	—	18.43	—	—
2.7.79	—	19.60	—	—
3.7.79	19.81	—	—	—
4.7.79	—	—	20.08	—
5.7.79	—	—	—	20.41
29.11.79	20.20	—	—	—
28.12.79	—	20.30	—	—
29.12.79	—	—	20.50	—
1.1.80	—	—	—	20.41
17.1.80	21.08	—	21.20	21.20
18.1.80	—	21.07	—	—
19.2.80	21.85	21.64	—	—
20.2.80	—	—	21.84	21.85
26.3.80*	23.75	23.54	23.74	23.75
17.5.80	—	—	—	24.35
21.5.80	—	—	24.29	—
23.5.80	24.13	—	—	—
24.5.80	—	23.92	—	—
3.6.80	24.66	—	—	—
7.6.80	—	24.61	24.63	24.66
5.7.80	24.28	24.23	—	—
9.7.80	—	—	24.28	—
13.8.80	—	—	—	23.90

Notes 1 1970 prices in shillings and old pence per gallon: 1971–5 prices per gallon: 1976–80 prices in pence per litre.
2 Asterisks show changes in excise tax.
3 Prices include duty, exclude VAT.

Source: R. M. Grant, 'Pricing behaviour in the UK wholesale market for petrol 1970–80: a "structure–conduct" analysis', *Journal of Industrial Economics*, vol. XXX, Mar. 1982

inability of the existing firms to prevent this entry led to the reduction in concentration we have already noted. This reduced both the incentive for firms to collude and the ease with which they could do so, and was a significant factor in changing the observed price behaviour in the industry.

4. Cost conditions

If one company had enjoyed a clear cost advantage it might have been tempted to compete actively with the others in an attempt to oust them from the market. This was not the case, however, since they all used similar technologies for producing oil and refining it into petrol, so that their costs were similar. This therefore tended to reduce the likelihood of competition and increased the likelihood of collusion.

5. Supply conditions

Over the period studied supply conditions fluctuated between periods of shortage and periods of abundance. During periods when supplies were short the Rotterdam spot market dried up as a source of supply for the independent wholesalers, severely curtailing their ability to penetrate the retail market. However, in the period of abundant supplies between late 1974 and 1977 there was a substantial increase in market penetration by independents.

All the foregoing considerations are relevant in the change in the structure of the industry which took place. The most dramatic evidence of this changed structure is the observed reduction in concentration, but as we have seen there are other aspects which were important. The change in structure brought about a breakdown of the pricing discipline which had been a feature of the industry in the 1960s. During that period the major suppliers (principally Shell-Mex and BP but occasionally Esso) had acted as the price leader with the other firms dutifully following any change in prices. As can be seen from Table 8.8, this behaviour continued until the end of 1973.

Between 1970 and 1973, as Table 8.8 shows, firms charged identical prices and changed prices by the same amount. The response to a price change in most cases occurred either the same day or the following day. This 'well-orchestrated parallelism' was a clear example of collusion. Any price competition that did occur during this period took place by way of the discounts which wholesalers granted to retailers rather than through the posted wholesale prices shown in Table 8.8. Since the magnitude of these discounts was confidential, any competition between the wholesalers was thus furtive rather than open.

The Arab-Israeli war of late 1973 brought a brief period of shortage of supplies of petrol and a rapid increase in prices which was followed by a period of plentiful supplies. With supplies obtained from the Rotterdam spot market, where prices had dropped dramatically because of the glut, the independents were able to undercut the existing firms and increase their market share. This increased the pressure on the major suppliers to defend their position by price competition and, as can be seen from Table 8.8, the collusive pricing behaviour degenerated into more open competition.

8.9 Predatory pricing? Big boys attack Virgin

In oligopolistic markets outbreaks of price competition are relatively uncommon – so uncommon in fact that they are newsworthy. In September 1984, under headlines which talked about 'price wars', *The Times* reported the allegation that new entrants into the transatlantic airline business were being subjected to 'unfair competition' from the established firms. The new entrants, Virgin Atlantic and People Express, had commenced operations earlier in 1984, undercutting the existing operators. The President of Virgin Atlantic complained vociferously when the existing airlines announced that they too would be lowering their fares. 'It is a bit of a coincidence,' he said, 'that British Airways, Pan Am and TWA are all announcing this low fare on the same day. I would just like to point out that when Laker Airways was around they did a similar thing at a similar time. And after he had gone out of business fares went right up again. This is the first time fares have gone down like this since that time.' British Airways defended their new low fares, however, saying that it was economic and covered costs (the new fare of £259 was some £19 less than the pre-existing one and only £1 more than Virgin's). Virgin complained that British Airways' high profits from safe routes would enable it to crush smaller but more efficient competitors. For a small airline, competing with BA was 'like getting into a bleeding competition with a blood bank'.[6]

8.10 The effects of buyer concentration

8.10.1 Seller power versus buyer power

In all the markets considered so far in this chapter the consumer has been faced with an oligopolostic market structure of varying degrees of concentration. The demand side of the market has, however, been atomistic – that is, there are lots of buyers no one of whom is large enough to influence the prices set by the sellers. Many products which consumers buy are however purchased through retailers who themselves buy from the manufacturers. In some markets these same retailers enjoy a large measure of buyer power by virtue of their size and concentration. This is particularly marked in the food industry. In the market for packaged food the sellers – that is, the food manufacturers – form an oligolopistic grouping. The manufacturers, however, sell direct to retailers – supermarkets, and other retail outlets – and the degree of concentration here is high and increasing. Thus these retailers can, and do, exert a considerable amount of buyer power, influencing the prices at which the manufacturers supply their products to retailers.

Table 8.9 Market shares in food retailing 1971–84 (%)

	1971	1979	Dec. 1981	Mar. 1983	Mar. 1984
Multiples	44	59	70	73	74
Co-op	13	15	17	15	15
Independents	43	26	13	12	11

Source: Industry sources made available to the author. The primary source is AGB (Audits of Great Britain) survey data.

Table 8.10 Breakdown of market shares March 1984 (%)

Multiples	
Sainsbury	16.7
Tesco	15.0
Asda	8.0
Argyll (Presto, Liptons)	5.4
International	3.0
Fine Fare/Shoppers Paradise	4.6
Kwiksave	5.7
Total Dee/Keymarket	5.2
Waitrose	1.4
Safeway	2.0
Other multiples	8.6
Co-op	14.9
Symbols (VG, Spar, Mace)	5.4
Other independent grocers	5.3

Source: Industry sources made available to the author. Figures quoted in the text are from the same source.

Table 8.9 illustrates the growth of concentration in food retailing during 1971–84, a growth which could legitimately be described as dramatic. The increased concentration of course results from the decline of the small independent grocer and the rise of the large supermarket chains (the multiples).
Among the multiples themselves the degree of concentration is large, as Table 8.10, shows but these figures tend to underestimate by a large margin the degree of seller concentration, since the multiples, for reasons of distributional efficiency, tend to concentrate their activities in particular geographical areas. For example, in 1984 Kwiksave had a 22 per cent market share in Lancashire, and in London where one might expect the degree of concentration to be higher, the top two firms, Sainsbury and Tesco between them had a 59 per cent market share. Many of the remaining independent retailers have formed voluntary groupings – the 'symbols' (VG, Spar, etc.) – so that the market share left for the remaining independents is almost negligible, at least as far as the food manufacturers are concerned.

Among the multiples there is intense compeitition for market share. A key element of this competition, though not the only one, is price. Clearly, therefore, each of the multiples will wish to secure supplies of a particular product as cheaply as possible so that they can undercut their rival retailers while still maintaining an acceptable mark-up to cover the overheads of the store. The market power of the multiples enables them to impose considerable pressure on the manufacturers and, it is alleged, they use this power to great effect in forcing down suppliers' prices and thus squeezing suppliers' profit margins. The threat to 'de-list' a product (that is, not to stock it on the supermarket shelves) is normally sufficient to persuade a manufacturer to accept the terms which the multiple dictates.

It would be wrong to suppose, however, that the multiples have the upper hand in all bargaining situations between manufacturer and retailer. If the good in question is more or less homogeneous – that is, if the products of rival manufacturers are indistinguishable or at least acceptable substitutes – then the manufacturer will be in a weak bargaining position. He will have no market power. If, on the other hand, the manufacturer can successfully differentiate his brand from that of his rivals, and establish loyalty with consumers, he will be in a strong bargaining position, that is, he will enjoy an element of monopoly power. The extent to which manufacturers are able to do this is referred to by marketing men as 'the strength of the brand'. For example, Nescafé instant coffee and Heinz tomato sauce are both strong brands. They enjoy a privileged position in their respective markets since they are the acknowledged market leaders. Since they are perceived by the consumer as being superior to rival brands they can be sold at a premium (that is, at a higher price than rival brands).

Table 8.11 Profitability of UK food companies 1981–82

	Sales 1981–82 (£'000)	Pre-tax Profits 1981–82 (£'000)	Profit Margin 1980–81 (%)	Profit Margin 1981–82 (%)
Kellogg of Gt Britain	178 694	29 599	12.2	16.6
Bovril	53 093	5 610	11.3	10.6
General Foods	157 153	16 250	6.8	10.3
H. J. Heinz	319 019	29 750	7.8	9.3
C. Shippam	22 184	2 002	8.9	9.0
The Ryvita Company	20 177	1 592	10.9	7.9
Van Den Berghs & Jurgens	298 469	23 072	6.5	7.7
Avana Group	125 578	9 488	6.2	7.6
Unigate	504 000	38 300	2.8	7.6
Mattessons Meats	76 286	5 389	6.9	7.1
Robertson Foods	82 902	5 724	2.8	6.9
Golden Wonder	89 079	6 025	8.2	6.8
Cadbury Schweppes	1 271 000	80 600	5.5	6.3
Campbell's Soups	35 304	2 126	11.2	6.0
J. Bibby & Sons	200 724	11 953	5.7	6.0
United Biscuits	1 026 000	60 900	5.6	5.9
HP Foods	80 827	4 450	4.5	5.5
Nabisco	57 548	2 421	2.9	4.2
Northern Foods	1 004 000	41 172	4.5	4.1
Burtons Gold Medal Biscuits	95 110	3 726	6.0	3.9
Batchelors Foods	84 435	3 096	4.5	3.7
Brooke Bond Group	996 328	35 314	5.1	3.5
J. Lyons & Co.	361 499	9 497	6.2	2.6
Haverhill Meat Products	84 561	2 083	3.9	2.5
Ross Foods	221 053	4 952	1.7	2.2
Rank Hovis McDougall	1 598 000	34 071	2.9	2.1
Tate & Lyle	1 950 000	40 100	1.7	2.1
Huntley & Palmer Foods	363 597	6 501	2.1	1.8
Findus	117 638	1 702	0.2	1.4

Table 8.11 continued

	Sales 1981–82 (£'000)	Pre-tax Profits 1981–82 (£'000)	Profit Margin 1980–81 (%)	1981–82 (%)
Kraft Foods	126 830	1 536	1.3	1.2
Weetabix	67 398	608	1.7	0.9
Adams Foods	145 747	1 237	0.7	0.8
Birds Eye Walls	384 743	2 531	4.3	0.7
William Jackson & Son	142 728	1 060	1.7	0.7
Danish Bacon Co.	207 843	580	– 0.1	0.3
Union International	1 097 000	2 472	– 0.5	0.2
Lovell & Christmas	136 551	320	– 0.6	0.2
J. B. Eastwood	164 595	159	– 3.3	0.1
T. Wall & Sons	98 549	– 2 422	– 0.2	– 2.5

Source: *World Food Report*, 21 Dec. 1983, based on ICC Business Ratios

The extra profit which this makes possible can be 're-invested' in advertising, further reinforcing the strength of the brand. The stronger the brand, the more than can be spent on advertising. The more that can be spent on advertising, the stronger the brand – a process of circular causation which protects the privileged position of the market leader and creates barriers to the entry of new firms.

A strong brand, then, is one for which there are no close substitutes. The extent to which the brand is perceived as being superior to rival brands is due partly to real differences in the product and partly to imaginary differences created by advertising. For example, it is well known that Heinz tomato sauce is a superior product containing more tomatoes and less of the cheaper ingredients than rival brands. Advertising serves to accentuate this difference. The most effective form of advertising is that which seeks to convince the consumer not just that the brand in question is superior to rival brands but that *no acceptable substitutes exist.* Such a technique is epitomized in the advertising slogan for Heinz baked beans: 'Beanz means Heinz'. That is, baked beans are identified exclusively with that particular brand: no acceptable substitute exists. The elasticity of demand is therefore lower so that higher prices for the Heinz beans do not cause consumers to switch to rival brands.

8.10.2 Buyer power squeezes producers' profit margins

The increased concentration among retailers and the market power which this gives them has resulted in an alleged squeezing of manufacturers' profit margins. These are shown in Table 8.11. Note that profit margin here is defined simply as the ratio of pre-tax profits to sales, which is a rather imperfect measure of profitability. A better measure would be profits as a percentage of capital employed but the difficulty here is to get an objective measure of the value of capital employed. A high return on capital employed can of course be achieved by opting for a strategy of high volume with low margins (low mark-ups). Some of the firms which show low profit margins according to the definition used in Table 8.11 undoubtedly come into this category (for example, Tate & Lyle, the sugar refiners, with sales of almost £2 billion in1981/82. It is interesting to note, however, that the firms near the top of the league in Table 8.11 are those with strong brands. This bears out the observations on brand strength which we made in the previous section.

8.10.3 Brands versus own-label

One of the most significant effects of the increase in buyer concentration in retailing has been the development of own-label products, sold under the brand name not of the food manufacturer but of the supermarket that sells them. Own-label products accounted for over half of Sainsbury's sales in 1984.[7] Figure 8.5 shows the penetration of own-label for a number of different products. These products are sometimes manufactured by the brand leaders themselves or, more often, by rival manufacturers. (For example, General Foods, the manufacturer of Maxwell House instant coffee, also manufacture own-label instant coffee for Sainsbury). The own-label product undercuts the manufacturer's brand by a sizeable margin, as Table 8.12 shows. Although this is an important consideration from the consumers' point of view, what is still more important for the retailer and the manufacturer is that manufacturers' profit margins are less on supplying own-label products than on supplying branded products. The manufacturers therefore would prefer to supply branded rather than own-label products but the strength of the retailers, coupled with the need to fill some manufacturing overcapacity, has compelled the manufacturers to enter into long-term contracts to supply own-label products to the retailers. From the retailers' point of view the attraction of own-label is threefold. Firstly, by charging lower prices they hope to steal market share from their rivals. Secondly, the mark-up (for the retailer) on own-label may be more than on branded goods. Thirdly, the fact that the own-label brand *becomes* the brand means that the retailer can begin to enjoy the sort of brand loyalty previously enjoyed by the manufacturer. This carries with it all of the advantages of a differentiated product and consequent barriers to the entry of new

Table 8.12 How own-label products undercut the brand leaders

	Price difference on standard sizes (%)							
	Safeway	**Sainsbury**	**Key Markets**	**Tesco**	**Fine Fare**	**Waitrose**	**Co-op**	**Average**
Cooking oil	9.4	12.6	4.2	8.5	15.7	12.6	9.4	10.3
Flour	5.5	10.2	13.6	7.7	11.9	15.0	—	10.7
Baked beans	10.2	10.2	10.2	10.2	8.3	7.7	10.2	9.6
Fruit squash	13.5	—	23.7	13.5	13.4	5.7	13.5	13.9
Instant coffee	17.6	23.0	27.5	13.3	13.9	12.8	38.3	20.9
Washing-up liquid	6.7	25.3	10.6	32.2	—	6.3	25.6	17.8
Margarine	7.9	17.0	—	23.5	8.6	18.4	—	15.0
Dog Food	32.2	4.8	21.0	11.8	23.7	12.9	21.9	18.3
Average	12.9	14.7	15.8	15.0	13.6	11.4	19.8	14.6

Source: *Marketing*, 8 Mar. 1984

firms which typify the aspirations of oligopolistic firms. This helps to explain why new firms that have recently entered food retailing, for example Marks and Spencer, have done so with an almost exclusively own-label range of products.

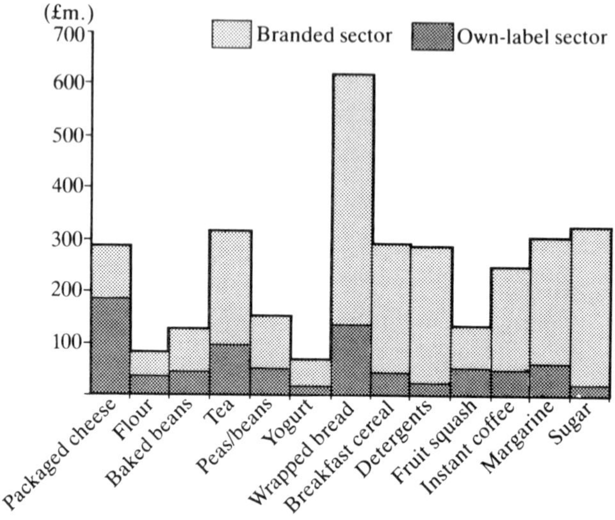

Fig. 8.5 The impact of own-label on the total market

(Source: *Marketing*, 8 Mar. 1984)

8.10.4 Countervailing power?

The extent and growth of concentration among retailers has led to a situation in which the oligopolistic power of the food manufacturers has been counterbalanced by the buying power of the retailers. This is an example of what the economist J. K. Galbraith has described as *countervailing power*. In his view there is a natural tendency in market economies for the existence of monopoly power to give birth to countervailing groups seeking to win some of those monopoly profits for themselves. He cites two examples: firstly, the growth of retailer power pitted against the power of the manufacturers; and secondly, the growth of trade union concentration, particularly in those industries where the firms enjoy monopoly power in the markets in which they sell their goods. An indication of the growth in trade union concentration is given in Table 8.13.

The growth of retailer power and the growth of trade union power are both phenomena which have occurred in the twentieth century. Most economists – including perhaps Galbraith himself in later works – would however stop short of seeing this as evidence for

Table 8.13 The growth of trade union concentration 1902–74

Year	**1902** (%)	**1919** (%)	**1930** (%)	**1948** (%)	**1957** (%)	**1974** (%)
C10*	4.2	15.0	12.0	22.0	21.5	27.4
% age of workforce unionized	11.0	40.3	22.9	41.8	40.8	46.4

*Percentage of total union membership accounted for by the ten largest unions.

Source: L. Hannah and J. A. Kay, *Concentration in Modern Industry*. Macmillan, 1977, p. 114.

the existence of a natural law of countervailing power. If there were such a natural tendency in market economies then this would be regarded by supporters of the market system (that is, capitalism) as one of the strengths of the system. A dynamic system of checks and balances which ensures that no one group gets too much power, and ensures that the abuse of a monopoly position carries with it the seeds of its own destruction, would indeed be a powerful justification for the market mechanism as an equitable way of allocating resources. What is more likely, however, is that the increase in buyer concentration among retailers is nothing more than an historical accident brought about by changes in social patterns (for example, the increase in car ownership and in the ownership of fridges and freezers which have brought a change in shopping habits).

Notes

1. See **Hart, P. E.** and **Clarke, R.**, *Concentration in British Industry 1935–75*, NIESR Occasional Paper XXXII, Cambridge, 1980, p. 44.
2. See **Davies, G.** and **Davies, J.**, 'The revolution in monopoly theory, *Lloyds Bank Review*, July 1984, No. 153.
3. The Monopolies Commission, *Breakfast Cereals: A Report on the Supply of Ready-Cooked Breakfast Cereal Foods*. HMSO, 1973.
4. Report by the Office of Fair Trading, *Ford Motor Co. Ltd: Licensing for the manufacture or sale of replacement parts*, 21 Mar. 1984.
5. Monopolies and Mergers Commission Report on Ford Motor Company Ltd. 'A report on the policy and practice of the Ford Motor Company Limited of not granting licences to manufacture or sell in the United Kingdom certain replacement body parts for Ford vehicles,' *HMSO*, Feb. 1985, Section 6.73.

6. *The Times*, 20 Sept. 1984.

7. '*Own Labels versus the Brands*', *Marketing*, 8 Mar. 1984.

Questions

8.1 If a competitive industry is replaced by a monopolistic one, which of the following statements are true? Correct the false ones.
(a) Prices in the industry will inevitably rise.
(b) The monopolist may choose not to maximize profits, so prices may not rise.
(c) The monopolist will have lower costs by virtue of his size so prices will fall.
(d) The monopolist may have lower costs by virtue of his size, but prices will rise if the monopolist exploits his market power.
(e) The MES in the industry may be quite small so that further concentration does not lead to significant cost reductions.
(f) Increased concentration at firm level will result in increased concentration at plant level. Unit costs will therefore fall.

8.2 Which of the following definitions of a 'monopoly situation' is used by the Monopolies Commission?
(a) one firm supplies the whole market
(b) one firm supplies over 50 per cent of the market for a particular good
(c) a single firm, or a group of firms acting together so as to restrict competition, controls over 25 per cent of the market
(d) the 3-firm concentration ratio exceeds 90 per cent

8.3 In addition to the current level of seller concentration, what other factors might be relevant in assessing whether a monopoly situation exists?

8.4 This question relates to section 8.3, on the Kellogg's Corn Flakes case.
(a) What form(s) of non-price competition were pursued by Kellogg? What was the principal purpose of such tactics?
(b) What was the impact of the introduction of own-brand cornflakes?

8.5 This question relates to section 8.4, on replacement body panels for Ford. The exercise by Ford of its artistic and design copyright constituted an anti-competitive tactic when applied to the replacement parts market but not when applied to the new vehicle market. Why?

8.6 If Boots the chemist took over a manufacturer of shampoo this would be an example of:
(a) vertical integration
(b) forward integration
(c) backward integration
(d) both (a) and (b)
(e) both (a) and (c)

8.7 If Boots the chemist started to sell package holidays in their retail outlets this would be:
(a) forward integration
(b) diversification
(c) 'a logical extension of their existing activity in retailing'

8.8 Suppose two former competitors merge and the subsequent profitability of the merged companies exceeds the profits that could have been expected if the two companies had remained separate. Consider whether the following statements are true.
(a) Since profits have increased the merger must have increased efficiency. Therefore the merger was in the public interest.
(b) If profits have increased it is evidence that market power has increased. Therefore the merger was against the public interest.

8.9 Of what relevance is the concept of MEPS in assessing the desirability of a proposed merger?

Questions 8.10, 8.11 and 8.12 relate to section 8.7.1, on European Ferries and Sealink.

8.10 The ownership by European Ferries of a number of cross-channel ports is an example of:
(a) not putting all your eggs into one basket
(b) vertical integration
(c) innovation

8.11 The ownership by European Ferries of these ports constituted:
(a) a threat to national security
(b) a better service to consumers as a result of scale economies
(c) a potential barrier to the entry of new firms

8.12 Why did the MMC allow the merger between the two hovercraft companies but disallow the proposed merger between European Ferries and Sealink?
(a) the MMC accepted that without rationalization hovercraft services would cease
(b) hovercraft were a British invention
(c) the relevant market (from the MMC's point of view) was seaborne cross-channel services. Hovercraft services did not constitute a market in themselves, merely one type of service, for which adequate substitutes existed.

8.13 What motivated the oil companies to re-introduce the branding of petrol in 1953? What was the reason for the introduction in 1969 of the star-rating of petrol by octane level?

8.14 Firms in oligopolistic markets are torn between the desire to compete and the opposing desire to collude. Consider each of the following factors and state whether it will increase or decrease the likelihood of collusion:
(a) the degree of seller concentration is high
(b) demand for the industry product is inelastic
(c) there are no effective barriers to the entry of new firms
(d) one firm enjoys a significant cost advantage

8.15 This question relates to section 8.9, on the Virgin Airlines case. Comment on the validity of the following statement:
'The action by British Airways is an example of cutthroat competition. Competition is good because it leads to lower prices which must be in the consumer's interest.'

8.16 List the scale economies which you think large supermarket chains enjoy. Which of these are real and which are purely financial economies of scale?

8.17 The following advertising slogans are all designed to convince the consumer that no acceptable substitute exists for the brand in question:

'Once you've tasted Perrier nothing else will do'

'Australians wouldn't give a XXXX for any other lager' (slogan for Castlemaine Four X)

What implications does this have for the elasticity of demand for the product and for prices and profits? Give examples of other advertising slogans which have the same intention.

8.18 Why do you suppose that Marks and Spencer, a firm with an established reputation as a retailer of good quality clothes, entered the food retailing business with an almost exclusively own-label range of products?

Chapter 9
Multinationals

In Chapter 8 we looked at the behaviour of firms operating in oligopolistic markets. A typical feature of such firms is their large size, but size in itself is not the only characteristic. A related feature of such firms is that they tend to be multinational. The word 'multinational' means something specific and is not merely a pseudonym for 'international'. A multinational firm (or MNE – multinational enterprise, or MNC – multinational company) is one that has production facilities in more than one country. Thus Ford, which has car plants all over the world, is, by definition, multinational. A company like British Leyland which produces in only one country and then exports part of its output is, however, by definition, not multinational. The difference, though seemingly trivial, is very important, as we shall see.

9.1 A brief history of the multinational company: the product life cycle

Multinational companies began to develop in a significant way in the inter-war period when companies based in America expanded their operations by establishing production facilities outside the United States, mostly (at that time) in Europe. There are several reasons why such companies adopted this strategy rather than choosing to export to Europe goods produced in America. Many of these reasons are illustrated by *Vernon's product life cycle theory*[1] (though there is no suggestion that a single rather simplistic theory can adequately explain the historical reasons for the growth and diversity of multinational activity). Vernon's theory suggests that all products go through a number of evolutionary phases during their life cycle. The cycle is initiated by the discovery or invention of a new product – for example, the telephone, the motor car, the microcomputer, and so on. The discovery is then refined to the stage where a product can be sold to the mass market. When Vernon first put forward his product life cycle theory, the United States economy had a position of pre-eminence such that most research and development work leading to the discovery of new products took place there. The American mass market was also by far the most important market because of its size and the level of income per capita. Hence new products were developed in America and the American market was the first to be exploited. The products which Vernon had in mind were consumer durable products. As the name implies, such products tend not to wear out very quickly so that the growth of sales of, say, vacuum cleaners would have a time profile rather like that in Fig. 9.1. That is, sales would increase more or less exponentially up to point A and then start to tail off as the market became satiated. At point B every household that wanted one would already own a vacuum cleaner, so that the potential for further sales was limited to replacing those that were worn out. Although with experience some manufacturers became more adept at making their products wear out more quickly, the scope for so doing was restricted since products which wore out too quickly would be perceived by consumers as being of low quality and sales of that brand would suffer as a result. 'Built-in obsolescence' could also be achieved by major technical advances which brought a significant improvement in the performance of new versions of the product, but there was little scope for this in vacuum cleaners or in many other consumer durables. 'Design improvements' were thus limited to cosmetic changes which failed to persuade even the most gullible of consumers that they should replace their old model with a new one.

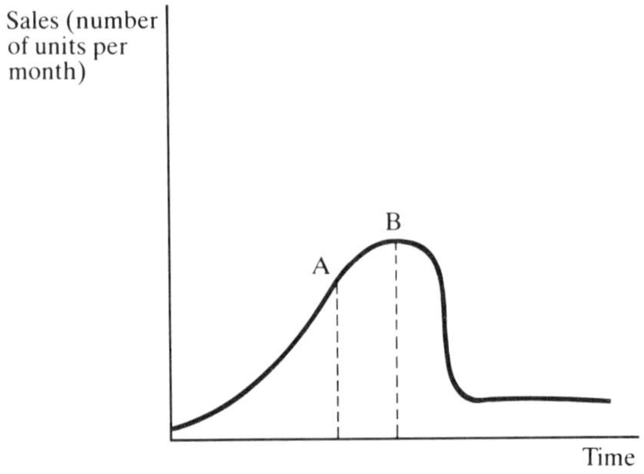

Fig. 9.1

With the domestic American market saturated, manufacturers sought new markets overseas – particularly in Britain and continental Europe. They could, of course, have exported to Europe products made in America. They preferred, however, to establish production facilities in those countries whose markets they wished to exploit. The advantages of so doing were many. Firstly, it overcame the problem of import restrictions which some governments had imposed. Secondly, it reduced transport costs. Thirdly, labour costs in Europe were generally lower than those in America so that products could be produced more cheaply. By establishing production facilities in Europe, American firms were able to compete not on equal terms with European rivals but on superior terms since the research and development expenditure associated with the new product had already been amortized (written off) in the American market. Because American firms in Europe had this significant advantage over their European competitors, they prospered. The age of the multinational had begun.

On the European market of course the growth of sales of a particular product had a time profile similar to that illustrated in Fig. 9.1. When the European market had been satiated therefore, the American multinationals had again to look around for new markets to exploit, and these they found in the Far East, in Africa, in South America and Australasia – in short, in all corners of the globe.

Although Vernon's theory is introduced here as a (partial) explanation of the emergence of the multinational company, it has a much wider and more general application since many products seem to experience a life cycle which can be broken down into three phases: rapid growth of sales, satiation and then stagnation. Some products, of course, have an extremely short life cycle – the hula hoop, the skateboard and the Rubic Cube are three examples of products with a life cycle of less than one year. It could be argued that these are just 'crazes', playthings which have no useful function. The same could also be said, however, about the cheap home computer which appears to have had a life cycle of about three years. Other products of course have a life cycle extending over several decades – the motor car for example. The current worldwide overcapacity in the car industry is partly the result of the approaching satiation in the demand for cars. In products like cars, however, the replacement demand is still substantial since obsolescence is built into the car, both because it is designed to wear out and because technical improvements, though modest, are sufficient to convince consumers that the new model is an improvement on the old. Note that cars could be designed to wear out more slowly but that this would generally lead to lower performance and higher cost. Finally, it should be noted that although certain products do appear to have a life cycle like that illustrated in Fig. 9.1, some writers argue that there is no empirical support for the theory. Clearly for non-durable products, and even for durable products where significant scope for design improvement exists, there is no reason why saturation should ever be reached. In other words, one is always operating on the upward-sloping portion of the life-cycle curve.

Table 9.1 The world's top fifty industrial groupings

Rank	Company	Headquarters	Main Activity	Sales (£m)	Year end
1	Exxon Corpn.	USA	Oil industry	66 705.2	31.12.82
2	Shell Transport & Trading/ Royal Dutch Petroleum	UK/Netherlands	Oil industry	54 776.0	31.12.82
3	American Telephone & Telegraph	USA	Telephone system operators	42 544.4	31.12.82
4	Mobil Corpn.	USA	Oil industry	41 251.0	31.12.82
5	Mitsubishi Corpn.	Japan	Conglomerate	40 182.1	31.03.82
6	General Motors Corpn.	USA	Motor vehicles	39 232.4	31.12.82
7	Mitsui & Co.	Japan	Conglomerate	36 183.3	31.03.82
8	British Petroleum	UK	Oil industry	34 583.0	31.12.82
9	C. Itoh & Co.	Japan	Conglomerate	33 750.1	31.03.82
10	Marubeni	Japan	Conglomerate	31 593.6	31.03.82
11	Texaco	USA	Oil industry	30 710.0	31.12.82
12	Sumitomo Corpn.	Japan	Conglomerate	29 998.2	31.03.82
13	Ford Motor	USA	Motor vehicles	24 226.9	31.12.82
14	Standard Oil Co. of California	USA	Oil industry	23 018.3	31.12.82
15	International Business Machines	USA	Business machine manufacturers	22 460.1	31.12.82
16	De Pont (E.I.) de Nemours	USA	Chemical and oil industries	21 785.0	31.12.82
17	Nissho Iwai	Japan	Conglomerate	20 334.3	31.03.82
18	Gulf Oil Corpn.	USA	Oil industry	20 020.0	31.12.82
19	Sears, Roebuck	USA	General merchandise retailers	19 620.8	31.12.82

20	Standard Oil (Indiana)	USA	Oil industry	18 348.4	31.12.82
21	Atlantic Richfield	USA	Oil industry	17 640.9	31.12.82
22	General Electric	USA	Consumer product & power system manufacturers	17 320.3	31.12.82
23	ENI	Italy	Oil and chemical industries, etc.	16 092.6	31.12.81
24	Shell Oil	USA	Oil and gas industries	13 585.6	31.12.82
25	Unilever PLC/Unilver NV	UK/Netherlands	Food, detergents, animal foods, toiletries	13 215.7	31.12.82
26	Veba	West Germany	Electricity oil, chemicals	13 023.7	31.12.82
27	United States Steel	USA	Steel and oil & gas producers	12 357.5	31.12.82
28	Occidental Petroleum	USA	Energy resources co.	11 903.4	31.12.82
29	Safeway Stores	USA	Supermarket operators	11 524.7	01.01.83
30	B.A.T. Industries	UK	Tobacco, retailing, paper, packaging, etc.	11 318.0	31.12.82
31	Française des Petroles	France	Oil industry	11 310.8	31.12.82
32	K Mart Corpn.	USA	Discount store operators	10 962.2	26.01.83
33	Petróleos de Venezuela	Venezuela	Oil industry	10 762.5	31.12.82
34	Toyota Motor	Japan	Motor vehicles	10 532.3	31.03.83
35	Sun Co., Inc.	USA	Oil industry	10 482.4	31.12.82
36	International Telephone & Telegraph	USA	Telecommunication & electronic equipment manufacturers	10 430.4	31.12.82
37	Siemens	West Germany	Electrical & general engineering	10 336.6	31.12.82
38	Philips Petroleum	USA	Oil industry	10 260.1	31.12.82

Table 9.1 Continued

Rank	Company	Headquarters	Main Activity	Sales (£m)	Year end
39	Toyo Menka	Japan	Conglomerate	10 164.5	31.03.82
40	Daimler-Benz	West Germany	Motor vehicles	10 027.1	31.12.82
41	Philips' Lamps Holding	Netherlands	Electrical & electronic products	9 883.0	31.12.82
42	Elf Aquitaine (Sté Nationale) -SNEA	France	Oil industry	9 859.0	31.12.82
43	Tenneco	USA	Oil industry, etc.	9 790.2	31.12.82
44	Volkswagenwerk	West Germany	Motor vehicles	9 647.9	31.12.82
45	Nippon Oil	Japan	Oil industry	9 637.7	31.03.83
46	Tokyo Electric Power	Japan	Electric utility	9 531.6	31.03.83
47	Fiat	Italy	Motor vehicles	9 019.8	31.12.82
48	Hoechst	West Germany	Chemicals, dyes & plastics	9 017.0	31.12.82
49	Bayer	West Germany	Chemicals	8 977.8	31.12.82
50	Renault	France	Motor vehicles	8 943.3	31.12.82

Notes: Exchange rates used at 30.6.83: France 11.645 Francs to £1; Italy 2300.5 Lira to £1; Japan 365.5 Yen to £1; Netherlands 4.35 Guilders to £1; USA $1.53 to £1; Venezuela 6.57 Bolivar to £1; and West Germany 3.88 DM to £1.

Source: *The Times 1,000*, 1983

9.2 The size of multinationals

The product life cycle helps to explain the reasons for the initial emergence of the multinational company. It is, of course, an over simplification and many of the most important multinationals do not fit into this model. Some are European-based multinationals like Unilever and Philips. Others are Japanese, like Mitsubishi, and many are oil companies whose activities naturally lend themselves to a multinational format. Multinationals have distinct advantages over purely national companies. These advantages (which are discussed in section 9.3) have resulted in the growth rate of such companies far exceeding that of companies which stick to national boundaries. A corollary of this is that companies which wish to grow rapidly are forced, sooner or later, to extend their activities beyond the frontiers of their native land. Initially they do this by exporting, but to secure the advantages of the truly multinational company they must eventually establish or take over subsidiary companies in other countries. Hence, when we look at the statistics we find that the growth rate of MNCs exceeds that of other companies both because existing MNCs have advantages over other companies, and because other companies are themselves forced to become multinational to secure these advantages.

There is therefore a resulting tendency for MNCs to become the dominant organizational form both in world trade and world economic activity generally. The world's largest multinationals are now very large indeed. Table 9.1 lists the top fifty industrial companies in 1982 which, with few exceptions, are multinational. The annual sales figures of these companies can be compared with the figures for gross domestic product (that is, annual output) for a selection of countries shown in Table 9.2. As can be seen, the annual sales figures of the largest companies easily exceed the GDP of middle-ranking countries like Denmark and Greece. A more telling statistic perhaps is that in 1982 the combined annual sales revenue of the top seven companies in the world came to about £320 bn – about $490 bn – somewhat larger than the entire annual output (GDP) of the UK. The large multinational companies therefore represent a concentration of economic power which, for many writers, is cause for concern and alarm.

The importance of the multinational enterprise in world trade is particularly striking. One author[2] has estimated that in 1981 just 72 firms accounted for half of Britain's exports, and only 18 per cent of Britain's exports were not accounted for by multinationals. In the following two sections we examine why MNCs have prospered. Section 9.3 considers some of the specific advantages they possess in comparison to national companies, and section 9.4 considers particular aspects of multinational activity.

Table 9.2 GDP of some 'middle-ranking' countries (billions of US dollars) 1982

Smaller than Exxon:	
New Zealand	23.8
Denmark	56.4
Finland	49.1
Greece	38.3
Ireland	17.6
Luxembourg	3.3
Norway	56.1
Portugal	23.4
Turkey	52.9
For comparison:	
USA	3041
Japan	1061
France	540
West Germany	659
UK	477

Source: *National Accounts of OECD Countries 1953–1982*, vol. 1
Note: Exxon – better known in the UK by the brand name Esso– had sales revenue in 1982 of $102 bn

9.3 The advantages of being a multinational

9.3.1 The advantages of size

Some of the advantages enjoyed by MNCs exist simply by virtue of the size of such companies rather than as a result of any particular organizational form. Size in itself facilitates further growth for a number of reasons. For example, the cost of acquiring funds for investment may well be lower for the large firm than it is for the small firm. This is so because large firms have access to privileged sources of funds only available to large, financially secure firms. One such source of funds is the Eurodollar market where large sums are borrowed and lent by multinationals at interest rates which are generally lower than elsewhere. Furthermore, there is no exchange rate risk since the funds are borrowed and lent in dollars and are never converted into any other currency. Large firms are also able to finance much of their investment through internally generated funds, that is, through retained earnings. Such advantages are, of course, just one of the economies of scale enjoyed by the large firm. It is important to distinguish however between *real economies* of scale and *pecuniary economies* of scale. Real economies benefit both the firm and society at large because there is a real saving in the resources required to do a particular job. Pecuniary economies, on the other hand, benefit the firm but are irrelevant from a societal point of view because there is no saving in resources resulting from increased efficiency. *Financial economies* are the most obvious example of a pecuniary scale economy which results from the large firm's market power or bargaining strength. This market power may enable it to negotiate more favourable credit terms on loans, or to purchase materials and other goods more cheaply than the small firm is able to do. These financial economies, then, are mostly pecuniary in nature rather than real. However, a not insignificant part of the financial economies results from the lower transactions costs per unit associated with the bulk purchase of materials or the negotiation of larger loans rather than small. These are real economies.

The decision as to whether a particular financial saving should be classified as 'real' or 'pecuniary' becomes more difficult when one recognizes that lending to large firms is less risky than lending to small ones. Large firms are less likely to default. The lower risk explains in part the cheaper interest rates available to the large firm. However, on reflection it can be seen that the reason that lending to large firms is less risky than lending to small ones is because large firms are able to internalize the risk within the firm and thus bear the risk themselves rather than impose it on the lender. Thus in the two cases the risk is borne by different parties – by the lender when loans are made to small firms and by the firm itself when loans are made to large firms. The risk inherent in the investment to which the loan relates is the same, however, regardless of who is undertaking it. This inherent risk depends on the nature of the investment project itself.

9.3.2 Risk spreading

The ability to spread the risk inherent in business activity, and hence to reduce its overall impact on the company is, of course, one of the major advantages conferred by size. The multinational company, however, can add an extra dimension to this risk-spreading activity by diversifying its activities over several countries and continents as well as over several product ranges and types of business activity. Thus the Ford Motor Company, an American multinational, has subsidiary companies (Ford would probably call them 'affiliates') in many parts of the world. The early 1980s saw a period when Ford of America was making heavy losses but was being supported by the profits being repatriated to it from Ford of Europe who at that time were highly profitable. By spreading risk in this way the multinational is thus less susceptible to the effects of cyclical fluctuations in economic activity. These fluctuations – recessions and booms – tend of course to be a worldwide phenomenon affecting all those countries linked by trade. However, the timing of these fluctuations and their magnitude differ from country to country. Moreover, the impact which these fluctuations will have on the multinational and its affiliates will depend on a complex set of factors, one of the most important of which is the behaviour of exchange rates.

9.4 Aspects of multinational activity

The important point to note is that a multinational format allows a company to take advantage of movements in economic activity. Being footloose and fancy free, without any ties or allegiancies, the multinational is able to turn to its own advantage those movements in economic activity which, for purely national companies, would present severe problems. These movements in economic activity may be cyclical, such as the short-term recessions mentioned above, or they may be secular – that is, part of a long-term trend.

9.4.1 Investment flows

The multinational will, for example, respond to secular movements in economic activity by adjusting its investment flows accordingly. That is, investment will flow to those areas where the rate of return is highest. If, for example, the American or the South African economy is growing faster and offering greater investment potential than the UK economy, then UK-owned multinationals will tend quite naturally to direct their investment flows out of the UK and towards the USA and South Africa. This investment in itself facilitates economic expansion, of course, and raises the growth rate of these other economies, thus confirming the multinational in its belief that the rate of return on investment overseas was greater than that in the UK. To the extent that this occurs, it clearly depresses the growth rate of the UK economy.

9.4.2 Sourcing

Multinational companies involved in manufacturing activity, such as the motor companies, frequently assemble their products utilizing components manufactured by their subsidiaries in other countries. Table 9.3 shows the sources of the components used in assembling the Vauxhall Astra, a nominally British car built by Vauxhall Motors, the UK subsidiary of the US multinational General Motors. This car can validly be described as a British car in the sense that it is assembled in the UK, and if one includes the cost of the manpower involved in its assembly then the local (i.e. British) content is estimated to be 62 per cent.[3] The remainder is sourced from a variety of GM subsidiaries in Europe and elsewhere.

The procurement of components and materials from subsidiaries in other countries is a common feature of multinational activity. It is sometimes referred to simply as 'sourcing'. One implication of sourcing is that products which appear (for example) to be British made may contain a high proportion of foreign-made components. This has implications for the balance of trade since if, for example, Vauxhall Astras are sold on export markets, the net benefit to the balance of trade is much less than the gross benefit since each car contains a high import content.

Table 9.3 Sources of components for Vauxhall Astra

Front doors	UK	Transmission	
Floor pan	UK	1.3 litre cars	Austria
Rear doors	WG	1.6 litre cars	Japan
Tailgate	WG	Automatics	France
Roof	WG	Electrical wiring	Eire/WG
Bonnet	UK	Wheels	UK
Glass	UK	Bumpers	WG
Radiator	France	Suspension	WG
Engine		Seat frames	WG
1.2 litre cars	WG	Upholstery	UK
1.3 litre cars	Austria/WG	Interior trim	UK
1.6 litre cars	Australia	Instruments	UK
1.8 litre cars	WG	Headlamps	WG
diesel	WG		

WG = West Germany

Source: *The Observer*, 21 Oct. 1984

9.4.3 Transfer pricing

Sourcing is, of course, a legitimate business practice. It has been alleged, however, that some multinationals source their products so as to maximize the profits of the group by engaging in *transfer pricing*. That is, the prices which are charged by one subsidiary to another for the transfer of components are such as to benefit the group, that is the multinational parent, possibly at the expense of one of the subsidiaries. To see how this could work out in practice, consider the following hypothetical example.

Suppose that, for example, two countries which we will label Hightax and Lowtax have different rates of corporation tax. Both countries are host to the subsidiaries of an American multinational car company. Both countries also assemble cars which are sourced both locally and abroad. The price at which components are transferred from one subsidiary to another will clearly affect the cost and therefore the profitability of the subsidiaries. Specifically, if components are transferred from the Lowtax subsidiary to the Hightax subsidiary at an inflated price, then this will increase the costs and reduce the profitability of the Hightax subsidiary. Similarly, the profits of the Lowtax subsidiary will be increased by an equivalent amount. Since the rate of corporation tax is lower in Lowtax than it is in Hightax, the overall tax liability of the group is therefore reduced.

It should be stressed that this is a hypothetical example and, for obvious reasons, little data exists to support the allegation that internal prices are deliberately distorted in this way by multinational companies. Given the informational requirement that needs to be satisfied for the practice to benefit the company, it seems unlikely that the practice is either widespread or carried out in a systematic way. Moreover, the discussion of costs in Chapter 5 illustrates the difficulty of defining how the cost of a particular component should be defined and therefore what constitutes a fair price to be used in internal transactions within the company. Having said this, however, it is clear that companies (and individuals) do take advantage of such things as differences in tax rates, investment incentives and the like, and that such behaviour will influence, to a lesser or greater extent, key macroeconomic variables like investment flows, growth rates and the balance of trade. However, it has been estimated[2] that the 30 per cent of Britain's exports are to related concerns – that is, to subsidiaries of UK parents or to other subsidiaries of foreign-based MNCs. The scope for engaging in transfer pricing is therefore considerable.

Notes

1. A survey of product-cycle theories is provided in Vernon, R. (ed) 'Technological and International Trade', *National Bureau Committee for Economic Research* 1970.
2. **Locksley, G.** and **Minns, R.**, 'Multi-nationals and the failure of economic management', *Guardian*, 3 Apr. 1985.
3. *The Observer*, 21 Oct. 1984.

Questions

9.1 'All multinationals operate on an international scale but not all international companies are multinationals.' Explain.

9.2 Assess the extent to which the product life cycle hypotheses can be applied to:
(a) video recorders
(b) home computers
(c) colour televisions
(d) washing machines
(e) coffee-making machines
To what extent have design improvements been able to stave off the day when the market for these products becomes satiated?

9.3 In 1986 the Nissan car company established a major production facility in the UK. Why did it do this rather than continue to export vehicles assembled in Japan?

9.4 What are the main advantages a company like Ford has over a company such as British Leyland?

9.5 A multinational sells cars in two national markets, Alphaland and Betaland. All cars are assembled by the Alphaland subsidiary using gearboxes produced by the Betaland subsidiary. Corporation tax is 40 per cent in Alphaland but only 30 per cent in Betaland. The following are the national prices which could be charged for internal transactions within the company:

price at which gearboxes are transferred from Beta to Alpha	300	250
price at which cars are transferred from Alpha to Beta	4000	5000

If the company wishes to maximize the post-tax profits of the group, which prices will it charge?

Chapter 10

The consumer

10.1 Diminishing marginal utility

For the last few chapters we have been concentrating on the supply side of the market. In this chapter we shall focus our attention on the demand side by considering in greater depth some of the points introduced in Chapter 2. Specifically, we shall be investigating the factors which influence consumption behaviour.

The concept of *utility* is central to the economic analysis of consumer behaviour. Utility, in an economic sense, means the satisfaction or pleasure which results from some act of consumption. Goods and services are therefore said to possess utility and consumers, if they are rational, will spend their income in such a way as to maximize their utility. This statement is a very general proposition, so general in fact that it is axiomatic. Nevertheless, it deserves some comment. Different people derive utility from different things and the statement is by no means inconsistent with the observation that while some crave a lifestyle of glamour, excitement and extravagance, others derive utility from solitude and contemplation – one man's meat is another man's poison. Neither is the assumption of rationality in any way inconsistent with the observation that some individuals engage in activities which to others appear to be acts of sheer lunacy. Rationality in this context simply means that when faced with a choice, the consumer will follow that course of action which will give him more utility rather than less.

Utility of course is not capable of being measured on a scale like temperature or barometric pressure. The Utilitarian school under John Stuart Mill, who introduced this concept, argued however that it was not in principle impossible to do so. A device for measuring utility – a 'hedonometer' or 'pleasure-meter' – has even been talked about. If it were possible to measure it on a scale, that is *cardinally*, the units of measurement would, of course, be *utils*. More realistically, utility could be measured *ordinally*; that is, one could rank consumption bundles in order of preference – first, second, third, and so on. Note that the distinction between cardinal and ordinal utility is the same as that between the cardinal numbers (one, two, three, etc.) and the ordinal numbers (first, second, third, etc.).

Goods generally are said to possess *diminishing marginal utility*, which means that the increments to utility provided by additional units of consumption become less and less as consumption increases. Consider Fig. 10.1, noting carefully the axes. The horizontal axis shows the total number of chocolate bars ('Zip') eaten per day, and the vertical axis the satisfaction or utility derived from them, measured of course in utils. Note that the curve shows the total utility derived, whereas the slope of the curve shows how much extra utility is derived from eating an additional chocolate bar. That is, the slope of the curve shows the *marginal utility*. (The relationship between total and marginal utility is of course the same as that between total cost and marginal cost, and total revenue and marginal revenue. It may be helpful to re-read section 5.3 if you are unsure about this.) It is easy to see from Fig. 10.1 that the extra satisfaction – the marginal utility – derived from the first bar is greater than that derived from the second. Similarly, the third and fourth bars yield less extra utility than those which came before. The marginal utility of the fifth bar is very small and beyond this point satiation is reached and additional units of consumption reduce rather than increase total utility – that is, marginal utility has become negative (the slope of the curve is negative).

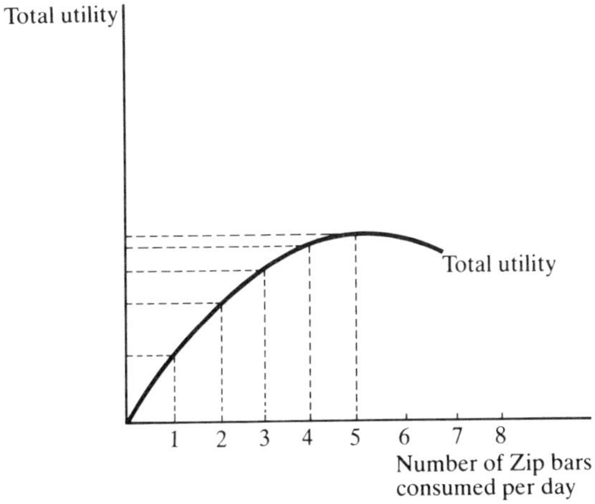

Fig 10.1

It seems not unreasonable to accept that all goods and services possess this property of diminishing marginal utility. It is perhaps a little more difficult to accept that income has diminishing marginal utility since additional large increments to income may make possible consumption experiences which were impossible previously and from which the individual may derive considerable satisfaction. This is not a proposition which can be refuted, of course, since utility in practice cannot be measured; at least, it cannot be measured cardinally. In passing it is worth noting what Shakespeare had to say on the subject of diminishing marginal utility. He of course pre-dated the Utilitarians by some two centuries so would not have been able to use the same terminology but, in *Antony and Cleopatra* he explains Antony's infatuation with the Goddess of the Nile with these words:

> Other women cloy the appetites they feed,
> But she makes hungry
> Where most she satisfies. (II. ii. 241)

For Antony then, Cleopatra had increasing rather than diminishing marginal utility.

10.2 Utility maximization

As we saw in section 10.1, the consumer is assumed to be a utility maximizer and as we argued there, the assumption that the consumer attempts to maximize his utility is axiomatic. It is another way of saying that people act rationally, not necessarily in a coldly calculating way, weighing up the amount of satisfaction derived from each pound's worth of expenditure, but rather they are rational in the sense that they do what they like doing. They buy those things, and engage in those pursuits, which give them satisfaction. In this section we shall derive the formal condition which needs to be satisfied in order that utility is maximized.

Consider an individual who spends all his income on just two commodities, cakes and ale, which are the only two things which give him satisfaction. Suppose the price of cakes, P_C, is 10p per cake and the price of ale, P_A, is 20p per pint. Both these goods of course possess diminishing marginal utility. At current consumption levels, however, suppose that the last cake yields an increase in total satisfaction of 5 utils and the last pint of ale yields an increase in total satisfaction of 8 utils. That is, at current consumption levels the marginal utility of cakes is 5 utils and the marginal utility of ale is 8 utils. In summary:

$$P_C = 10 \qquad P_A = 20 \qquad MU_C = 5 \qquad MU_A = 8$$

Has the consumer arranged his consumption spending in such a way that he is maximizing his utility? Clearly not, for if he reduces his ale consumption by one pint he can afford two more cakes. As a result of the drop in ale consumption his total utility will fall by 8 utils but the additional cakes he buys will increase his satisfaction by (almost; see below) $2 \times 5 = 10$ utils, thus giving him a net increase in total utility of 2 utils. By transferring expenditure from ale to cakes he will therefore increase his total utility.

Since both cakes and ale have diminishing marginal utility, the increase in cake consumption will however reduce the marginal utility of the last cake consumed (to somewhat less than 5 utils) and the reduction in ale consumption will increase the marginal utility of the last pint of ale consumed (to somewhat more than 8 utils). The increase in the marginal utility of ale and the reduction in the marginal utility of cakes thus sets a limit to the extent to which total satisfaction can be increased by substituting cakes for ale in consumption. If this were not the case of course, that is, if the goods in question did not possess diminishing marginal utility, then the rational consumer should give up ale altogether and spend all his income on cakes.

A few moments' reflection will show that the consumer maximizes his total utility when he arranges his consumption set in such a way that the ratio of marginal utility to price is the same for all goods. That is, the following condition must be satisfied:

$$\frac{\mathrm{MU_A}}{P_\mathrm{A}} = \frac{\mathrm{MU_C}}{P_\mathrm{C}} \qquad [10.1]$$

In other words, what this means is that total utility is maximized when the last penny spent on cakes yields the same increase in total satisfaction as does the last penny spent on ale. If the condition is not satisfied, the consumer can increase his total satisfaction by substituting cakes for ale in the way described above, and this process of substitution should be continued until eqn 10.1 is satisfied. Clearly eqn [10.1] can be extended to any number of goods, not just cakes and ale. In a more general form it can be rewritten as:

$$\frac{\mathrm{MU_A}}{P_\mathrm{A}} = \frac{\mathrm{MU_B}}{P_\mathrm{B}} = \ldots = \frac{\mathrm{MU}_n}{P_n} \qquad [10.2]$$

where A,B, ..., n are all the goods and services in the economy.

10.3 Income and substitution effects: the choice of family size

The previous section showed how the rational consumer could maximize his utility when faced with a choice between cakes and ale. In the real world of course, consumers have to make choices between an enormously wide range of goods and services, all of which make some claim on their income and have the potential for yielding utility. The consumer, in short, is faced with what in the jargon is called a *choice problem*; and economics is about making choices.

An area of application of economic analysis recently explored is that of fertility rates. Underlying this analysis is the notion that family size is the result of a choice process, or, in other words, couples choose whether or not to have children, when to have them and how many to have.

The question of family size may seem an improbable area of application of economic analysis. Can the cold logic of the economic calculus really be applied to this most fundamental of human desires? What about unplanned pregnancies? Should one really analyse reproductive behaviour as if people acted in a rational and considered manner? If one considers the question more deeply, however, it is clear that these objections are not valid. In a biological sense, birth follows conception, which follows intercourse in a natural sequence. In a social or a statistical sense, however, they are not linked in this strict sequence. Most acts of intercourse are not followed by conception – the birth rate would be very much higher if they were. This is not to deny of course that there are some unplanned pregnancies. However, the dividing line between planned and unplanned pregnancies is not easy to draw. Some pregnancies are planned but do not occur due to infertility. Some pregnancies are planned by one partner but not by the other. But all pregnancies occur because effective contraceptive measures are not taken, and herein lies the choice. If you choose not to take a raincoat when going out you run the risk of getting wet, not normally a serious risk. If you choose not to take waterproof clothing with you when going hill-walking you run the risk of getting wet and chilled, a more serious risk which may even prove fatal. Since most people would be more likely to take seriously the consequences of getting wet when hill-walking than when walking down a city street, they are more likely to guard against that eventuality. The perceived seriousness of the consequences will determine how carefully you plan against those consequences occurring. Similarly, women for whom conception is seen as extremely undesirable will take effective contraceptive measures, even to the extent of sterilization in certain circumstances.

Of course, in individual cases the best-laid plans often go awry. Some pregnancies do occur which were not 'planned' and other pregnancies which were 'planned' do not occur. That is why the economic analysis of choice behaviour cannot predict or explain the size of any one particular family. It can however attempt to explain the size of families on average or, if you like, it can be applied to the study of fertility *rates*.

Children as a consumption good

Children, at least in developed Western societies, can to some extent be regarded as a consumption good. That is, parents derive utility or satisfaction from the rearing of children in much the same way as they derive utility from their material possessions such as their house, car, TV and from the services which they consume such as holidays or going to the zoo. The amount of satisfaction derived from child rearing depends of course on personal tastes and circumstances. Some people like children, others do not. Other things being equal, therefore, those individuals that like children will tend to have large families. Other individuals will prefer to spend their time and income in different ways. In formal terms of course this implies that the utility-maximizing consumer will arrange his consumption set such that:

$$\frac{MU_A}{P_A} = \frac{MU_B}{P_B} = \dots = \frac{MU_K}{P_K} = \dots = \frac{MU_n}{P_n} \qquad [10.3]$$

where A and B are any two other goods from the *n* goods available and good K is the consumption good, children. In words, the last pound devoted to children will yield exactly the same increase in total satisfaction as does the last pound devoted to consumer good A, good B, and so on for all *n* goods. In reality, of course, the utility-maximizing consumer will have a much more difficult task than if he were simply choosing between cakes and ale. Children are more akin to a consumer-durable good like a house which yields a stream of services through time, as opposed to goods which yield immediate satisfaction, like cakes and ale, and are then used up. Moreover, the consumer will have to base his decision on very imperfect information – he will probably already have tasted cakes and ale and be contemplating repeat purchases. He (or she) may never have experienced parenthood and the complete experience takes a lifetime to acquire. Nevertheless, even though our rational individual will not achieve the condition set out in eqn [10.3] above, we could argue that if he is rational he will strive towards it.

The price of children

Children of course do not have a purchase price but child rearing does involve a cost. Certain complementary goods have to be acquired – a cot, a pram, nappies, toys – but the cost of these items is normally fairly insignificant in comparison to the main item in the cost of having a child, which is the *income forgone* by the parent who stays at home to look after the child rather than engage in paid employment. Thus the main cost of having a child is the *opportunity cost* of not working during the child's pre-school years (and possibly the difficulty of re-entering the labour market thereafter). This realization immediately leads to two interesting and possibly testable predictions. Firstly, following the birth of one child the cost of producing a second child is low. The necessary capital equipment has already been acquired (pram, cot, etc.) and this can be used for more than one 'unit', thus lowering the unit cost. Moreover, if the parent is already staying home to look after one child the further loss of earnings involved in rearing a second child is comparatively small –

perhaps six years' lost earnings instead of four. There are, in short, economies of scale in child rearing. Thus we might expect to find that very large families were commonplace were it not for the fact that, along with other consumption goods, children possess diminishing marginal utility – the more you have of them the less you want more of them. Secondly, we might expect to find that family size is related to socio-economic variables but in a rather complicated way. For example, as income increases would we expect couples to have more children or less? The answer, it turns out, depends on the strengths of the *income and substitution effects*. Assuming that children are not an inferior good (that is, assuming that their income elasticity is positive – a reasonable assumption) then as income rises we would expect couples to have more children, other things being equal. Other things are not equal, however, because the cost of children also tends to rise as income rises, since the major element in the cost of having children is the income forgone by the parent. Thus children become more expensive relative to other consumer goods as one rises up the socio-economic scale and hence we would expect the rational consumer to 'consume' less children and to consume more of the substitutes whose price is falling relative to the price of children.

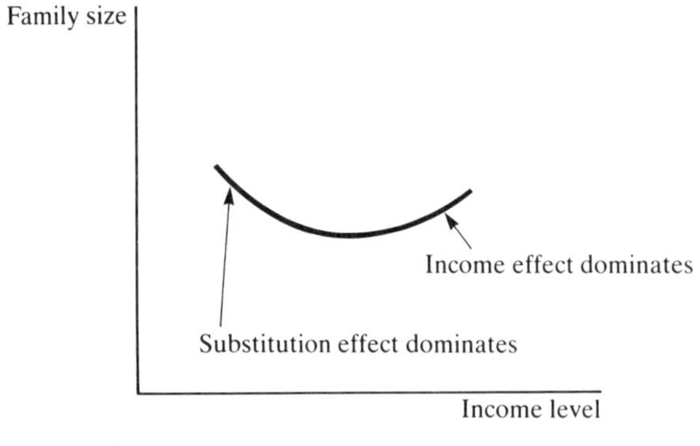

Fig. 10.2

This may produce the result that both low-income and high-income families tend to be somewhat larger than those families in the middle of the income range. This is illustrated in Fig. 10.2. The distribution shown in Fig. 10.2 results from the fact that initially as income rises the substitution effect dominates – children become more expensive relative to other goods and therefore the utility-maximizing individual chooses to consume fewer children and more of the cheaper substitutes. As income continues to rise beyond a certain level, however, the income effect begins to dominate and families, by virtue of their high income, can afford more of everything, including children. Very high-income families may even be able to afford to employ a nanny to look after them.

The reason for illustrating the income and substitution effect in the context of the analysis of fertility rates is to show that the analysis of choice behaviour can be applied to many situations which initially appear to be beyond the scope of economics. Note the important (but rather disappointing) result we derived, which was that the substitution effect and income effect potentially working in opposite directions produced a result that was indeterminate.

Questions

10.1 Which of the following statements illustrates the concept of diminishing marginal utility?
(a) 'When I've eaten one choc-o-crunch bar I don't like the second one as much as I did the first. But I still like it.'
(b) 'Once you get the taste for choc-o-crunch bars it's difficult to stop eating them.'
(c) 'When I've had one choc-o-crunch bar I go right off them.'

10.2 A consumer buys only two commodities, Seven-up and crisps, both of which have diminising marginal utility. At current consumption levels the marginal utility of crisps is 10 and the marginal utility of Seven-up is 14. The price of crisps is 10p and the price of Seven-up is 16p. Which of the following are true?
(a) The consumer is maximizing his utility.
(b) The consumer would probably increase his utility by buying more Seven-up and less crisps.
(c) The consumer should buy more crisps and less Seven-up to increase his total utility.
(d) If the consumer eats more crisps he will get even more thirsty so the utility of Seven-up will rise.

10.3 An electrical retailer records the prices and sales volumes of both colour and black-and-white television sets for 1982 and 1985.

	Price		Sales	
	Black & white	**Colour**	**Black & white**	**Colour**
1982	£70	£250	100	400
1985	£60	£250	80	500

Consider whether the drop in sales of black-and-white sets (despite a drop in price) could be explained in terms of income and substitution effects. (Incomes rose between 1982 and 1985.)

Chapter 11
The Price System as an allocative mechanism

11.1 Markets and the allocation of resources

Economics, as the reader should now be aware, is about how resources are allocated. One way in which resources can be allocated is by a system of state planning such as that used in the countries of the Eastern bloc. In what is basically a capitalist or free enterprise economy such as that of Britain, however, most resources tend to be allocated by the market mechanism or what we call the *price system*. The purpose of this chapter is to examine how the market mechanism does this in theory and to consider whether the theory is a reasonable description of reality. The analysis which we will present forms the basis of what is known as *welfare economics* and it provides a theoretical underpinning to many microeconomic policy decisions. The analysis was formulated originally by the Italian economist Vilfredo Pareto.

We saw in Chapter 10 how a rational economic man will divide his consumption spending such that the following condition will be satisfied (eqn [10.2]):

$$\frac{\mathrm{MU_A}}{P_\mathrm{A}} = \frac{\mathrm{MU_B}}{P_\mathrm{B}} = \dots = \frac{\mathrm{MU}_n}{P_n}$$

That is, he will allocate his spending in such a way that the last penny spent on purchasing good A yields exactly the same increase in total satisfaction as does the last penny spent on good B. If this were not the case, we argued, he could always reallocate his spending so as to produce a net increase in his overall level of satisfaction.

Assume now that the goods which our rational consumer buys are sold on markets in which prices reflect production costs. Specifically, assume that in each market, price is equal to marginal cost. This condition will of course be satisfied in perfectly competitive markets but may not be satisfied in markets where elements of monopoly are present. If price *is* equal to marginal cost in all markets, however, then we can rewrite eqn [10.2] as

$$\frac{\mathrm{MU_A}}{\mathrm{MC_A}} = \frac{\mathrm{MU_B}}{\mathrm{MC_B}} = \dots = \frac{\mathrm{MU}_n}{\mathrm{MC}_n} \qquad [11.1]$$

simply by replacing P_A by MC_A, and so on. This equation represents a very fundamental statement about the way in which resources are or should be allocated. If this condition is satisfied for all consumers – and for us to make this statement all consumers must act rationally and all goods must be sold on markets in which price is equal to marginal cost – then we can make the following statement: such a system produces an allocation in which the last pound's worth of society's resources devoted to the production of good A (that is, MC_A) yields exactly the same increase in total satisfaction as does the last pound's worth of resources devoted to the production of good B (MC_B), and that the same is true for all goods.

It is not easy for the reader coming to eqn [11.1] for the first time to understand its full significance. It is impossible however to underestimate its importance since it is a statement to the effect that the price system allocates resources – that is, solves the economic problem – in a way which is *Pareto optimal*. That is, the allocation of resources which results is the 'best' that it is possible to attain. Any other allocation of resources would be 'sub-optimal' in the sense that a *reallocation* of resources is capable of producing a Pareto improvement – that is, a reallocation is capable of producing an increase in society's welfare. Of course, a reallocation which shifts resources towards one particular individual at the expense of others will be seen from the point of view of that individual as a preferred or improved allocation of resources. The term 'Pareto improvement', however, refers to a reallocation in which one individual is made better off and no one else is made worse off. A Pareto optimal allocation of resources therefore is a situation in which nobody can be made better off without at the same time making someone else worse off. The key conclusion is that the market mechanism, that is, the unfettered operation of the laws of demand and supply, ultimately produces an allocation of society's scarce resources which is, in the restricted sense of the term employed here, optimal: it cannot be bettered. As such it represents a strong case for private enterprise.

Before we go on to consider the validity of the analysis presented above, it is worth elaborating on its main points.

Firstly, the role which prices play in the resource allocation process is central. Prices act as signals to which both producers and consumers respond. We saw in the previous chapter how the utility-maximizing consumer would respond to a change in relative prices by modifying his consumption pattern. For example, if the price of cakes rose relative to the price of ale, the rational consumer would then buy fewer cakes and more ale. In a similar way, producers respond to changes in the prices of the factors of production which they use. For example, if the price of steel rises relative to the price of plastic then producers will tend to replace steel components by plastic ones where it is technically feasible to do so. In this way they minimize their production costs in an attempt to maximize profits, in the same way that the consumer attempts to maximize utility.

Prices, then, convey information about relative scarcity. Goods which are in scarce supply and for which there is a high demand, will command a high price; goods which are abundant and for which there is little demand, a low price. This is what is meant by 'scarcity' in economics. It is the supply relative to the demand which determines the economic scarcity of a good. For example, the drawings and paintings of Pablo Picasso are quite numerous but there is a high demand for them so they command a high price. In contrast, I myself have produced relatively few drawings and paintings but even for this small number the market demand is zero and hence they command a zero price.

The economic problem exists because scarcity exists. Not everybody can have everything they want, so choices have to be made. The poor man has to choose between bread and potatoes, the rich man between a new yacht and a villa. Choices have to be made not only in consumption, however, but in all other situations characterized by scarcity – the individual has to decide how to allocate his time between work and leisure, the investor how to allocate his funds, the firm how to produce its goods and what and where to sell. All of these decisions have two things in common. Firstly, they are decisions based on the information about relative scarcities which is provided by the set of relative prices. Secondly, each decision is goal-orientated. It has some purpose to it. The consumer seeks to maximize his utility, the firm seeks to maximize its profits. In all cases, however, decisions are motivated by self-interest rather than by philanthropy. In pursuing their selfish ends, however, individuals inadvertently bring about an allocation of society's resources which is 'optimal'. They do good by doing well, since the price system channels and co-ordinates their myriad selfish actions in such a way that society as a whole benefits.

11.2 Market failure

If the analysis of the previous section is correct, then it does indeed seem that the market mechanism will produce an allocation of society's resources which is 'optimal' in the restricted sense that we have used this term. Indeed, advocates of the free market mechanism have used Pareto's analysis to support their contention that the greatest happiness of the greatest number can be secured if the state refrains from intervening in the market and simply allows market forces to rule. On the other hand, those who believe in some state intervention have pointed to the very restrictive – and unrealistic – assumptions under which such a Pareto optimal allocation of resources will be produced. There are four key criticisms which can be levelled at these underlying assumptions.

1. Price not equal to marginal cost

In perfectly competitive markets price will be equal to marginal cost. Such markets are, however, rare. In most markets, in practice, price will diverge from marginal production cost (even assuming that marginal cost can be identified) and in many cases price will bear almost no relation to production costs – see for example section 7.4 on sailboard prices. The extent to which price could diverge from marginal costs obviously depends on the extent to which the firm enjoys monopoly powers. Monopolists – or to be more correct, oligopolists – are price makers rather than price takers, so their price need not reflect the element of economic scarcity embodied in the marginal cost concept.

2. Income distribution

A Pareto optimal allocation of resources is predicated upon a particular initial distribution of society's resources or, in other words, upon a particular distribution of income. Different income distributions will produce different Pareto optimal allocations of resources. In other words, there is not just one Pareto optimal allocation of resources but many Pareto optima. When consumers spend their income, each pound they spend is like one vote cast for the production of a particular commodity. A pound spent on cakes is a vote for cake production. Suppose, for the purpose of this example, that society is composed of two groups, those who like cakes and a second group who like ale. If the cake lovers are rich and the ale lovers poor then the allocation of society's resources will be heavily biased towards cake production. If, on the other hand, the ale lovers become rich and the cake lovers poor then the resulting increased expenditure on ale would result in a shift in society's resources away from cake production and towards ale production. The allocation of society's resources which results from the operation of the market mechanism is therefore clearly dependent on the initial distribution of income.

3. Untraded goods

Some goods which affect consumers' utility are not traded. That is, not only are they not sold on perfectly competitive markets, they are not sold on markets at all. Thus, for example, a consumer's utility may be affected by the level of noise pollution to which he is exposed, by oil pollution on holiday beaches or by the level of street violence. None of these things are traded on markets. Hence the amount of society's resources devoted to producing them – or in this case controlling them – is not the result of a set of preferences expressed in the market. In other words, the consumer cannot vote for more resources devoted to reducing pollution by spending more money on reducing pollution. In summary, there is an area in which the market does not work.

4. Public goods

A further area in which the market works only imperfectly, if at all, is known as the *public good* area. The term 'public goods' as used by economists refers to certain goods and services often but not invariably supplied by the public sector rather than the market sector. Services such as policing, street lighting, roads and flood protection schemes can be considered as public goods. Because such goods possess the characteristics of non-excludability and non-rivalness (to be explained in section 13.3) they may not be supplied efficiently by the market mechanism. That is, they may not be supplied in the quantities which consumers' preferences would dictate because consumers cannot effectively express their preferences by purchasing or not purchasing the good in question.

Two related conclusions follow from the foregoing analysis. Firstly, the operation of the market mechanism may not produce a Pareto optimal allocation of resources because of the ability of some sellers in oligopolistic markets to set prices which diverge from marginal cost. Secondly, even if the allocation of resources in society were Pareto optimal there might be some citizens, or indeed a majority of citizens, who would prefer a different allocation of resources – for example, one which allowed for a different distribution of income and which allocated resources to areas which the market mechanism did not adequately serve.

Questions

11.1 A Pareto optimal allocation of resources is one where:
(a) nobody can benefit from a redistribution of resources
(b) resources cannot be transferred from one use to another without causing a reduction in somebody's welfare
(c) resources cannot be transferred from one use to another without causing a reduction in society's welfare

11.2 Say which of the following are correct:
A Pareto optional allocation of resources:
(a) cannot be achieved under a planned system
(b) is automatically achieved in a market system
(c) is never achieved in reality
(d) could be achieved if prices conveyed information about relative scarcities

11.3 Suppose the price of aluminium rose relative to the price of nylon. Which of the following statements are correct?
(a) The government would have to instruct firms to use less aluminium.

(b) Manufacturers would try to use nylon rather than aluminium where it was feasible to do so. The demand for aluminium would go down.
(c) Products which used aluminium would become more expensive. People would buy less of them so the demand for aluminium would go down.
(d) Only those consumers who knew that aluminium was becoming scarce would economize on its use. The rest would not.

11.4 In a market system, in pursuing their selfish ends individuals 'do good by doing well'. Why was this not true of Al Capone (the gangster who was so successful in America in the 1930s)?
(a) It was true. Al gave people what they wanted.
(b) Because the statement does not apply to things like alcohol and gambling.
(c) Because people were not free to choose whether they dealt with Al Capone or not.
(d) Because, by acting selfishly, people cannot possibly do good.

11.5 Market failure occurs because:
(a) not everyone has heard of the concept of Pareto optimality
(b) the distribution of incomes is unequal
(c) market prices do not always reflect the true resource costs involved.

Chapter 12
Planning

12.1 Economic planning in peace and war

State planning stands in contrast to the market as a mechanism of resource allocation. In this chapter we shall look at planning in two distinct, though related, contexts. Firstly, we shall consider the way resources are allocated in the centrally planned or command economies of the Soviet type. Secondly, we shall look at the planning methods used in capitalist economies in wartime, the focus of our study being the British economy in the Second World War. These two examples of planning, though distinct, in fact share the common features that they do not use prices and profitability as a means of indicating where resources should flow. In a market system, as we have seen, the myriad decisions of economic agents – firms and consumers – are co-ordinated by the unseen hand of the price mechanism. Decisions are decentralized but the basic questions which have to be resolved – what is to be produced, by what method and for whom – are resolved because economic agents respond to price signals. Thus, ultimately the allocation of society's resources is the result of decisions which are decentralized and diffused. This is the way of the market.

In a planned system, in contrast, decisions are taken centrally by some state planning agency. This agency, in effect, dictates the way in which society's resources are allocated in pursuit of some objective which may be either the maximization of economic growth (as in the case of centrally planned economies) or the winning of a war (as in the case of wartime economies).

It may seem strange that a book about the operation of market economies should discuss planning, which is in effect the antithesis to market allocation. There are a number of valid reasons for so doing, however. Firstly, a sizeable proportion of the world's population – between a third and a half – live in economic systems which are characterized by central planning: the Soviet bloc, China and many third-world countries. Secondly, in both the First and Second World Wars the combatants resorted to planning as a means of more effectively promoting the war effort. Thirdly, a study, even a brief one, of the operation of economic planning gives an invaluable perspective to the study of the operation of market economies. The market economy does work; it does allocate resources, but there is an alternative way of doing so – planning. Since planning is a preferred development strategy in some countries and is used extensively by market economies in wartime, it will be instructive to consider the rationale for economic planning, the mechanisms involved and the experiences of such policies.

12.2 Soviet planning

Words like 'socialist', 'communist' and 'Marxist' are all adjectives used loosely in the West to describe economies the essential feature of which is economic planning. Confusingly, however, these terms mean different things to different people. For example, in America the word 'socialist' is applied to many European countries, among them Sweden, France and even Britain, which are essentially capitalist in nature. They are capitalist because even though there may be some state-owned industries, most resources are privately owned and economic decisions are for the most part taken on the basis of market signals. In command economies, by contrast, the means of production tend to be owned by the state, and decisions about resource allocation are based on administrative fiat. Some centrally planned economies are more 'planned' than others, however. The USSR is probably the most centralized of the command economies. Even today there is comparatively little private ownership of productive resources and even though prices may be used as part of the allocative mechanism these prices do not necessarily reflect relative scarcities. By contrast, Yugoslavia, which stands geographically and ideologically on the edge of the Communist bloc, has introduced a sort of 'market socialism'. In this evolving system factories and other production facilities tend to be owned and run by workers' co-operatives and the decisions of the factory managers about what to produce, in what quantities and by what techniques, are based on market prices.

12.2.1 The history of Soviet planning

It is difficult to appreciate why Soviet central planning developed in the way it did without knowing something of the historical context within which it occurred. In 1917, the date of the Russian Revolution, Russia was a backward country whose attempts to industrialize had faltered. Between 1914 and 1921 war with Germany and the ensuing civil war had caused a catastrophic worsening of an already bad situation. Industrial output in 1921 fell to a third of what it had been in 1913.[1] Some recovery occurred under the New Economic Policy (NEP) instituted by Lenin in 1921 which reintroduced elements of the free market. However, Lenin's policy of reforms was reversed by Stalin when he came to power in 1928. The Stalin era, 1928–53, marks the period in which the full mechanism of state central planning was constructed. In 1928 Russia felt herself vulnerable, firstly because she was economically weak in comparison with the capitalist economies and secondly because, being the only communist country, she felt isolated and under threat. Thus it was imperative to build up her economic strength quickly to enable her to withstand the assault which she felt sure would come from the capitalist countries. The promotion of rapid economic growth requires that resources that would otherwise have been used to produce consumer goods be diverted into investment – investment in machines, factories, roads, communications, power generation and so on – as well as investment in the human capital required – the trained technicians, doctors, teachers, scientists and all the other specialists that an advanced industrial society requires.

In a market economy, as we have seen, the consumer is sovereign, in theory at least. He ultimately dictates what is produced and he also dictates what proportion of annual output will be devoted to investment. He does this by refraining from consumption, that is, by saving part of his income, thus freeing resources to build up the economy's stock of capital goods. The rationale for central planning, then, was to remove from private individuals the ability selfishly to consume almost all of annual output. Central planning would lower consumption levels in the short term in order to increase the stock of capital assets in society and thereby raise production possibilities in the longer term. Thus during the Stalin era the proportion of Russia's resources devoted to investment (in heavy industry and infrastructure) was comparatively high. Consequently, the rate of economic growth was high in comparison to previously achieved Russian levels and in comparison to most capitalist countries at the same time. This then was – and is – the rationale for economic planning in the Soviet Union.

12.2.2 The nature of Soviet planning

A Soviet economic plan starts from a set of macro aggregates – the target output of steel, of cement, of men's suits, of trained doctors, and so on. Each of the economic enterprises producing, say, steel is then given an individual production target, the production targets both at the individual (micro) level and at the aggregate (macro) level being related to past years' realized performance. Each of the individual enterprises is then allocated the resources deemed to be both necessary and sufficient to meet its production quota. At this stage inputs and outputs are decided upon in physical terms rather than in terms of the money values of those inputs and outputs. Thus, for example, the target output for steel is *X* million tonnes rather than *X* million pounds' worth of steel; coal input into steel making is *Y* million tonnes of coal rather than *Y* million pounds' worth of coal; and so on for all the other inputs including labour. The physical plan is then translated into monetary terms using prices deemed appropriate by the central planners. Each individual enterprise then purchases the inputs it has been allocated, at the prices decided upon by the central planners, and sells the output it produces, again at the prices decided upon by the central planners.

Note that in this system the performance (the efficiency) of an enterprise is gauged by its success in meeting its production target (which is based on previous achieved levels). Profitability is not a meaningful measure of efficiency, nor indeed is it a relevant concept since it depends on an arbitrarily imposed set of prices. Moreover, there is no incentive to the firm to economize on the use of the resources it has been allocated since if it were to do so the resulting surpluses (of income over expenditure) would be appropriated by the state and the firm's allocation of inputs for subsequent years reduced. The incentive to exceed current production targets is slight since this results in increased targets in subsequent years.

12.2.3 An evaluation of Soviet planning

The foregoing account of Soviet planning is based on methods used in the Stalin era, but contemporary methods are essentially the same. However, early attempts at planning were characterized by an emphasis on physical planning – the use of prices as part of the planning process was eschewed altogether. The measurement of output in physical terms (often in weight) frequently led to absurdities. Some of the stories which emanate from the Soviet Union about central planning in the Stalin era may be apocryphal, but the deficiencies of the system are well known and acknowledged by the Soviets themselves. A famous cartoon, much emulated even in the official Soviet press, shows a crane lifting an enormous button. The caption, which loses nothing in translation from the original Russian, read: '. . . and with this single button we can fulfil our production quota for the next three years.'

The reforms of the 1950s reintroduced prices into the planning system but the prices used were not market prices in the sense that they did not reflect scarcity. That is, they did not reflect consumers' evaluation of the desirability or otherwise of the products, so that there was no incentive for producers to improve the quality of the goods produced. In the West goods which are perceived as being of higher quality command a higher price. In the Soviet system prices are administered centrally. The system therefore has an inbuilt inflexibility which does not readily permit price differentials between high-quality and low-quality goods. Moreover, innovation and technical change were, and are, extremely slow to occur in the Soviet system. Both in terms of techniques used to produce a given output and in terms of the range of outputs produced, the Soviet system was ossified. One of the strengths of a free enterprise system is its ability to exploit market opportunities, to fill gaps which entrepreneurs spot in the market and to create entirely new markets. Thus, for example, Sir Clive Sinclair created a market for cheap home computers with the ZX81 and Spectrum computers. The market did not exist before he created it. He also attempted to create another new market with the Sinclair C5 electric tricycle, which appears to have been a resounding failure. The essential point, however, is that the dynamic of the free enterprise system is based on the rewarding of success and the punishing of failure. This in turn is based on profitability, and profits flow from producing things which people are prepared to buy. The deficiencies of the Soviet system stem from the lack of any feedback mechanism from consumers to producers, a mechanism we referred to earlier as consumer sovereignty. In a market economy, as we noted in Chapter 11, consumers influence (and, arguably, determine) what is produced. They do this by the purchasing decisions they make. Prices are the link between the wishes of consumers and the actions of producers. In the Soviet system planners decide what is produced. There is no need for prices.

Prices of course do exist in the Soviet Union, both for producer goods and for consumer goods, but they do not necessarily reflect relative scarcity. Since prices are officially controlled rather than market determined, excess demand gives rise to shortages. These are choked off not by a rise in price but by queueing which then becomes merely an unofficial form of rationing. To get the good in question you have to be prepared to wait. Goods have a time price as well as a money price. Similarly, excess supply results in the production of surpluses – goods which cannot be disposed of at the official prices – just as food surpluses are created under the European Community's Common Agricultural Policy.

The fact that consumer sovereignty does not exist even in a weak form in the Soviet system is not in itself surprising. The concept of the market as an allocative mechanism in which resources are allocated in accordance with consumer preferences – in short, the mechanism described in section 11.1 – is not a concept with which Marx would have been familiar. Marx, on whose writings the Soviet system is founded, predates those economists like Marshall, Jevons and Pareto who fully worked out the view of the price mechanism described above.[2] Thus, for Marx, planning must be better than no planning because no planning – that is, the market – was simply chaos. The idea that the function of prices might be to bring order out of chaos is not one that Marx would have heard of: nor, incidentally, it is an idea which would be acceptable to latter-day Western Marxists or Soviet economists. Since the concept of optimal resource allocation is Paretian in origin, the concept of a misallocation of resources can only be understood within the framework of welfare economics which Pareto originated. Thus the economic inefficiencies of the Soviet system represent misallocations of resources only if one is first prepared to accept the framework of Paretian welfare economics. In other words, in pointing to the economic inefficiencies of the Soviet system and identifying these as misallocations of resources, we tend to assume implicitly that no such misallocations occur in a free market system. That is, we assume the market allocates resources 'correctly' or optimally. This is far from true, however, for the reasons set out in section 11.2 (and other reasons besides). Many people would question, for example, whether the resources devoted to advertising in a capitalist society really do fulfil a socially necessary or even socially useful function. Moreover, some of the most highly skilled and highly paid members of the labour force are engaged as accountants, lawyers and tax experts whose sole function is to minimize the contribution that companies make to the Exchequer through the payment of taxes. Two examples, it could be argued, of resource misallocations.

There is another significant failing of market economies to which planned economies are less susceptible, namely the cycles in economic activity which periodically produce deep recessions. In the depression years of the 1920s and 1930s, for example, and again in Britain in the early 1980s, resources lay idle – surely an extreme form of resource misallocation. However, although one could argue that recessions are endemic to a capitalist society, it could also be argued that they result from the application of incorrect policies at a macro level. In other words, governments could prevent recessions from occurring by boosting the overall level of demand in an economy as and when necessary.

12.3 Planning in wartime

In the Soviet Union the rationale for central planning was to divert into investment those resources which would otherwise have been used up in consumption. Similarly, in wartime there is a need to divert resources into the production of munitions. Since society's productive potential is limited these resources must be drawn away from the consumption-goods sector. The industries producing consumption goods will only produce what people are able to buy. Thus, people's ability to purchase consumer goods must be reduced. In the Second World War in Britain this was achieved in two ways. Firstly, by raising income taxes so that post-tax incomes were reduced. Secondly, a system of rationing – limiting demand to the reduced supply then available – was introduced. In this way the government took command of those productive resources needed to produce munitions without at the same time generating demand inflation in the consumer goods industries.

The extent to which the government was able to divert resources is shown in Table 12.1 which, interestingly, casts doubt on the popular belief about the German economy being an all-out war machine. Throughout the course of the war, as can be seen, the British government was relatively more successful in diverting resources away from consumption than the German government.

Table 12.1 Civilian expenditure on consumption in Germany and the UK 1938–44

(Indices based on constant prices – 1938 = 100)

Year	Germany (Pre-war area)	UK
1938	100	100
1939	108	100
1940	100	87
1941	97	81
1942	88	79
1943	87	76
1944	79	77

Source: N. Kaldor, 'The German war economy', in *Essays on Economic Policy*, vol. II, Duckworth, 1965

The operation of the system of rationing and price controls in wartime Britain is something which has been well documented and may even be within the range of personal experience of some readers (rationing was finally brought to an end in 1954). The aspect of economic planning which we want to focus on here is the way in which the output of munitions was planned. The methods used resemble the techniques of Soviet planning described in section 12.2.2. They were not in any sense modelled on Soviet experience, since literature documenting Soviet planning experience in the pre-war period was sparse. Rather, the techniques of planning evolved as the war progressed, with pragmatism rather than dogma being the guiding principle. There does not seem, moreover, to have been a single co-ordinated master plan for wartime production. Ely Devons[3], one of the wartime planners in Britain, writes:

In the early years of the war there was little attempt at the central direction of production. As far as I am aware no-one worked out, or attempted to work out, what resources would be left after meeting the minimum needs of the civilian population, and how these resources should be divided between the armed forces and the production of aircraft, army and naval supplies. It is true that general decisions were taken about the size of the Army, Air Force and Navy to plan for, but these decisions were by no means clear cut and did not in any case take account of the interrelation between the size of the armed forces and the production of munitions that would be needed for them. Each supply department was left to proceed with its plan for expansion in the light of the requirements that were put to it by the appropriate Service Department. It was only later, as the war proceeded, and these various plans came into conflict that a system of central direction to solve these conflicts was evolved; and by that time the general outlines of the plans of the various departments concerned were already determined, at least for a substantial period of time ahead. (Devons p.73)

In fact, a system of separate committees was established, each one responsible for different aspects of the war effort. There was at first no central co-ordination between these various committees. Individuals on these committees, Devons writes, 'were often out of touch with what individuals on the other co-ordinating committees were doing'. Central direction emerged, however, through the medium of the *production plans* of the various departments:

The main link and co-ordinating mechanism between the various allocating committees was provided by the production programmes of the individual supply departments. It was by the effect on the plans of the individual departments of the decisions of any one of these allocating committees, and the further reaction of these altered plans on the decisions of the other committees, that the whole planning process was kept in motion. Thus, if the man-power committee cut the allocation of labour to the Ministry of Aircraft Production, as a result MAP would reduce its aircraft programme; this would, in turn, reduce MAP's requirements for steel, timber, building capacity etc., and these reduced requirements would be taken into account by the appropriate allocating committee at the next quarterly review. It might be that at such a review MAP's steel allocation was cut even further, and this would involve a further re-adjustment in its programme, which would again have its effects in MAP's demand for other factors. (Devons p.74)

In today's terminology we would describe this as an iterative process. Of course, given the speed at which committees worked, the process of iteration had not been completed before action pertinent to the prior decisions of committees had already been taken. Often, however, some of the more cumbersome aspects of the formal planning procedures were overcome by *ad hoc* and informal consultative arrangements between individuals on related committees. Individual initiative made the system workable.

The wartime planners did not, of course, have access to the high-speed data processing capabilities of modern computers, but it is difficult to see that they would have been assisted in their task had such computers been available. In the post-war years mathematical techniques were developed to cope with complex resource-allocation problems involving interrelations between inputs and outputs, such as the situation described by Devons above. The most important of these techniques, input-output analysis, was developed by Wassily Leontief[4] in the 1940s and is used to some extent in the centrally planned economies today. The technique in effect speeds up the process of iteration by solving simultaneously a set of equations showing the interrelationships between all of the major inputs and outputs in an economic system. Had the technique been available to the wartime planners, however, the outcome would probably have been little different. The system of planning evolved as the war progressed and became more efficient as a result of human initiative and ingenuity. As Devons says, 'It would be quite mistaken to conclude that the process by which government economic planning operated in wartime in any way resembled the theoretical structures of the overall planners.'

While the divergence between practice and theory is undoubtedly a feature of all planning systems – using the term 'planning' in its widest sense – the reader should not take away the impression of British wartime planning as consisting of Whitehall civil servants muddling through in the face of an ultra-efficient German war effort organized from the centre and characterized by utter ruthlessness and superb organizing ability. In reality very little central planning took place in Germany until the Speer administration took control of the production of munitions in 1942. The success of the Speer administration in increasing the output of munitions occurred rather late in the war and too late to affect the outcome. Table 12.2 gives some illustrative figures of British and German armaments production.

Probably the most important of the munitions production programmes was that concerned with aircraft. In Britain this was the responsibility of the MAP (Ministry of Aircraft Production). The MAP's responsibilities covered not just those factories assembling the airframe itself but also those factories manufacturing the principal component parts – the engines, undercarriages, propellers, turrets, etc. Obviously, components had to be manufactured in the correct

Table 12.2 Comparison of output of particular classes of armaments in Germany and the UK 1940–44

	1940		1941		1942		1943		1944	
	Germany	UK	Germany	UK	Germany	UK	Germany	UK	Germany	UK
Military aircraft										
Fighters	3 100	4 300	3 700	7 000	5 200	9 800	11 700	10 700	28 900	10 500
Bombers	4 000	3 700	4 300	4 700	6 500	6 300	8 600	7 700	6 500	8 100
Other types	1 800	1 900	2 100	1 800	1 800	1 600	2 800	3 000	1 100	5 000
Trainers	1 300	5 100	900	6 600	1 200	5 900	2 100	4 800	3 100	2 900
Total (numbers)	10 200	15 000	11 000	20 100	14 200	23 600	25 200	26 200	39 600	26 500
Bombs (filled weight '000 tons)	n.a.	48	245	143	262	241	273	309	231	370
Tanks	1 600	1 400	3 800	4 800	6 300	8 600	12 100	7 500	19 000	4 600
Heavy guns (75 mm and over)	6 300	1 900	7 800	5 300	13 600	6 600	38 000	12 200	62 300	12 400
Light guns (over 20 mm and under 75 mm)	n.a	2 800	3 400	11 400	9 600	36 400	8 100	25 800	8 400	3 600
Small arms:										
Infantry rifles ('000)	1 350	81	1 358	78	1 370	594	2 244	910	2 585	547
Infantry machine guns ('000)	170	30	320	46	320	1 510	440	1 650	790	730

Note: United Kingdom figures refer to UK production only. German figures include all deliveries to the Wehrmacht.

Source: N. Kaldor, 'The German war economy', in *Essays on Economic Policy*, vol. II, Duckworth, 1965

quantities for the number of completed aircraft coming off the production line. In addition, the requirements for spare parts had to be satisfied. The problem of co-ordination between the component manufacturers and the airframe manufacturers was solved via the MAP using the medium of the production plan referred to earlier. Each of the individual representatives on the co-ordinating committee knew the planned output of Spitfires, Hurricanes, etc., and the likely demand for spare parts for the next quarter. From this the component manufacturers could estimate the requirement for components. In the event that the *planned output* of, say, propellers was insufficient to meet the *planned requirements* for them, then a combination of two things would happen. Either planned requirements for propellers would be reduced by scaling down the planned output of aircraft or more resources would be diverted away from other areas and into propeller production.

The MAP was actively instrumental in the resource allocation programme at all levels. It would have been possible of course to leave it to the market as is done in peacetime, but there were considerable drawbacks with such a system. Consider how such a system would have worked. The MAP would have issued contracts to aircraft manufacturers to purchase given numbers of aircraft at prices which the MAP determined. The manufacturers themselves would then have been free to enter into contracts with the component suppliers to purchase components that would do the job as cheaply as possible.

The drawbacks of such a system are twofold. Firstly, the speed of adjustment of the output of components in response to changes in the output of final aircraft, and vice versa, would almost certainly have been slower if it had relied upon price signals to indicate relative scarcities. Certainly there was a widespread belief that this was the case and a widespread acceptance therefore that the MAP should intervene. The MAP, that is, had to be seen to be doing something actively to promote the war effort rather than just leaving it to the market. The second drawback of leaving the aircraft manufacturers to purchase the components they required at the best prices they could obtain was that the contract price of the aircraft (paid by the MAP to the aircraft manufacturer) would determine the quality of the components fitted to it. In effect, the price would determine the specification of the aircraft. The higher the price the better the specification.

> *For example, an extra £1,000 for a Spitfire would enable the Spitfire manufacturers to command the best Merlin engines, and a reduction of the price for the Hurricane would have forced manufacturers of the Hurricane to engine their aircraft with second best Merlins. (Devons p.68)*

Now it might have been possible for the MAP to set the relative price of Spitfires and Hurricanes in such a way that this outcome was achieved (assuming this was what the MAP desired). But it was much easier to achieve this outcome if the MAP *directed* the output of the engine manufacturers in the way that it saw fit. The desired allocation of resources (in this case engines) was achieved more quickly and with a greater degree of certainty through a system based on the physical direction of resources rather than through a mechanism in which producers responded to prices.

We began this chapter by defining planning as being a system of resource allocation which stands in contrast to a market allocation. The reader may by now be aware, however, that to present the situation as a choice between two stark alternatives – planning or the market – is misleadingly simplistic. In producing a complex manufactured product such as an aircraft, co-ordination of the various aspects of production (in other words, planning) is a technological necessity. The problems of co-ordination in aircraft production in peacetime are no less acute than in wartime. They are simply less urgent. Companies like British Aerospace are the modern-day equivalent of the MAP. They have production plans, extending several years into the future, for the various types of aircraft they produce. These plans must be co-ordinated with the planned production of components, whether these components are produced in- house (within BAe itself) or by independent suppliers. The process of planning is no different from that carried out in wartime except that it is carried out by different people – BAe employees rather than Whitehall civil servants. The only substantive difference is that the resource cost of this indispensable planning – the salaries of the planners – is incorporated in the price of the aircraft rather than paid out of general taxation.

Notes

1. **Dalton, G.**, *Economic Systems and Society*. Penguin, 1974.
2. **Alfred Marshall 1842–1924**. (His famous *Principles of Economics* was published in 1890); William Jevons 1835–82; Vilfredo Pareto 1848–1923; Marx's *Das Kapital* was first published in 1867.
3. **Devons, E.**, 'Economic planning in war and peace', in *Essays in Economics*. Greenwood Press, 1980.
4. **Leontief, W. W.**, *The Structure of the American Economy 1919–1939* (2nd ed). OUP: Fairlawn N. J., 1951.

Questions

12.1 'What's in a name?' The words we use to describe economic systems are not value-free. They reflect, to a lesser or greater extent, approval or disapproval of that system. Study the following two lists of names:

price system	central planning
capitalism	socialism
free enterprise	state planning
market mechanism	communism
private enterprise	planned economy
free-market system	command economy

Now re-arrange each list so that it starts with terms which reflect approval of the system and finishes with terms which reflect disapproval of the system.

12.1 In Bogravia, an Eastern European satellite of the USSR, consumers wishing to buy a car must put down their names on a waiting list and pay a deposit. The most sought-after model is the Lada 1200, for which there is a four-year waiting list. There are no demonstration models in the showroom, only photographs. Which of the following statements are correct?
(a) The size of the waiting list is evidence that the price charged is too low. The price should rise to choke off the excess demand.
(b) By keeping the price down the authorities ensure that everyone who wants a car can buy one.
(c) The price of the Lada in Bogravia reflects what the Bogravian consumer thinks about the desirability of the product.
(d) At least it's better than just giving cars to members of the Communist Party.
(e) The Lada is a technically advanced car so everyone wants it.
(f) The Lada is a copy of a model that Fiat stopped making in Italy years ago.
(g) There are no waiting lists for cars in Britain.
What could you predict about the price of second-hand (nearly new) Ladas in Bogravia?

12.3 In Britain the price of a new Skoda car (manufactured in Czechoslavakia) is less than the price of a new Ford manufactured in Britain or a Toyota from Japan. Why?

Chapter 13

State intervention in market economies: public spending

13.1 A welfare economics framework?

In Chapter 11 we looked at a theoretical model of the way in which resources are allocated by the market, and in Chapter 12 we looked at planning both in the context of Soviet-type economies and in the context of wartime capitalist economies. A *mixed economy* such as that of the UK is fundamentally a market economy but with a significant amount of state intervention. This intervention takes a number of broad forms, namely:

1. Spending on goods and services.
2. Spending on income maintenance programmes e.g. unemployment benefit.
3. State ownership and control of certain industrial resources, e.g. nationalized industries.
4. Legal controls on the behaviour of firms.

Within a Paretian welfare economics framework these forms of intervention can be seen as ways of tackling the various forms of market failure identified in section 11.2. Thus the framework of welfare economics sketched out in Chapter 11 forms a sort of overarching theory which can be used to explain and justify these various forms of state intervention. The modern tendency, however, is to place less emphasis on the overarching theory of welfare economics and to adopt a more piecemeal approach to the analysis of intervention. The reason for this may be a suspicion that the all-encompassing nature of welfare theory explains everything, but in such broad generalities as to explain nothing. A second reason, possibly, is the acknowledgement that the all-pervasive existence of market failure in the real world makes a Pareto optimal allocation of resources impossible to attain no matter how much one tries to patch up the system with bits of intervention here and there. We shall adopt the piecemeal approach, though recognizing that all forms of state intervention do have a welfare-theoretic base.

In this chapter we shall look at public spending (the first two forms of intervention mentioned above). In Chapter 14 we shall consider the third form of intervention mentioned above – national ized industries. The final form of intervention mentioned is mostly concerned with policy towards monopolies and mergers, which we considered in section 8.7.

13.2 Public spending: transfer payments

Table 13.1 presents an analysis of public spending in the UK broken down into broad categories. As can be seen, over one-quarter of government spending is on transfer payments. The major expenditure in this category is on retirement pensions, unemployment benefit and supplementary benefit, but also included are things like maternity benefit, child allowances, student grants, family income supplement and death grant. From the cradle, as you might say, to the grave. Such transfer payments constitute the cash part of the income maintenance programme which all market economies provide to a greater or lesser extent for their citizens. The non-cash part of the income-maintenance programme is the income-in-kind provided by free health care, education, and so on. The objective quite clearly is to redistribute income in favour of those on low incomes and to prevent their standard of living slipping below some 'acceptable' level.

Table 13.1 Analysis of UK public spending 1983

	Broad categories (%)
Social security and welfare (transfer payments)	27.8
Defence	13.1
Education	12.8
Health	13.2
Housing and environmental services	9.5
General public services	5.7
Other community and social services	8.2
Economic services	9.7

Source: Compiled by the author from *National Income and Expenditure* (Blue Book) 1984

Approximately three-quarters of government spending – that is, that part of total government spending which does not go on transfer payments – is on goods and services. The rationale for the public provision of certain goods and services is related to the 'public good' characteristics of certain goods. These characteristics, which were mentioned in section 11.2, are non-excludability and non-rivalness. We shall first explain the meaning of these terms in section 13.3 and then consider in section 13.4 the extent to which they provide a rationale for public provision.

13.3 Non-excludability and non-rivalness

'Non-excludability' means that those who do not pay cannot be excluded from consuming the good in question. Thus defence-of-the-realm is a non-excludable public good. Even if you pay no taxes at all, and thus make no contribution towards the cost of provision, you cannot be excluded from enjoying the benefits of being defended. Neither of course can you choose not to consume the good in question. Whether you pay for it or not – and whether you like it or not – you consume the benefits of living under the nuclear umbrella. Declaring your house and garden a nuclear-free zone does not alter this basic fact.

'Non-rivalness' is the second characteristic of public goods. It means that if a good or service is provided for one person then it can be provided for everyone at no extra cost. In other words, the goods are not rivals in consumption. Radio and television broadcasts are an example of a non-rival public good. By tuning to a particular broadcast I do not diminish the signal strength in any way. My consumption in no way diminishes the supply available to my neighbours.

Radio and television broadcasts are also intrinsically non-excludable public goods of course, though attempts are made through the legal system to render them excludable. In other words, in Britain at least, the law requires you to purchase a television licence in order to use a television set. The enforcement of the law is difficult, however, since broadcasts are intrinsically non-excludable – television sets work just as well whether you have paid your licence fee or not. Thus, in order to catch and prosecute the 'free riders' – those who do not pay their television licence fee – the authorities are forced to incur substantial administrative costs: the cost of advertising campaigns designed to persuade people to buy a licence and the cost of TV detector vans to catch those who do not. When attempts are made to render excludable those goods which are intrinsically non-excludable, the administrative and other costs of so doing are often large. Roads, for example, are by their nature more or less non-excludable. In Britain, however, cars used on public roads must be licensed but, as with the television licence fee, there is widespread evasion.

13.4 Public spending: goods and services

The market will fail to provide an adequate supply of public goods – those goods which possess to some degree the characteristics of non-

Table 13.2 Detailed analysis of public spending – central and local government

		1983 (£m)	1983 (%)	1952 (%)	1920 (%)	
Military defence		15 904	13.1	30.3	36.5	
Civil defence		59	—	1.5	—	
External relations		2 415	2.0	1.5	—	
Roads and public lighting		3 147	2.6	2.2	7.2	
Transport and communication		2 029	1.7	1.8	—	
Employment services		2 917	2.4	0.3	2.4	
Other industry and trade		3 087	2.5	1.0	—	
Research		1 067	0.9	—	—	
Agriculture, Forestry, Fishing Food		2 292	1.9	6.9	0.2	
Housing	*6 665*		*5.4*	—	—	
Water, sewerage, refuse disposal	*1 510*		*1.2*	—	—	
Public Health services	*423*		*0.4*	—	—	
Land drainage/coastal protection	*230*		*0.2*	—	—	
Parks etc.	*1 080*		*0.9*	—	—	
Miscellaneous local government services	*1 673*		*1.4*	—	—	
Total housing and environmental services	11 581		9.5	11.6	3.4	
Libraries, museums and arts		798	0.7	0.2	—	
Police		3 063	2.5	1.5		
Prisons		652	0.5	0.3	6.4	
Parliament and law courts		1 152	0.9	—		
Fire service		676	0.6	0.3	—	
Education		15 583	12.8	8.7	17.0	
School meals, milk and welfare foods		564	0.5	1.4	—	
National Health Service		16 016	13.2	9.6	7.2	health
Personal Social Services		3 028	2.5	—	—	
Social Security benefits		33 741	27.8	15.9	6.7	pensions and poor relief
Finance and tax collection		1 810	1.5	1.7	—	
Miscellaneous		—	—	2.5	12.2	General admin.
Total expenditure excluding debt interest		121 581	100	100	100	

Sources: Estimates for 1983, 1952 from *National Income and Expenditure* (Blue Book)

Estimates for 1920 from C. H. Feinstein, *National Income and Expenditure 1855–1965* C.U.P., 1977

Note: Total may not sum to 100 due to rounding.

excludability and non-rivalness. Table 13.2 presents a more detailed analysis of government spending in Britain in 1983 together with some historical figures for comparison. It can be seen from this table that some of the areas of public spending can be explained in terms of the 'public good' argument. Defence, for example, which consumes about 13 per cent of total public spending, is a pure public good. If the government did not provide it, no one else would because no private-sector company is capable of 'selling' £16 bn worth of defence to the 52 million consumers in the UK. Defence is either provided for everyone or for no one. It cannot be divided up into 52 million separate lots and sold to individual consumers, because each consumer would choose to be a 'free rider'. If they had a choice, no rational consumer would pay.

Although the public-good argument explains why defence is not provided by the market, it cannot, of course, be used to justify so much – or so little – public expenditure in this area. The decision to devote 13 per cent of public spending to defence is essentially a political decision. It does not result from a set of consumer preferences expressed in the market in the same way that the quantity of washing machines produced ultimately depends on the purchasing decisions of consumers. Hence where the market fails because of the existence of public goods there is no mechanism whereby consumers can express their preferences, that is, make known their views, except by the very imperfect means of voting for a political party in an election.

Some of the other areas of public spending shown in Table 13.2 are goods or services which possess the characteristics of non-excludability and/or non-rivalness to a greater or lesser extent. For example, most of the expenditure on environmental services – roads, parks, coastal protection – comes under this heading. No private company could have 'sold' the Thames Flood Barrier to the millions of consumers who could potentially have benefited from it. Thus if it were not provided by the government and financed out of general taxation it would not have been provided at all.

It is clear that two of the largest spending areas – education and health care – are not really public goods at all. Between them these two areas comprise about one-quarter of total public spending, yet they are neither non-excludable nor non-rival. A hospital bed occupied by a psychiatric patient cannot simultaneously be occupied by a heart transplant patient. They are rival goods. Resources devoted to screening for cervical cancer cannot simultaneously be employed in finding a cure for AIDS. Similarly, because health care and education are essentially personal services they are excludable by their nature. Schools and colleges can decide which students to admit and which to exclude. Doctors decide which patient is to receive a transplanted kidney. There are exceptions of course. For example, some of the output of the Open University (the broadcasts) is a pure public good and fluoridation of the water supply (to prevent dental decay) constitutes a non-excludable good. The bulk of the output of the education and health-care sectors is both excludable and rival, however. The implication of this is that there is no reason in principle why both education and health care could not be provided by the market. The existence of private health care and private schools in Britain bears witness to this fact. Moreover, some countries have a much smaller state provision of education and health care than we do in the UK (though some have much larger). Since the provision of health care and education cannot be justified in terms of the public-good argument, some other justification is required. This is provided by the *merit good* argument. Certain goods and services are so important, it is argued, that every individual should be able to consume an adequate amount of them no matter what his income. In effect, by subsidizing certain goods, or by providing them at a zero price to the consumer, the state attempts to persuade consumers to consume a larger quantity than they would do if they were forced to pay the full cost of production. This argument extends to a range of goods like school meals, libraries, museums and the arts, as the following conversation between two high-ranking civil servants illustrates:

> Sir Humphrey Appleby: . . . *and what about greyhound racing? Should dog tracks be subsidized as well as football clubs for instance?*
> Bernard: *Well, why not if that's what the people want?*
> Sir Humphrey: *Bernard, subsidy is for* art. *For culture. It is not to be given to what the people* want. *It is to what the people* don't want *but* ought to have. *If they want something they'll pay for it themselves. No, we subsidize education, enlightenment, spiritual uplift – not the vulgar pastimes of ordinary people.*
> *(Extract from 'Yes Minister – the Middle Class Rip off')*

In addition, certain goods and services provided by the state give benefit not just to the direct recipient of the good in question but to society at large. For example, inoculation against communicable disease benefits the patient himself but also those with whom he is likely to come into contact. In this case *positive external benefits* are said to exist and their existence can be used to justify the provision of treatment below cost or at zero price.

Finally, some areas of public spending, particularly that on education and health care, can be considered as investment spending – in this case investment in human capital. The return yielded by this investment is in the form of a more productive workforce. It is argued that through ignorance or myopia individuals will tend to underinvest, preferring immediate consumption benefits. The state, taking a longer view, channels resources away from immediate consumption (by taxing people's incomes) and towards investment in those areas which increase the productive capacity of the economy in the longer term.

Questions

13.1 State which of the following constitute expenditure on goods and services, and which are transfer payments:
unemployment benefit
supplementary benefit payments
student grants
teachers' salaries
salaries of social workers
spending on the school dental service
spending on research (e.g. the Economic and Social Research Council)

13.2 Consider the extent to which the following are either non-excludable or non-rival or both:
television broadcasts
the M1 motorway
the River Thames
McDonald's hamburgers
the pavement outside McDonald's
navigation buoys

13.3 The Arts Council receives considerable amounts of public money. How can this be justified?

Chapter 14
Public Corporations

14.1 Public corporations and nationalized industries

In section 13.1 we identified a number of broad areas of state intervention in market economies. One of these was the ownership and control of certain industrial resources – the nationalized industries. It is to this form of state intervention that we now turn.

The term 'public corporation' is the official designation given to bodies that are publicly owned (i.e. state owned) yet are outside the sectors controlled directly by central government or by local authorities. Public corporations engage in commercial activities but are independent of the government and Parliament in the day-to-day management of their commercial and financial affairs, though they are subject to constraints on their borrowing. Table 14.1 gives a list of public corporations in existence at 31 December 1984.

Within this list only those marked with an asterisk are officially designated as 'nationalized industries' the remainder being referred to officially as 'other public corporations'. The distinction is somewhat arbitrary, however, since corporations such as the Royal Ordnance Factories, the Royal Mint and HMSO are essentially trading corporations in the same sense as the National Coal Board and British Rail. In this chapter, however, we shall adhere to the official usage of the terms – that is, the term 'public corporations' will refer to all those institutions listed in Table 14.1 and the term 'nationalized industries' will be restricted to that subset designated as such (i.e. those marked with an asterisk).

Lest any confusion exists in the mind of the reader over the use of the word 'public', it should be pointed out that it is used in two different – and opposite – senses. A public corporation is a state-owned corporation in which the public cannot own shares (or can own only a minority interest). A public limited company (plc), in contrast, is a private-sector company whose shares are held by the public. Confused? Well, just remember that in Britain a 'public school' is in fact a private school. Private schools are open to the public, except that you have to pay. There are also things called private companies. The public owns shares in these but they are not traded on the Stock Market. It should be quite clear by now that

Table 14.1 Names of public corporations in existence at 31 December 1984

Audit Commission

Bank of England
* British Airways Authority
* British Airways Board
British Broadcasting Corporation
* British Gas Corporation
* British National Oil Corporation
* British Railways Board
* British Shipbuilders
* British Steel Corporation
* British Waterways Board

* Civil Aviation Authority
Commonwealth Development Corporation
Covent Garden Market Authority
Crown Agents & Crown Agents Holding & Realisation Board

Development Board for Rural Wales

* Electricity Council (together with the Central Electricity Generating Board and Area Electricity Boards in England and Wales)

General Practice Finance Corporation

Highlands and Islands Development Board
H.M. Stationery Office
Housing Corporation

Independent Broadcasting Authority

Land Authority for Wales
* London Transport Executive

* National Bus Company
* National Coal Board
National Dock Labour Board
National Film Finance Corporation
New Town Development Corporation and Commission
* Northern Ireland Electricity Service
Northern Ireland Housing Executive
Northern Ireland Transport Holding Company
* North of Scotland Hydro-Electric Board

Passenger Transport Executives
Pilotage Commission
* Post Office
Property Services Agency (Supplies)

Table 14.1 continued

*	Regional Water Authorities in England & Welsh Water Authority
	Royal Mint
	Royal Ordnance Factories
	Scottish Development Agency
	Scottish Special Housing Association
*	Scottish Transport Group
*	South of Scotland Electricity Board
	Trust Ports
	Urban Development Corporations
	Water Authorities Association
	Welsh Development Agency

*'Nationalized industries' – see text

Source: *National Income and Expenditure*, 1985, Section 16

'privatization' means selling off parts of the public sector to members of the public, that is, transferring them to the private sector.

As can be seen, the public corporations form a heterogeneous group whose only common feature is their status as commercially independent but publicly owned corporations. The histories of these corporations, and the reasons for their existence, are as varied as their trading activities. Many, such as the National Coal Board, were set up by the post-war Labour government. Others, such as the Regional Water Authorities, were set up to administer functions previously carried out by local authorities. Some were set up as regulatory bodies to cope with newly emerging needs – for example, the Independent Broadcasting Authority and the Civil Aviation Authority. Others, such as the Bank of England and the Post Office, had been in existence as government departments for many years before being officially transferred to the public corporations sector.

As a group the public corporations form a significant sector of the national economy. In 1983 they accounted for 10.7 per cent of GDP and 16 per cent of Fixed Capital Formation (Investment). They employed about 1.7 million people (about 7 per cent of the labour force). The size of this sector is, however, shrinking as the Conservative government proceeds with its plans to 'privatize' or denationalize large parts of the public sector. This process of privatization is already well under way, as Table 14.2 shows.

14.2 Reasons for nationalization

This chapter will be principally concerned with various aspects of the privatization debate. It is first necessary, however, to consider the

Table 14.2 Privatization in the UK 1979–84

Company	Business	Date of sale	Remaining Government holding (%)	Net proceeds (£m)
British Petroleum	Oil	Oct. 79 Jun. 81 Sep. 83	 31.7	276 8 543
British Aerospace	Aerospace	Feb. 81	49.4	43
British Sugar Corporation	Sugar refiner	Jul. 81	nil	44
Cable & Wireless	Telecommmunications	Oct. 81 Dec. 83	 23.1	182 263
Amersham International	Radio-chemicals	Feb. 82	nil	64
National Freight Co.	Road haulage	Feb. 82	nil	5
Britoil	Oil	Nov. 82	48.9	627
Associated British Ports	Seaports	Feb. 83 Apr. 84	 nil	46 51
International Aeradio	Aviation communications	Mar. 83	nil	60
British Rail Hotels	Hotels	Mar. 83	nil	51
British Gas Onshore Oil Assets (Wytch Farm)	Oil	May 84	nil	82
Enterprise Oil	Oil	Jun. 84	nil	380
Sealink	Harbour and Ferry	Jul. 84	nil	66
Jaguar	Cars	Jul. 84	nil	297
British Telecom	Telecommunications	Nov. 84	49.8	3916
British Technology Group and other sales	Miscellaneous	—	—	716

Source: *The Economist* 23 Feb. 1985

reasons why the present nationalized industries were originally taken into public ownership. As we have already indicated, these reasons vary from case to case. On a general level, however, it is well known that Clause 4 of the Labour Party's Constitution talks of 'the public ownership of the means of production, distribution and exchange' as a specific political objective. Taken literally, this means nationalizing everything, and while some members of the Labour Party would support this objective, most would not. More usually, the Clause is interpreted to refer to the nationalization of certain key industrial and commercial sectors – the 'commanding heights' of the economy. This provided the justification, if not the rationale, for the post-war acts of nationalization.

The economic case for public ownership of certain industries rests on a number of general principles. Keynes, the acknowledged founder of modern macroeconomics, talks in his *General Theory*[1] of the stabilizing influence that a sizeable public sector would have on the economy. It is well known that a market economy without a significant public sector is prone to suffer cycles in economic activity which periodically produce booms and slumps. This is principally because the investment behaviour of private-sector firms is very volatile. In periods when the growth in sales appears to falter, firms cut or delay their investment in new productive capacity. The reduction in investment demand which this brings about induces a further decline in demand. The economy enters a recession from which it will not automatically extricate itself. The investment spending of the public sector would be less volatile, Keynes argued, and this would tend to damp down the oscillations in economic activity. Moreover, control of the public enterprise sector would allow it to be used by the government for countercyclical demand management. That is, investment spending in the public sector could be boosted to take up the slack in private-sector demand when necessary. This then is the macroeconomic case for a public sector in general and, by extension, the case for public ownership of key industrial sectors.

In addition, certain of these key industrial sectors are what are known as natural monopolies. That is, they are industries which can only be run efficiently if one firm supplies the whole market. To allow competition between rival firms would result in wasteful duplication of services. Examples of natural monopolies are electricity distribution (it would not be sensible to allow rival companies to erect transmision lines for electricity), gas distribution, postal deliveries, the railways, water supply and sewage disposal. If such a monopoly were in private hands, it is argued, it could operate against the public interest. A monopolist who is pursuing the objective of profit maximization will use his market power to raise prices and restrict supply. Since by definition barriers to the entry of new firms exist, super-normal profits will continue to accrue to those private individuals who own the monopoly firm. Therefore, it is argued, the private-sector monopolist should be taken into public ownership so that prices can then be controlled and output expanded.

Moreover, many of the natural monopolies are thought to have some strategic significance, in the sense that they are important to the defence and security of the state – for example, energy supplies and communications. This reinforces the case for some state control of such industries. Ownership, through nationalization, ensures this overall control. In addition to their strategic significance, these industries also form an important part of the infrastructure of the economy – transport, communications, energy supplies, and so on. Since infrastructure is an important prerequisite for the growth and development of the economy, the state may wish to direct investment resources into those areas as a means of promoting economic growth in the economy as a whole.

The foregoing arguments apply to many of the industries which have been taken into public ownership. The specific circumstances of each individual case are as important as the general case for public ownership, however. For example, in 1948 the railways were nationalized because they were then in dire straits and would not have been able, in private hands, to attract the necessary investment capital for modernization. Many of the nationalized industries had an equally inauspicious start in life. In 1967, for example, the British Steel Corporation was formed from 13 separate steel companies which were 'already in a difficult and deteriorating position. In 1957–58 they had earned a net profit of over £400 m; by 1962–63 this had fallen to around £200 m, and during 1967–68, which was the Corporation's first year, the figure was less than £60 m. This represented a return of only 0.5 per cent on net assets at replacement cost.'[2]

The British Steel Corporation came into existence because the government of the day wished to increase concentration in the industry as a means of promoting efficiency. The government was instrumental in the mergers which gave birth to BSC. Similarly, the government was instrumental in promoting the merger activity in the motor industry which eventually produced British Leyland in 1968. (BL remained in private ownership until 1975.) Similarly, British Aerospace was formed in 1977 as a result of a government-sponsored merger between Hawker Siddley and the British Aircraft Corporation, firms which had both received substantial amounts of government money in the past.

14.3 Reasons for privatization

It is probably true to say that the Labour Party never really knew what to do with the nationalized industries – how they should be regulated, what pricing and investment policies they should pursue, and so on. Mrs Thatcher, however, when she came to power in 1979, knew exactly what to do with them. The Conservative government's plans for the nationalized industries became increasingly clear in the early 1980s, as the following three quotations show.

> *It remains our purpose, wherever possible to transfer to the private sector assets which can be better managed there. (Sir Geoffrey Howe, Chancellor of the Exchequer, Budget speech, 9 March 1982.)*

> *Privatisation represents by far the most effective means of extending market forces, and in turn of improving efficiency and the allocation of resources.* (Lord Cockfield, then Minister of State, Treasury, 19 November 1981.)
>
> *It must be right to press ahead with the transfer of ownership from the state to private enterprise of as many public sector businesses as possible . . . The introduction of competition must, whenever possible, be linked to a transfer of ownership to private citizens and away from the state. Real public ownership – that is, ownership by the people – must be and is our ultimate goal.* (Mr Nicholas Ridley, Financial Secretary to the Treasury, 12 February 1982.)

From these statements, which were all quoted in the May 1982 *Economic Progress Report* published by the Treasury, one is left in no doubt that the intention is to privatize large parts of the public sector, particularly public corporations, and the rationale for so doing rests on the following two propositions. Firstly, privatization ensures competition, and secondly, competition ensures efficiency.

14.3.1 Privatization ensures competition?

The first of these two propositions is clearly wrong, or at least is correct only in a restricted context. A nationalized industry that monopolizes the market which it serves and is returned to the private sector intact is still a monopoly. A state monopoly has merely been replaced by a private-sector one. In the market for its product there has been no increase in competition as a result of privatization. The term 'liberalization' has been coined to refer to the introduction of competition into an erstwhile protected monopolistic industry. Clearly, privatization does not ensure liberalization. The two things are quite distinct. Moreover, while it is relatively easy to privatize an industry, it may be much more difficult to liberalize it. Some of the existing and former nationalized industries are natural monopolies, as we have already noted. It is absurd to suggest that these industries could be split up into atomistically competitive firms – indeed, any sort of competition is wasteful in industries such as water supply and electricity distribution because scale economies are such an important feature of those industries. Thus the privatization of British Telecom did not in itself increase competition in the industry since it was sold off as a single entity. BT's statutory monopoly had been rescinded some years earlier and this did more to liberalize the industry than was achieved by privatization *per se*. Similarly, it is proposed that British Gas should be sold off as a single entity. To split it up is, supposedly, neither economically desirable nor feasible.

Although it is clearly wrong to equate privatization with an increase in competition in the market for its product, a privatized industry is in a sense exposed to competition on the Stock Market. That is, its shares are in competition with the shares of all other companies and those shares reflect the profitability of the company. Nationalized industries, on the other hand, are not subject to the discipline of the market. They can never suffer the ultimate sanction – liquidation – since their losses will always be made good by the government. It is in this sense, and in this sense only, that privatization *per se* exposes the industry to competition.

Although the foregoing applies whether or not the industry is a monopoly, it loses much of its force if the firm faces no competition in the market for its product and if barriers to the entry of new firms exist – that is, if the firm is a monopolist – since in this case the firm can make profits, not by increasing efficiency and cutting costs, but by raising prices. A firm's Stock Market valuation, that is, the price of its shares on the Stock Exchange, reflects not its efficiency but its profitability. Efficiency and profitability are two different things.

14.3.2 Competition ensures efficiency?

The second proposition on which the justification for privatization rests – that competition ensures efficiency – is also open to question. Even if we assume that the industry can be liberalized, such liberalization will clearly not result in a market structure which is anything like a perfectly competitive market. Rather, it will be an oligopolistic market. As we saw in Chapter 8, the behaviour of firms in oligopolistic markets may be competitive, but it may also be collusive. If competition does emerge, it is unlikely to be price competition: non-price competition is much more usual.

We cannot, however, make any general statements on the basis of our analysis alone about the efficiency of firms in oligopolistic industries. A crucial problem is that we have not yet defined what efficiency is. The debate about the efficiency of nationalized industries relative to private-sector firms is, however, a debate which predates the current spate of privatizations. Nor is the debate confined to the UK, since all market economies have some state-owned industries. What we shall do in section 14.5 is to summarize the evidence that has been collected on this issue. Before we can do this, however, we need to say something about the pricing strategies adopted by nationalized industries and the objectives they pursue.

14.4 Pricing strategies in nationalized industries

The pricing strategies pursued by nationalized industries and the objectives they pursue are clearly related issues. If a private-sector company pursues profit maximization, this has clear implications for the prices it will charge. They will be profit-maximizing prices, not necessarily in the sense that the firm consciously equates marginal cost to marginal revenue, but in the sense that the firm feels its way by a process of trial and error towards prices that maximize the firm's profits. For a nationalized industry, however, particularly a monopolistic one, the pursuit of maximum profit is not necessarily an appropriate objective.

With the growth of the nationalized industry sector in the post-war period it was recognized that guidelines needed to be laid down governing the nationalized industries' pricing and investment strategies. Economists at the time were closely wedded to the idea of *marginal cost pricing* for nationalized industries. Prices, they argued, should be set equal to the marginal production cost of the good or service in question. The reason for their advocacy of marginal cost pricing stemmed from a rather literal interpretation of the Pareto welfare analysis set out in section 11.1 Recall that, according to this analysis, if all goods were sold on markets where price was equal to marginal cost, then a Pareto optimal allocation of society's resources would result. Therefore, argued the economists, nationalized industries should set their prices equal to marginal costs, since this would lead society as a whole to gain the maximum benefit from the operation of these industries.

14.4.1 Limitations of marginal cost pricing

The guidelines for pricing and investment were set down in a series of government White Papers in 1961, 1967 and 1978. (A White Paper is a document which lays down in general terms the policy to be followed.) For a number of reasons however, it came to be realized that a strict adherence to the marginal cost pricing principle was neither desirable nor feasible. These reasons stemmed both from developments in the theory of welfare economics itself and from an increasing realization of the impracticality of applying the policy prescriptions which emanated from it.

On the theory side, economists recognized that nationalized industries operated in an environment where most firms' prices were not equal to marginal cost. If nationalized industries set price equal to marginal cost when prices were above marginal cost in the private sector, this would lead to a misallocation of society's resources. Consider the following hypothetical example of an economy in which there are only two sources of energy, both indigenous. The oil industry is in private hands and the gas industry is state owned. Prices are set equal to marginal cost for gas, but are above marginal cost for oil. Table 14.3 summarizes this. Consider the choice facing the consumer who is considering how to heat his home in winter. He will base his decision on the set of relative prices – in this case the price of oil relative to the price of gas – but in this instance relative prices do not reflect relative scarcities. The price of gas is too low relative to the price of oil so that the price ratio between the two does not reflect the relative cost of producing gas in comparison to the cost of producing oil. Because prices for gas are 'too low', demand for gas will be higher than it would otherwise have been. Too large a proportion of society's resources will flow into gas production, and too small a proportion into oil production. Recognizing this, economists developed the general theory of the 'second best'. In a first-best world (in which all other prices are equal to marginal cost) nationalized industries should also set price equal to marginal cost. But in a second-best world, where in the private sector price exceeds marginal cost, nationalized industries should emulate the behaviour of private-sector firms. In other words, if prices in the private sector exceed marginal cost by 10 per cent then nationalized industries should set their prices on the same basis. In this way a Pareto optimal allocation of resources is still assured, even in this second-best world.

Table 14.3 Example: energy pricing

Private sector	Public sector
Oil	Gas
$P > \text{MC}$	$P = \text{MC}$

Although the general theory of the second-best clears up a problem in welfare theory, it leaves untouched the thorny problem of how marginal cost is to be measured. It is not at all clear what 'marginal cost' means in practice. Economists know what it means in theory. It is the first derivative of the total cost function. Less mathematically, it is the increase in total costs which results from the production of one extra unit of output. In the real world, however, there are *indivisibilities*. For example, in British Rail's case, the marginal cost of carrying an extra passenger when there are still empty seats on its trains is virtually zero. When the train is full, however, the marginal cost of carrying an extra passenger is the cost of putting an extra coach on the train, or of running an extra train. To adhere strictly to marginal cost pricing would result in most passengers paying almost nothing, and one extremely unfortunate passenger paying a very high price indeed. In addition, in calculating marginal costs some account must be taken of capital costs. In electricity generation, for example, the short-run marginal cost of power generation is the fuel cost alone. But if prices to the consumer took into account only fuel costs, then the industry would not be raising sufficient revenue to cover the depreciation of its generating capacity, nor to pay for new capacity. A related point is that firms which are subject to substantial scale economies cannot hope to cover all their operating costs if they set price equal to marginal cost. To see why this should be so, consider Fig. 14.1, which shows a typical declining cost firm (or industry). The downward sloping long-run average cost (LRAC) curve indicates that unit costs fall as the level of output rises. Such cost conditions are typical in capital-intensive industries such as electricity generation and telecommunications. It can be demonstrated (see section 5.3) that if average costs are declining then marginal cost must be less than average cost, as in Fig. 14.1 (LRMC – long-run marginal cost). If the firm sets price equal to marginal cost and charges a price of P_1, then losses will result. This is because the firm's total revenue which is equal to the rectangle OP_1CD is less than its total costs represented by the rectangle OABD. (Remember that total revenue is equal to the revenue per unit, OP_1, multiplied by the number of units sold, OD. Similarly, total costs are the costs per unit, OA, multiplied by the number of units produced, OD). The firm therefore makes losses equal to the rectangle P_1ABC.

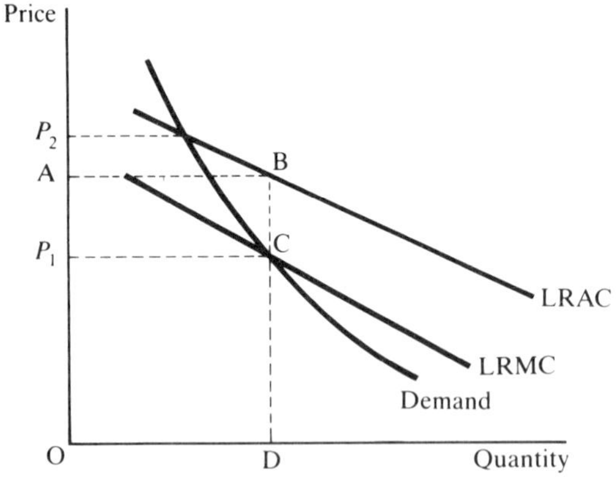

Fig. 14.1

In order to 'break even' the firm must set price equal to average rather than marginal cost and charge a price of P_2 (Figs 14.1 and 14.2). At this price and with output restricted to OZ, both toal revenue and total cost can be represented by the rectangle OP_2YZ. This seems to mean that the firm is making zero profits. If we remember, however, that our definition of cost includes a normal return to capital, it means that the firm is making zero super-normal profits (see section 6.5).

14.4.2 Controls on pricing and investment

For the reasons set out above, successive White Papers on the nationalized industries have tended to move away from an advocacy

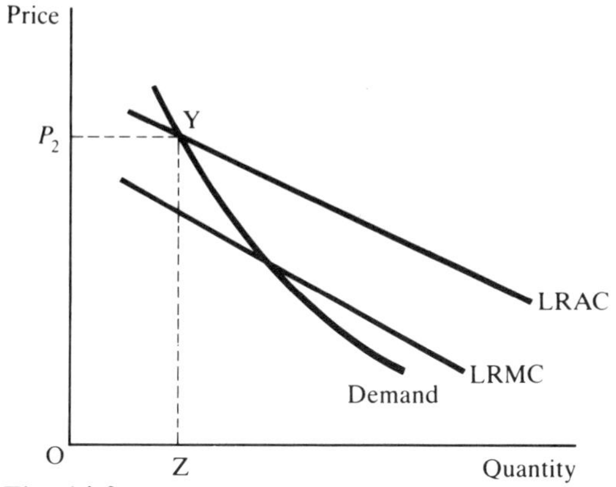

Fig. 14.2

of marginal cost pricing. In its place they have substituted the requirement that nationalized industries should set their prices in such a way that the industry meets the *financial target* imposed upon it. This financial target is in the form of a prescribed rate of return on the value of the assets employed in the industry. This rate of return can obviously be varied from time to time by the government. A problem exists, however, in that the *valuation* of the assets employed in the industry is by no means straightforward. Different approaches produce different estimates of the value of assets and it is not possible to say objectively which is 'correct'. The major area of disagreement centres around whether assets should be valued at their historical cost (minus an allowance for depreciation) or at their replacement value. The latter would normally give a much higher value.

In addition to financial targets, nationalized industries are now also subject to two additional controls. Both these controls affect the industry's investment, and therefore, indirectly the prices it can charge. The first requirement is that an investment project can only be undertaken if it will yield the required rate of return (RRR). This RRR is normally 5 per cent in real terms (that is, after allowing for inflation and using standard discounted cash flow techniques). Additionally, the borrowing which the industry undertakes to finance its investment is subject to an external financing limit (EFL). This effectively puts a ceiling on the amount of capital that the industry can raise on the capital market in any one financial year. The implication of this is considered in more detail in section 14.6.

14.5 The efficiency of public-sector industries

We saw in section 14.3 that the advocates of privatization argued that the efficiency of the nationalized industries would be increased if they were transferred to the private sector. Implicit in this view is the belief that nationalized industries are inherently less efficient than similar industries in private hands. It also implies, in particular, that the record of the nationalized industries in Britain shows evidence of inefficiency.

In this section we shall review some of the evidence on the relative efficiency of public- and private-sector firms, drawing on the work of Pryke and that of Millward.[3] We have already noted that profitability is a poor measure of efficiency. Profits depend, among other things, on the prices charged and these have often been held artificially low in nationalized industries as part of government anti-flation policy. An alternative measure of efficiency therefore needs to be found, and several writers have used 'productivity' indexes as yardsticks. Labour productivity can be calculated by dividing output by labour input. That is:

$$\text{output per employee} = \text{labour productivity} = \frac{\text{value of output}}{\text{labour input}} \qquad [14.1]$$

The denominator in the expression 'labour input' can be measured by the number of employees. The numerator, however, is measured in value terms, rather than in volume terms. (It would be possible to measure output in volume terms if it were homogeneous – for example, tons of coal – but comparisons of labour productivity in different industries would not then be possible.) This immediately casts doubt on the validity of the index as a true measure of efficiency since variations in prices will affect the value of output and hence labour productivity.

A more serious objection is that other factors of production in addition to labour are involved in the production process. The most important of these is, of course, capital. Capital-intensive industries, like telecommunications and electricity generation, therefore have high levels of labour productivity in comparison to labour-intensive industries like ports, but this says nothing about their relative efficiency.

A better measure of efficiency would take account of both the labour and capital used in production. These factor inputs would perforce have to be measured in value terms. Although the value of labour input can be measured quite simply by the wages bill, the value of capital input is much more difficult to determine. Usually some arbitrary assumption is made. For example, the value of capital input is equal to 10 per cent of the value of the industry's capital stock. In this way a (somewhat questionable) measure of the value of total factor inputs is obtained and from this a measure of *total factor productivity*, so called, can be derived. Thus:

$$\text{total factor productivity} = \frac{\text{value of output}}{\text{value of labour input} + \text{value of capital input}} \quad [14.2]$$

Alternatively, the *rate of growth* of either labour productivity or total factor productivity can be used. Pryke used such measures in his two studies of the UK nationalized industries covering the periods up to 1968 and from 1968 to 1978. Although he reached a generally favourable verdict for the earlier period, concluding that the nationalized industries had performed rather better than British manufacturing industry as a whole, his later study is much more critical of the performance of the nationalized industries. Table 14.4 reproduces Pryke's calculations for the period since 1968.

Millward, however, is critical of the use of the sort of 'productivity' measures discussed above. He argues that they are meaningless as productivity measures, essentially because they are influenced by price movements in both outputs and inputs.

A further difficulty is apparent from Table 14.4, namely that the nationalized industries do not form a homogeneous group. The first three, British Telecom, British Airways and British Gas have apparently secured large increases in 'productivity'. These three industries were in a particularly favoured position, however. They are capital- intensive industries and during the period studied, improvements in technology enabled large improvements in productivity to be secured. British Airways, for example, benefited from the introduction of wide-bodied jets; British Gas benefited from the exploitation of North Sea gas; and British Telecom from the general advances in electronics. Moreover, the demand for the output of these industries was increasing, as can be seen. The Central Electricity Generating Board was similarly favoured, though not to the same extent, as demand was not increasing as fast and unit costs were rising. In contrast, as can be seen from Table 14.4, all of the other nationalized industries were suffering a decline in the demand for their output. Costs were, in most cases, rising, necessitating price increases which further depressed demand.

A conclusion that emerges from Table 14.4 is that some nationalized industries did 'better' than the average for manufacturing industry generally, and others did 'worse'. Those that did better were the industries with generally favourable demand and cost conditions. Those that did worse had unfavourable demand and cost conditions. No general conclusion can therefore be reached about the relative

Table 14.4 Changes in output, employment and productivity in public enterprise and manufacturing 1968–78

	Growth in output (%)	**Growth in employment** (%)	**Growth in labour productivity** (%)	**Growth in total factor productivity** (%)
Telecommunications	129	2	120	66
British Airways airline activities	129	22	86	71
British Gas	82	– 18	126	—
British Electricity Boards	23	– 26	68	7
Postal services	– 12	– 1	– 12	—
BL: vehicles UK	– 17	– 1	– 17	—
British Rail	– 18	– 24	8	—
National Freight Corporation	– 22	– 39	31	—
BSC: iron and steel	– 26	– 26	– 2	– 22
National & Scottish Bus Groups	– 33	– 27	– 5	– 13
NCB collieries	– 36	– 28	– 7	– 13
Manufacturing, all industries	10	– 12	28	16
Manufacturing, excluding BSC (1968–78) and BL (1973–78)	12	– 12	30	18

Source: R. Pryke, *The Nationalised Industries: Policies and Performance since 1968*. Martin Robertson, 1981, p. 238.

efficiencies of public ownership versus private ownership, even if we accept Pryke's view that his 'productivity' indexes do in fact measure efficiency.

A more satisfactory approach to the general question of whether public ownership affects efficiency is to compare the performance of public- and private-sector firms operating in the same industry. Opportunities for doing this are relatively rare, but Millward reports the results of a number of such studies. In Canada there are two main railway companies, the publicly owned Canadian National and the privately owned Canadian Pacific, operating in competition with each other over many routes. The major conclusion Millward draws is that there is no significant evidence that productivity is lower in Canadian National than in Canadian Pacific. A study of Australian airlines where a public firm Trans-Australian Airways coexists with a private firm (Ansett Transport Industries) produces broadly similar conclusions. Millward's third case study is that of electricity supply in the United States, where a large number of firms, some public and some private, supply the nation's power. Because of its relevance to the general issue of whether public ownership affects efficiency, this industry has been subject to scrutiny by a number of authors. In reviewing these studies, Millward concludes that 'none of the cost studies support the proposition that public electricity firms have lower productivity or higher unit costs than private firms', allowing for differences in factor prices and the size of plant. Similar conclusions emerge from studies of unit costs in areas such as water supply and refuse collection. (Economists, as Millward once remarked, always end up talking rubbish.)

14.6 Privatization and the PSBR

The empirical studies of the previous section were all addressed to the central question of whether public as opposed to private ownership materially affects the managerial efficiency of firms. At the very least, one could conclude that there is no strong evidence to support the proposition that privatization *per se* will increase efficiency. Since the British Government and Treasury are presumably familiar with this evidence, their support for privatization must therefore be explained in one of two ways. Either their interpretation of the available evidence is different from the one we have made, or they are motivated by factors we have not yet considered. This second possibility leads us into a consideration of two possible motives. Firstly, a general ideological desire to roll back the frontiers of the state, which we shall discuss in the next chapter. And secondly, the impact which privatization has on the Public Sector Borrowing Requirement (PSBR), which we discuss below.

A full analysis of the PSBR takes us into the realm of

macroeconomics and hence is outside the scope of this book. Broadly speaking, however, the PSBR is equal to the financial deficit of the public sector, which is composed of central government, local authorities and public corporations. The financial deficit of the public corporations sector is the excess of its expenditure over its income in any one year. This excess is met by borrowing from the public, that is, from private individuals and financial institutions, by the issue of bonds and other debt instruments.

The Public Sector Borrowing Requirement, of which the Public Corporations Borrowing Requirement forms a part, is a key target of the present government's macroeconomic policy. They wish to reduce it to as low a level as possible, basically because they see it as a burden on the economy. Whether or not this is a sensible interpretation of the PSBR will not be considered here. However, given that the government is pursuing the objective of reducing the PSBR, privatization is an excellent way of doing so.

This follows for three reasons. Firstly, any public corporation which is incurring a deficit adds an equivalent amount to the government's spending and hence to its borrowing requirement. Secondly, and more importantly, borrowing by public corporations to finance future investment is treated as part of the PSBR even though this borrowing is really little different from the borrowing which private-sector firms undertake to finance investment. Because they are treated differently, however, borrowing by a nationalized BT, for example, increases the PSBR and is a burden on the economy. Borrowing by a privatized BT does not increase the PSBR and is not a burden on the economy. This seems nonsensical but, like all sophistry, there is a grain, but only a grain, of truth in it. Private-sector companies, the argument runs, are ultimately subject to the discipline of the Stock Market. Investments must produce a return which in the long term is no less than the average return in the company sector generally. If not, the company's shares will fall in value and it will eventually be taken over or go into liquidation. Public-sector companies, on the other hand, are not subject to such discipline. Although their investments are required to earn a specified return, they do not suffer a fall in their Stock Market valuation if they fail to do so. Their investments are, in a sense, underwritten by the government. They cannot go bankrupt. This therefore is the argument which is used to justify the inclusion of public corporations' borrowing as part of the PSBR and to view it as 'a burden on the economy'.

Clearly the smaller the public corporations sector, the smaller the 'burden' it can impose on the economy. This, in part, is the rationale for privatization. It is also the rationale for the imposition of External Financing Limits on the nationalized industries which we mentioned earlier.

By far the most important reason for privatization, however, if one takes a cynical view, is that the proceeds from the sale of public assets reduce the PSBR directly. The sale of BT raised £3.9 bn. British Gas, according to some estimates, could fetch as much as £9 bn. This clearly makes a very sizeable impact on the PSBR which was running at around £10 bn in 1984–85.

Notes

1. **Keynes, J. M.**, *The General Theory of Employment, Interest and Money*. 1939.
2. **Pryke, R.**, *The Nationalised Industries: Policies and Performance since 1968*. Martin Robertson, 1981, p.183.
3. **Pryke R.**, *Public Enterprise in Practice*, MacGibbon and Kee 1971, and Pryke (1981) op.cit.; Millward, R. *et al.*, *Public Sector Economics*. Longman 1983.

Questions

14.1 Which of the following statements are correct?
(a) All nationalized industries are public corporations but not all public corporations are nationalized industries.
(b) The public sector stands in contradistinction to the private sector.
(c) Public limited companies (PLCs) are part of the public sector.
(d) PLCs are part of the private sector.
(e) Public corporations are state-owned enterprises.

14.2 In 1983 the public corporations accounted for 16 per cent of total investment but only 10.7 per cent of output. Suggest reasons why this discrepancy exists.

14.3 Consider the extent to which the nationalized industries (listed in Table 14.1) constitute 'natural monopolies'.

14.4 Which of the following necessarily results from the privatization of a nationalized industry?
(a) Selling off assets brings a windfall gain to the Treasury.
(b) Privatization increases competition in the industry.
(c) Privatization increases efficiency in the industry.

14.5 How might one best measure 'efficiency' in the operation of a nationalized industry which monopolizes the market which it serves? An 'efficient' industry is one which:
(a) achieves a specified output level at least cost
(b) uses the minimum amount of resources to produce a particular output
(c) charges low prices
(d) achieves the highest profits
(e) has the greatest return on assets employed
(f) none of the above is a satisfactory definition of efficiency.

14.6 Suppose state-owned industries compete with private-sector companies whose prices exceed marginal cost. What does the theory of the second-best advocate about prices in the state owned industries?

(a) The nationalized industries should still set price equal to marginal cost.
(b) The state-owned industries should merely try to cover their total costs.
(c) Prices in the state-owned industries should be above marginal cost.
(d) The ratio of price to marginal cost should be the same in the nationalized industries as it is in the private sector.
(e) Nationalized industries should behave commercially and try to maximize profits.

14.7 The Central Electricity Generating Board has a 'merit order' of power stations. Stations with low fuel costs per unit of electricity generated – that is, low marginal costs – are at the top of the merit order. Hydro and nuclear stations have low marginal costs, followed by coal-fired and oil-fired stations. Given that electricity demand varies during the day, explain why 'off-peak' electricity is sold to the consumer more cheaply than 'on-peak' electricity?

14.8 The following could all be used to try to measure the 'efficiency' of a nationalized industry. What are the drawbacks of each of these measures?

(a) profitability
(b) labour productivity, i.e. $\dfrac{\text{value of output}}{\text{labour input}}$
(c) rate of return on capital employed
(d) total factor productivity

Chapter 15

The producer, the consumer and the state

This is a concluding chapter only in the sense that it comes at the end of the book. It does not purport to come to any conclusions. The issues are too complex, the questions are too large and an introductory textbook is not the appropriate forum within which to state any conclusions, definitive or otherwise. It is not an indictment to say, as Shaw did, that if all the economists in the world were laid end to end they still would not reach a conclusion. Rather it is a reflection of the complexity of the issues involved.

Nor does this short chapter attempt to summarize what has gone before, since any summary would be overly superficial. What it does do is to restate and highlight some of the issues raised in this book. The reader can if he wishes form his own conclusions. Be warned, however. If you think you know the answers it is probably because you do not fully understand the question.

An undercurrent in this book, implicit up to now, has been the relationship between the three dramatis personae in the economic system – the producer, the consumer and the state. The form of the relationship between these three characterizes the mixed economy. On the one hand we have presented a model – that of Pareto welfare theory – which portrays the individual consumer as being sovereign. Producers – that is, firms – merely respond passively to his wishes. There is no need for the state to intervene except in those few areas of market failure, principally those areas concerned with pure public goods like defence. Clearly this view is untenable, however. Producers do not passively respond to consumers' wishes. Rather they shape and manipulate those wishes through advertising and through the exercise of market power. Typically markets in the real world are not atomistically competitive. They are oligopolistic, and virtually the whole of Chapter 8 was devoted to a study of cases in which producers attempted to use and abuse their market power. The pursuit of self-interest by such firms does not, as Pareto claimed, lead to an allocation of resources which is optimal in any sense. It does not lead to the greatest happiness of the greatest number. There is a need for state intervention to curb the power of large firms when that power is abused.

Market failure – in the sense of externalities and public goods – is characterized in a Pareto model as a minor blemish on an otherwise perfect system. In fact it runs through that system, touching every part. Externalities are all-pervasive in an industrialized, urbanized society. The public-good area is of major significance, shaping as it does the physical and social environment within which individuals live out their lives. The market mechanism cannot by definition provide an adequate supply of those public goods like universal health care and education and environmental services which become more important as society becomes more affluent. Again, there is need for state intervention in the provision of public goods and to address the problem of externalities.

There is, I would guess, an overwhelming consensus that some state intervention in these areas is both appropriate and desirable. There never can be any consensus, however, in deciding exactly how much state intervention is desirable. To what extent should private producers be free to pursue their selfish ends? To what extent, indeed, should society's productive resources be in the hands of private individuals who are free to pursue those ends? And to what extent should the state intervene to correct for market failure? These questions are of course – as if you had not already realized it – political. Economics is political economy. It can never divorce itself from that no matter how much it pretends to be an objective, value-free science.

There is of course a political tide in Britain in 1985. That tide, which has been running in Britain for several years, has been referred to as 'rolling back the frontiers of the state'. It is about shifting the emphasis of our mixed economy away from increasing reliance on state intervention and towards greater reliance on market forces. Supply-side economics, it is sometimes called. What characterizes this policy is the view that an economy actually functions better – that is, is more productive – if individuals both as consumers and producers are motivated by the rewards and punishments that are an essential feature of the market mechanism. This view is, of course, based on a particular interpretation of how the market mechanism works. In this book we have tried to give an analysis of how that market mechanism works. The reader should by now be aware that our analysis is not characterized by a world of competitive markets where price is determined by demand and supply (whatever that is), where producers passively respond to consumers' wishes and in which market failure is only a minor defect.

We have not set out in our analysis to persuade the reader into accepting any particular view about the appropriate role of the state. We shall not have failed, however, if the reader has been brought to a more informed agnosticism.

Index